THE PRACTICAL GUIDE TO KEEPING

CHICKENS

DUCKS, GEESE & TURKEYS

THE PRACTICAL GUIDE TO KEEPING
CHICKENS
DUCKS, GEESE & TURKEYS
A DIRECTORY OF POULTRY BREEDS AND HOW TO KEEP THEM

FRED HAMS

LORENZ BOOKS

CONTENTS

Introduction   **6**
The Evolution of
   Domestic Fowl   8
Breeds, Strains, Varieties
   and Hybrids   12
Poultry Anatomy   14
Combs   16
Other Ornaments and
   Appendages   18
Feather Structure   20
Feather Patterns   21
Feather Colour   22
The Life Cycle of Poultry   24

Buying Poultry   **26**
Deciding How to Buy   28
Choosing Hybrids   30
Choosing Pure Breeds   31
Choosing Rare Breeds   32
Rehoming Battery Hens   34

Housing Your Poultry   **36**
Creating the Ideal
   Environment   38
Choosing Appropriate
   Housing   40
Types of Housing   42
Building Your Own
   Chicken House   48
Additional Essentials   54
Hygiene   57
Housing Young Poultry   58
Security   60
Routine Cleaning
   and Maintenance   62

**Caring For Your
   Poultry**   **64**
Poultry Behaviour   66
Handling Poultry   68
Feeding Poultry   70
Introducing New Birds
   to a Flock   74
Transporting Poultry   75
Pests and Diseases   76
Egg Problems   82

Breeding Poultry   **84**
Setting Up a Breeding
   Program   86
Auto-sexed and
   Sex-linked Breeds   88
Rearing Chicks Under a
   Broody Hen   92
Hatching Using an
   Incubator   94

Exhibiting Poultry   **100**
The Breed Standard   102
The Poultry Show   104
Exhibiting Poultry   105
Preparing for the Show   108
Exhibiting Eggs   112

**Keeping Other
   Domestic Fowl**   **114**
Keeping Ducks   116
Caring for Ducks   118
Breeding Ducks   121
Keeping Geese   122
Caring for Geese   124
Breeding Geese   126

Keeping Guinea Fowl   127
Keeping Turkeys   128
Breeding Turkeys   133

**A Directory of
Foundation Breeds**   **134**
What is a Foundation Breed?   136
British Foundation Breeds   **138**
   Hamburg/Hamburgh   138
   Old English Pheasant Fowl   140
   Derbyshire Redcap   140
   Dorking   141
   Sussex   142
   Scots Grey   144
   Scots Dumpy   144

European Foundation Breeds   **146**
   Appenzellar Spitzhauben   146
   Sultan   147
   Poland/Polish   148
   La Fleche   149
   Campine   150
   Lackenvelder   150
   Thuringian   151
   Vorverk   152
   Friesian   152

**Mediterranean Foundation
   Breeds**   **153**
   Minorca   153
   Dandarawi   154
   White-faced Black Spanish   155
   Blue Andalusian   156
   Sicilian Buttercup   157
   Leghorn   158

Ancona	159	Japanese/Shabo	188		
Fayoumi	159	Rosecomb	189		
		Pekin/Cochin Bantams	190		
Asian Soft-feather		Sebright	192		
Foundation Breeds	**160**	Serama	193		
Cochin	160				
Brahma	162	**A Directory of**			
Langshan	164	**Manmade Breeds**	**194**		
Java	166	What is a Manmade Breed?	196		
		American Manmade Breeds	**198**		
Game Birds and Asian		Dominique	198		
Hard-feather	**167**	Jersey Giant	199		
Old English Game	167	Plymouth Rock	200		
Oxford Game	168	Wyandotte	202	**A Directory of Other**	
Carlisle Game	169	New Hampshire Red	204	**Domestic Fowl**	**230**
Aseel/Asil	170	Buckeye	205	Ducks, Geese and Turkeys	232
Shamo	171	Rhode Island Red	206	**Ducks**	**234**
Malay	172	Araucana	208	Aylesbury	234
Modern Game	173			Pekin	235
Old English Game Bantams	174			Cayuga	235
Indian/Cornish Game	176	**European Manmade Breeds**	**209**	Muscovy	236
Rumpless Game	177	Houdan	209	Rouen	236
		Barnevelders	210	Silver Appleyard	237
A Directory of		Welsummer	211	Black East India	237
True Bantams	**178**	North Holland Blue	212	Khaki Campbell	238
What is a True Bantam?	180	Faverolles	213	Saxony	238
Sablepoot/Booted Bantam	182	Marans	214	Hook Bill	239
Belgian Bantams	183	Russian Orloff	215	Indian Runner	239
Barbu d'Uccle	183			Call	240
Barbu d'Anvers	184	**British Manmade Breeds**	**216**		
Barbu d'Everberg	184	Orpington	216	**Geese**	**241**
Barbu de Grubbe	185	Buff Orpington	218	Embden	241
Barbu de Watermael	185	Australorp	219	African	242
Dutch Bantam	186	Lincolnshire Buff	220	Chinese	242
Nankin	187	Norfolk Grey	220	Brecon Buff	243
		Marsh Daisy	221	American Buff	243
		Ixworth	221	Pilgrim	244
				Pomeranian	244
		Long-tailed Japanese Breeds	**222**	Sebastopol	245
		Yokohama/Phoenix	222	Toulouse	245
		Ohiki	224		
		Kuro Gashiwa	224	**Turkeys**	**246**
		Sumatra	225	Black	246
				Bronze	247
		Modified Feather Breeds	**226**	Cröllwitzer	247
		Silkie	226		
		Frizzle	228	Glossary	248
		Transylvanian Naked		Index	251
		Neck/Turken	229	Acknowledgements	256

INTRODUCTION

There are many reasons to keep poultry, and plenty of people take pleasure in looking after these rewarding birds. Like any other pet, poultry will require your time and attention. They will also need space to exercise, a secure, draught-free home, and daily fresh food and water.

A regular source of truly fresh, quality-assured eggs is the motive for an increasing number of people to keep poultry. The appeal may be driven in part by concern about food production and animal welfare. Knowing where our food comes from and what it, in turn, has eaten are important factors in many buying decisions today, as are knowing how it has been treated and whether it was reared according to its natural instincts. By keeping our own hens, we know exactly what they have been fed. We have also taken responsibility for providing them with a suitable environment in which to live and thrive. It is not necessary to keep a rooster if you require eggs to eat. A rooster is only essential if you want fertile eggs, either to hatch and nurture the chicks, or to pass to someone who does.

▼ *If you choose the correct breed, hens can make ideal pets for children.*

▶ *If you keep enough hens, they will produce a surplus of eggs that you can sell or give away.*

Keeping poultry as productive pets

Nurturing any bird or animal, whether it is poultry, a cat or dog, makes us live life at a different pace, partly because the animal is dependent upon us for its welfare and requires our time and attention. Poultry can add immensely to our enjoyment of time spent in the garden as well as promote the garden economy. Their comical and inquisitive behaviour can be highly entertaining, and many will become tame enough to handle, even by young children. Taking time to enjoy the presence of the pet and its behaviour, to care for it and reap the rewards, are the pleasures of owning poultry. Additionally, watching a hen turn broody, then sit and hatch chicks naturally, can provide a family with a magical insight into part of life's cycle.

Keeping pure and rare breeds

For some, owning a pure breed of poultry is nostalgic – the equivalent of owning a piece of living history, and the opportunity to keep an old-fashioned breed that may have been familiar to our grandparents. Usually, eggs are a secondary consideration for this type of poultry keeper, since many of the old pure breeds are not such prolific egg-layers as today's modern hybrid birds.

There will be others who, having seen pictures of exotic-looking fowl in early poultry books, are amazed to find that the descendants of those

fowl are still bred. The popularity of exotic breeds is currently booming. Often purchasing such an unusual bird creates a sense of duty to perpetuate and select future generations of fowl in order to ensure the survival of the breed in as good order as possible.

Keeping poultry for exhibition

Few beginners keep poultry with the sole intention of exhibiting them. However, those who have chosen a pure breed because of its shape, character or feather markings will be inclined to compare birds that they have bred themselves with others of the same breed or variety. Exhibiting can add much to the poultry breeder's experience. Poultry owners who exhibit at their local show meet and exchange notes with others, and will often try to rear a bird as close as possible to the written standard for their breed.

Keeping poultry as a business proposition

Poultry keeping can become a small-scale business, should you decide to keep poultry as breeding stock. The fertile eggs, or the resultant young birds, can be sold on either for hatching, for pets, or for future egg-laying. However, poultry keepers engaged in breeding poultry and artificially incubating them to sell for profit carry a responsibility to future generations of fowl and their keepers.

Some breeders may set out to supply a local requirement for free-range, or organically fed, poultry and their eggs. Stringent regulations govern such activities. Unless you have bred the pullets (young birds) for such a business from your own stock, it is likely that you will need to buy them in. Many such birds may have been bred and reared in intensive bio-secure conditions. Finding a supplier that has bred birds in a way that you find acceptable will take time.

Very dark brown eggs, which are perceived to be healthy, or blue eggs, which seem unusual and therefore an appealing business prospect, are produced almost exclusively by pure-breed utility strains. However, utility strains of pure breeds are rare. Today most pure breeds are reared and selected for exhibition purposes at the expense of their utility value. Pure

▼ *Collecting the eggs is always an appealing job. Everyone can find magic in the discovery of a newly laid egg.*

▲ *As well as adding interest to the garden, some enjoy exhibiting their poultry at local or national shows.*

breeds that have utility value do not lay eggs in such large numbers as hybrid birds, and generally cost more to keep; therefore, the eggs produced will necessarily require a higher selling price than standard hybrid eggs. Utility strains of pure breeds are rarer than exhibition strains, adding to the difficulty of locating breeding stock. Few breed clubs have interest in the utility roots of the breeds they represent. However, club utility breeders are likely to be aware of other vendors, and may be able to provide you with details of breeders in your area. Would-be breeders may have to rely on the expertise of just a few utility enthusiasts.

HOW TO USE THIS BOOK

This volume is intended as a reference for those who are considering keeping chickens, or who already own poultry and wish to learn more. It is also suitable for those who wish to develop their interest in poultry breeding or exhibiting. The book is divided into two halves. The first section looks at all the different aspects of setting up as a poultry keeper; with information to help clarify the most likely reasons for buying poultry, whether to choose a pure breed or a hybrid, and the benefits of each.

Buying housing is a significant financial outlay, and choosing the correct type for the breed of bird is essential: dedicated chapters explain all the choices available. Responsible ownership is key for healthy poultry, and every aspect of poultry management is looked at here in detail, including feed types, health issues, poultry behaviour and egg problems. For keepers who wish to develop their interest further, there is expert advice on setting up a breeding program, incubating eggs and caring for young

birds. For poultry owners interested in exhibiting their prized breed or indeed, eggs, there is advice on how to begin showing, and a guide to what to expect at the poultry show.

The second half of the book provides a detailed look at more than 100 popular breeds of poultry, including ducks, geese and turkeys; some breeds with worldwide popularity. The breeds are arranged according to type, primarily whether they are an old foundation breed used to create other newer breeds, or whether they are an artificially created crossbreed, developed from interbreeding other pure breeds. Within each category, the breeds are arranged according to their geographic point of origin in much the same way as they would be organised if exhibited at a show. The true bantams of the poultry world have their own chapter, as do ducks, geese and turkeys. An essential characteristics panel accompanies each breed, listing the key features, egg yield, temperament and housing requirements of each breed to help you decide if it is the right breed for you.

THE EVOLUTION OF DOMESTIC FOWL

Domestic fowl belong to the order Galliformes, which includes guinea fowls, peafowls, pheasants, turkeys, grouse, chickens and quail, among others. These are all heavy, ground-feeding birds. Domestic and wild jungle fowl are descended from the genus *Gallus*.

Four species of wild jungle fowl have been considered as ancestors of all domestic chicken breeds (*Gallus domesticus*): *Gallus gallus* (red jungle fowl), *Gallus lafayette* (Ceylon or Sri Lankan jungle fowl), *Gallus sonneratii* (gray jungle fowl) and *Gallus varius* (Java or green jungle fowl). The wild jungle fowl still exists, although it is known to be endangered in its natural range. It is distinctly recognizable as poultry, but is small and light in weight compared to many modern breeds.

The main issue dividing poultry breeders and scientists is whether or not a single species of wild jungle fowl is the progenitor of all domestic fowl. Charles Darwin was one of many scientists to favour the view that the red jungle fowl is the

▼ It is thought most likely that poultry originated in Asia and that they were spread out across the globe by traders, who carried them for food and to sell.

ancestor of all modern poultry. Poultry fanciers (the name given to all those who keep and breed poultry, often on a small scale), particularly those keeping the older strains of game fowl, are more likely to favour the view that domestic poultry have more than one jungle fowl species as an ancestor.

▲ Gallus lafayette, the Sri Lankan jungle fowl, has been shown to produce fertile offspring when crossed with domestic fowl.

Early migration of poultry

Domestic breeds of poultry have been known to humans for thousands of years. It was originally assumed that domestication of poultry could be traced to the Indus Valley, a vast area that covered parts of Afghanistan, Pakistan and northwest India, around 2000BC. Cockfighting was known to have taken place there at that time and continued to be a significant reason for keeping poultry up to the mid-19th century. It was thought that domesticated poultry spread to Europe via Persia (modern-day Iran) and Asia Minor from this region. Archaeological evidence has since shown that domestication of poultry occurred in China around 6000BC. The 4,000 additional years would have provided plenty of opportunity for different types of fowl to develop

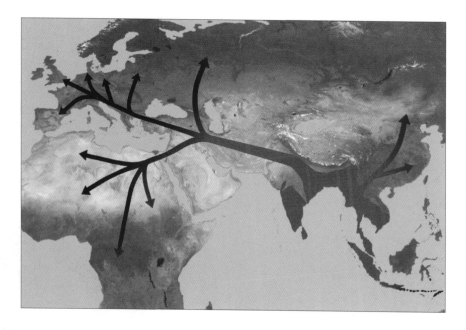

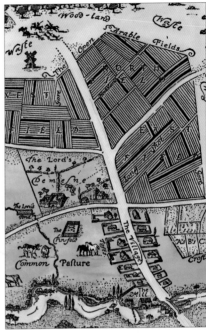

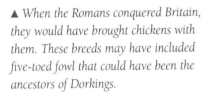

▲ *When the Romans conquered Britain, they would have brought chickens with them. These breeds may have included five-toed fowl that could have been the ancestors of Dorkings.*

within a sophisticated civilization, and with significant differences in size, shape, visual appearance and characteristics.

Poultry spread to America in the 17th century, taken by emigrants from Europe. Turkeys, which are native to that continent were brought back to Europe from America at around the same time.

The development of farming

From the 13th to the 19th centuries most of the developing world lived an agrarian life. Peasants were tied to a manorial system, in which they were protected by the lord of the manor. Strips of land around the estate were parcelled out to workers who lived on

▶ *The traditional farmyard scene in which poultry co-existed with other livestock developed from the feudal system of land tenure.*

the produce they grew. Each worker had several strips of land ensuring that each got a share of the good land as well as that which was less productive. In return for the land, peasants paid a tax either giving a portion of their labour or produce to support the manor house. Additionally common land, not owned by the manor, was used by everyone for growing crops and grazing animals. With the agricultural

▲ *During the middle ages game birds were kept for cockfighting. Tenants may have kept animals including poultry on the strips of land that they tended as well as on common land.*

revolution, the system of working strips of land disappeared as fields became enclosed in order to become more productive, and to keep grazing animals within the boundaries. As understanding of crop rotation grew,

the land was made more productive. Labourers were given land around their cottages, rather than strips of land, and from this a system of subsistence farming developed. Each peasant would farm his own land and keep on it the animals and fowl he required to keep his family. With improved production, surplus crops could be sold, changing the nature of the relationship between landowner and tenant.

The 19th century

It was in the 19th century that animal husbandry developed on a greater scale, producing surpluses to feed the growing numbers of people migrating to towns and cities as the industrial revolution took hold. The poultry industry as we know it evolved at this time. Prior to this date, apart from keeping a few birds for eggs, feathers or for the pot, most owners kept birds for cockfighting.

Cockfighting

Keeping birds for sport-fighting was once universally popular the world over. Julius Caesar wrote that the Britons kept fowl for pleasure and as a diversion. This "diversion" is

understood to mean cockfighting. Early references to cockfighting suggest that for most of the last thousand years it has had a dominant influence on how poultry was selected and bred.

The attendance at cockfights may have included all classes of society, but breeding and creating fighting strains remained under the patronage of the nobility as part of the feudal system. Initially these breeding programs would have built on the inherent hardiness of the fowl.

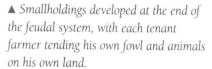

▲ *Smallholdings developed at the end of the feudal system, with each tenant farmer tending his own fowl and animals on his own land.*

Bred for fighting

Britain had early contact with India, and Indian breeds with more muscular stature were crossed with English breeds to develop offspring with a heavier build. Families of cockfighting game developed in the hands of individual breeders. Over time these differences effectively became separate breeds, as breeders selected game for specific features.

Game fowl bred for sport were reared free range and at worst died in maturity. It was probably between the 16th and early 19th centuries that cockfighting reached its greatest refinement. Fights, brawls and unruly behaviour at cockfights had as much to do with cockfighting being made illegal, as any cruelty considerations. A series of laws passed between 1835 and 1849 finally ended legal cockfighting in Western Europe.

◄ *An ill-matched and probably impromptu cockfight – many still take place in Southern and South-East Asia.*

Poultry mania

In 1843, a huge poultry breed was brought to Britain from Asia by British naval officer Sir Edward Belcher. Belcher had just returned from a mission to survey the waters around China, but on arrival, he found that the area had already been surveyed. He therefore sailed on into Indonesian waters, making a fleeting visit to Vietnam, bypassing the northern Chinese ports, before picking up fowl from the northern point of what is now Sumatra.

Compared to local breeds these Asiatic Cochin-Chinas, as they became known, were heavy-boned and clothed in fluffy feathers. They were completely different in dimensions and appearance from any poultry known or seen in Europe. Exhibition of these fowl created massive public interest on an unprecedented scale. In fact, by the time the breed came to general notice at the Birmingham Poultry Show of 1850, the public had already displayed a keen interest in everything Chinese. Writing in 1880 in his *Illustrated Book of Poultry*, Lewis Wright captured the scene and public mood. "Every visitor went home to

tell of these wonderful fowls, which were as big as ostriches, and roared like lions while as gentle as lambs: which could be kept anywhere including a garret and took to petting like pet cats. Others crowded in to see them and the excitement grew, and even the streets outside the show were crammed."

▼ *The Asiatic birds were feathery, and had a far greater body size than poultry known in the West, as well as tiny wings positioned high up on their backs.*

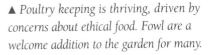

▲ *Poultry keeping is thriving, driven by concerns about ethical food. Fowl are a welcome addition to the garden for many.*

Later developments

Led by much hype and publicity, there followed a popular interest in poultry keeping on both sides of the Atlantic. American entrepreneurs started breeding from and crossing the various types of fowl that could be imported either via England or directly from the Far East.

Brahma fowl arrived in Britain from 1852 at the height of the "Cochin boom" when astute breeder and dealer George P. Burnham sent nine birds to Queen Victoria. The case holding the birds was painted purple and gold and addressed to Queen Victoria. *The Illustrated London News* reported their arrival and described them as Grey Shanghais from China.

The imported birds introduced a host of new and useful genetic traits to the Western world, including winter egg production, and the previously unseen brown egg. The possibility of hybrid vigour was to become an invaluable tool to the poultry breeder, later heralding the creation of the modern hybrid.

BREEDS, STRAINS, VARIETIES AND HYBRIDS

What constitutes a breed? In poultry terms it has come to mean the type, or shape, and collection of genetic features that are linked closely enough to be described as a type. There are more than a hundred pure breeds of poultry in the world, many specific to geographical regions.

The diverse visual appearance and characteristics of poultry, such as the inherent ability to tolerate cold or heat, have partly developed in response to the environment in which each breed originated. They are also the result of selective breeding by farmers. Breeders would have prized different characteristics, such as feather patterns or perhaps productivity of the hen, and would have developed these features in their breeding programs.

While few people would have trouble identifying poultry in general, it is likely that many of us will have seen only a few breeds in our local environment. It is the sheer variety of these birds, their differing temperaments and utility or aesthetic qualities, that appeals to poultry fanciers and exhibitors today.

Pure breeds

Nearly all of the important poultry breeds that we now think of as being "pure" have their origins in the 18th century. Pure breeds have distinct physical and visual characteristics. Later "manmade breeds" developed out of crosses between pure breeds. These incorporated various combinations of heavy-boned Asiatic fowl and the tiny ancient fowl of Northern Europe or the

► *In some long-tailed Japanese varieties, feather length can extend to several metres.*

Mediterranean in the breeding pen. As a result, modern breeds are capable of much variation. These variations will continue to evolve with the environment in which poultry live as well as from human intervention.

Bantam versions have often been developed in parallel with the exhibition strains. These now often out-number their full-size counterparts.

Few pure breeds rival the egg production of their modern hybrid counterparts, and some are kept to add beauty and completeness to gardens rather than for their output of eggs. It is wonderful that, albeit in some breeds in a miniature or bantam form, so many of the traditional breeds are still here to be studied, understood and reared.

It is these pure breeds that attract many people who see keeping poultry as a fulfilling hobby, an added bonus being a supply of fresh eggs. Today, most hobby or specialist breeders are attracted to a particular breed for its standardized show points, such as intricate feather patterns, modified silky or frizzled

▲ *Feathered feet are generally an Asian characteristic, which can vary from the outer shank feathering to fully feathered feet, where feathering extends to the middle toe.*

feathering, great height and reach or very short legs.

The term "light breed" refers to bone structure and body shape. It is derived from an earlier "sitter" and "non-sitter" classification (meaning those likely or unlikely to go broody and rear their own chicks).

Strains

Different strains of breeds also exist. A strain of a pure breed is one that has been developed by a breeder's family for generations, and has been reared and selected from a closed flock. A closed flock does not allow for any other poultry, including any of the same breed, to be introduced into the flock. In this way the bloodline remains pure through the generations, and the ancestry of the birds can be clearly traced. A strain of poultry may also refer to specific characteristics that a breeder has developed within

► *Modified feathering in the Naked Neck breed can extend to a complete absence of feathers on the neck.*

breeding. Historically, breeds may have existed in just a few colourways, or combinations of colours. In order to introduce new colours to one breed, poultry keepers include genetic material from other breeds with the requisite shades. Colours such as Wheaten, Buff, Columbian and Silver, for example, have specific breed requirements. Birds may feature more than one colour, and the breed standard may require that a colour be specific to certain parts of the bird, or predominate in a given area. Varieties are also thus standardized, and criteria must be accepted by a relevant body.

In breeds such as Poland, variety is defined by beard or lack of beard. The standard also takes into account different feather structures. When buying imported breeds and new colour varieties with the intention of selling future offspring, check first with an accredited poultry club that the characteristics are to standard.

Hybrids

Often the birds that we see on poultry farms are known as "hybrids" rather than as pure breeds. These are fowl that are in effect artificially bred. They have been developed in response to market pressures to produce the

◄ *True bantams, the dwarves of the poultry kingdom, often have a low wing carriage and a jaunty stance.*

maximum quantity of eggs for the smallest amount of feed. It was enthusiasts, rather than commercial breeders, who began experimenting with the creation of hybrids more than a hundred years ago. Through observation they determined which hens laid the largest number of eggs, and bred from those individuals. All hybrids have pure breeds in their ancestry. As the industry progressed, hybrids were created by selecting desirable features from different breeds and adding them to the gene pool. Only in a few instances do these hybrids bear any resemblance to the earlier standard-bred utility flocks. Such birds may lay 20 per cent more eggs than their pure-bred counterparts, and are ideal for many domestic situations.

his own flock. To the untrained eye all strains of the same breed may look identical. After all, they all must adhere to a written standard for that breed that has been defined and approved by an officially recognized body. Strains may, however, have subtle variations such as egg-producing capacities, or some strains may consume more grass than others.

Varieties

The term "variety" is usually reserved for colour variations within a breed. There are many colours of poultry, a number of which are from selective

▼ *These hens are typical of those hybrids that lay brown eggs.*

▼ *Muffs and beards often inhibit wattle development.*

▼ *Very short legs are the result of a creeper gene.*

POULTRY ANATOMY

Pure breeds of poultry can be vastly different in visual appearance as well as in temperament, yet all are easily recognized as such. The small head with comb, longish neck and large body make poultry distinctive and easily identifiable, but smaller differences in shape vary with breed.

The skeleton supports and protects the internal organs, and, in poultry as with most birds, provides a relatively light and rigid structure to aid flight. A relatively small head is essential for a bird that flies, since a large head would be a hindrance. The long neck aids pecking and acts as a shock absorber for the head when landing.

Build, legs and feet

Some lightweight breeds such as the Hamburg and Appenzellar Spitzhauben have a bone structure that is not dissimilar to that of their wild jungle fowl ancestors. Heavier breeds such as Cochin and Indian Game have a correspondingly heavy bone structure. Breeders have sometimes been blamed for exaggerating the shape and structure of their breeds. However, none of this development causes distress to the breed in any way comparable with the distress caused to broiler strains when birds are fattened rapidly and unable to stand at a few weeks old. The fact that many breeds seldom or never fly is rather related to the increasingly heavy build as well as to the domestic bird's placid nature.

Like other birds within the order Gallinae, poultry have relatively short legs and toes. The hock joint, where the feathered thigh hinges on to the clean shank, may be compared to the human ankle. Most poultry have four toes: three pointing forwards and one backwards. This arrangement provides a strong support for the bird's body weight. Some breeds have a fifth, non-functional toe. Roosters are armed with spurs on the lower inside flank.

Muscles and digestion

The muscular system enables the bird to move. It also aids the flow of air and blood within the internal organs. Environment and management regimes have an effect on poultry muscle development. Huge differences are found between the muscle distribution of breeds such as Aseel and Indian/Cornish Game and breeds that have retained much of the shape and balance of their jungle fowl ancestors, such as the Hamburg. The shape and musculature of the breastbone varies from breed to breed, and also helps to determine the general build. Muscle distribution is assessed by breeders and judges as part of the breed standard. Different forms of Old English Game are handled differently because of this.

The digestive system includes gullet, crop, proventriculus or true stomach, gizzard, pancreas, liver, intestines, ceca and cloaca. Its function is to process food and water ingested via the beak, breaking down nutrients for absorption into the bloodstream and eliminating waste. Food is stored in the crop, and then digested constantly to provide the bird with nutrition and energy. The gizzard equates to the stomach of mammals. Food is digested by the slow expansion and contraction of the gizzard, and is reduced to fine particles with the assistance of fine grit, which the bird takes in as part of its diet.

Circulation and respiration

The circulatory system transports essential compounds through the body as well as eliminating waste from tissues. It includes the heart, spleen, blood, bone marrow, blood vessels and lymphatic system.

The respiratory system takes in oxygen and eliminates carbon dioxide. Responsible for cooling the body as well as facilitating oral communication between birds, it includes the nasal cavity, trachea, lungs and air sacs. The air sac is a significant feature of a bird's anatomy, providing air spaces within the body cavity that are enclosed by thin membranes. These are connected to the lungs and marrow cavity of certain bones. Holding variable amounts of air, they act as a reservoir for the entire respiratory system. Inhaling bacteria and moulds which are often present in poorly ventilated poultry houses causes the growth of yeast-like fungi within these sacs. The fungi were once described as aspergillus, but are now correctly diagnosed as mycoplasma.

▼ *External indications of health include glossy plumage, clear round eyes, a clean bottom, a healthy red face, and nostrils free from discharge and congestion.*

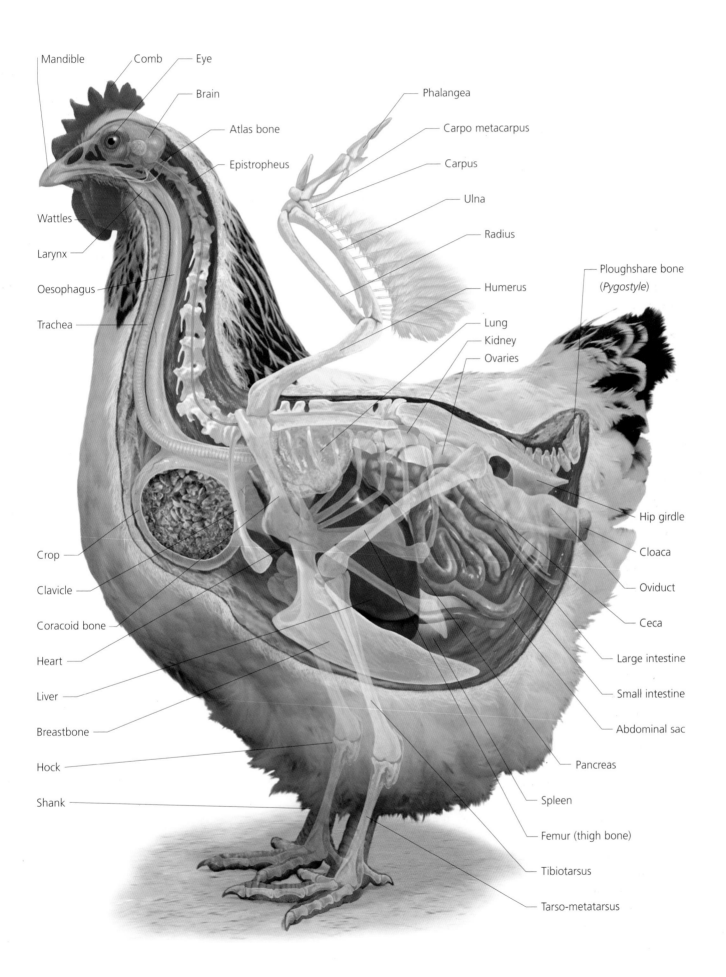

Mandible
Comb
Eye
Brain
Atlas bone
Epistropheus
Wattles
Larynx
Oesophagus
Trachea

Phalangea
Carpo metacarpus
Carpus
Ulna
Radius
Humerus
Lung
Kidney
Ovaries

Ploughshare bone
(*Pygostyle*)

Hip girdle
Cloaca
Oviduct
Ceca
Large intestine
Small intestine
Abdominal sac

Crop
Clavicle
Coracoid bone
Heart
Liver
Breastbone
Hock
Shank

Pancreas
Spleen
Femur (thigh bone)
Tibiotarsus
Tarso-metatarsus

COMBS

It is the comb that distinguishes the genus *Gallus* from other bird breeds. Since the domestication of the ancestors of modern domestic fowl (all of which had combs) there have been a number of mutations affecting the visual appearance of combs.

There are a number of distinct comb types – buttercup, horned, mulberry or walnut, pea, rose, single and strawberry.

Buttercup comb

The buttercup comb is specific to the Buttercup breed of poultry. It is a fleshy comb shaped like a goblet, that sits centrally on the head and is smooth in texture.

Horned combs

V-shaped or horned combs are specific to some European breeds. The two prongs of the V are joined at the base of the comb which starts at the top of the beak. The Houdan, La Fleche, Sultan and Polish breeds all have horned combs.

Mulberry or walnut combs

The mulberry or walnut comb is small, broad and relatively flat, and sits low on the front of the head. It is

▼ *The buttercup comb is unique to the Sicilian Buttercup breed. It should look like an upturned buttercup flower.*

▲ *The mulberry or walnut comb of the Silkie is the shape and colour of the fruit.*

relatively smooth on all sides. Silkies and Yokohama breeds exhibit walnut combs.

Pea combs

The short pea comb is standardized in just five true poultry breeds, including the Sumatra and the Indian or Cornish

▼ *The horned comb of La Fleche accompanies cavernous nostrils, and occasionally a few raised feathers.*

breeds. It was first described in 1850 as being similar to a pea blossom and is a medium-length comb that starts at the top of the beak and finishes at the front of the head. Each comb has three lengthwise serrations.

Rose combs

The rose comb is clearly identifiable by its leader, a spike at the end of the comb that may, depending upon

DOMINANCE IN COMB TYPES

Much of the work into the genetics of comb types was carried out by William Bateson in 1902. He crossed a Wyandotte, which has a rose comb, with a Leghorn, with a single comb, and a Brahma, which has a pea comb. All the offspring (the F1 generation) had walnut combs, an entirely new comb type. When the F1 generation were mated, the resulting F2 generation showed a 3:1 segregation, which was said to have shown that pea and rose combs were dominant over the single combs, thus proving that Mendel's laws of genetics extended to the animal kingdom as well as plants. However, Bateson had chosen Wyandottes, which were the result of earlier unions between breeds with different combs, and this fact could have skewed the results. Comb genetics can be confusing, but fascinate exhibitors and hobbyists, some of whom make the occasional experimental cross. The fact that the purest bred Wyandottes continue to produce a percentage of single-combed offspring could again be the result of their own mixed ancestry.

▲ *Pea combs were thought to resemble the shape of an open pod of peas, or that of the pea flower.*

▲ *A rose comb may terminate in a leader (spike) that extends straight back from a wide front, or may follow the neck line.*

▲ *Single combs with even serrations are expected to stand upright in both sexes, in heavy breeds such as the Sussex.*

breed, be long, short or almost horizontal. The rest of the comb contains fleshy nodules. Several well-known breeds have a rose comb including Leghorns, Dorkings, Hamburgs and Derbyshire Redcaps.

Single combs

Most of the economically significant domestic breeds have single combs, as have *G. gallus*, *G sonneratii* and *G. lafayettii*. With the exception of the Javanese jungle fowl, all the probable

ancestors of domestic fowl have single combs. The large single comb should stand boldly upright in an exhibition rooster, while the comb of its female counterpart may flop gracefully to one side, or may also stand upright. When viewed from the side, the single comb forms a semi-circular head ornament that begins at the top of the beak and travels centrally over the top of the head, finishing at the back. Most combs have serrations, with those at the centre of the comb

standing taller than those at each end. In order to stand upright, the tall rooster comb needs a wide and strong base. To flop to one side the female comb needs to be relatively slim.

Strawberry combs

As its name suggests, the strawberry comb has the appearance of half a strawberry sitting on top of the head at the top of the nose. The Russian Orloff, for instance, has a strawberry comb.

▼ *In some breeds, the single comb should flop gracefully to one side on the hen bird, while standing upright in the rooster.*

▼ *The strawberry comb of the Malay may result from the breed's development in Cornwall, not its Malaysian ancestry.*

▼ *The Russian Orloff breed has a strawberry comb, which starts directly above the beak.*

OTHER ORNAMENTS AND APPENDAGES

Feathered feet, extra toes, crests, beards and ear muffs are fascinating, and are standardized features of many fancy domestic poultry breeds. Only the Sultan breed possesses all of these additional features, as well as an unusual comb.

Distinctive appendages such as crests and extra toes are difficult to perfect in poultry and often appeal to experienced breeders, who thrive on the challenge.

Crests

Crests that consist of feathers on the head, sometimes enhanced by an enlarged skull, seem to fascinate many of today's breeders and exhibitors. The distinctive enlarged skulls are formed by a type of cerebral haemorrhage, and are generally confined to breeds with full crests such as Poland, Sultan and some Houdans. The cranial distortion is sufficiently different in rooster and female birds to allow the sex of chicks to be determined at hatching. Single combs are rarely associated with full crests; instead comb types vary from broad and almost circular in Silkies, through leaf-shaped in Houdans, to practically non-existent in Polands.

▼ *The Houdan crest should be accompanied by a horn-shaped comb, which is small in this female.*

▲ *The profuse muff and beard of the Russian Orloff may be the result of a genetic quirk.*

Beards and muffs

These are additional feathers grouped on the head area. Found in Houdans, Faverolles, and some Polish and Belgian bantams, beards and muffs are caused by an incomplete dominant gene. Fanciers and exhibitors have selectively bred fowl to emphasize this feathery combination.

▲ *The Barbu de Watermael has a muff and triple-lobed beard.*

Vulture hocks

These appendages consist of stiff, downward-pointing feathers that almost resemble flight feathers on the heel of the tibia, at the point where most fowl have soft or downy feathers. This feature has been found to be recessive, and helps to emphasize the amount of effort breeders have undertaken to preserve and enhance appendages that may well have no utility value.

Feathered feet

While feathered feet are an Asiatic trait, there is little evidence that many of the original breed imported in the 1850s had heavily feathered feet, apart from an early reference to Burmese bantams having wing-like feathers on their feet. It fact, there is

◄ *The Appenzellar Spitzhauben crest should sweep forward like that of a Roman centurion's helmet.*

indication that the Cochins of 1855 had little more than feathered shanks. Through selective breeding, by 1895 Cochins had evolved into fowl with the feathers on both middle and outer toes that we see today in the breed. This variation of shank and foot feathering in the original Asiatic imports explains the limited amount of shank feathering on breeds such as Modern Langshans and the occasional appearance of foot feathers – a fault, in breeds like Sussex, that is inherited in part from these earlier imports.

Shortening of the outside toe (brachydactyly) is often found in those birds with the most completely feathered feet. The Sussex breeders who incorporated a percentage of feather-legged ancestry into their birds managed, by 1900, to have standardized a completely clean-legged fowl. However, breeders of the French Faverolles retained some proportion of the leg feathering, along with crests and beards inherited from Houdans, and five toes – a feature of their Dorking ancestry. While all are fancy traits, the Faverolles' utility strains retained

▼ *The Booted Bantam or Sapelpoot breed from the Netherlands has fully feathered feet.*

▲ *The pea comb and daw (pale) eye of the Asil or Aseel are still evident in its Indian Game descendants.*

many of their table qualities, which are still being selected today by hobbyists and some French farmers.

Five toes

The fifth toe (polydactyl) is an important feature of the Dorking and Silkie breeds. The extra toe must have dated from the genesis of domestic poultry keeping, though to some extent these features have been selectively encouraged and are part of the breed standard criteria. In Dorkings, judges and breeders will expect five very well-placed toes. In

▼ *Vulture hocks are stiff flight-like feathers that are attached to the hock, just below the thigh.*

▲ *The Sultan breed has all five appendages: crest, muff, beard, vulture hocks and five toes.*

breeds such as the Faverolles, the feature will have to compete with beards, and in Sultans, with a whole range of standardized appendages. Multiple spurs may be unique to Sumatra game, but as both multiple and single spurs are standardized, they are no more important than the breed's other characteristics.

▼ *Five toes are a breed standard in Dorkings. They are also found in Faverolles, Lincolnshire Buffs and Silkies.*

FEATHER STRUCTURE

Feathers are unique to birds. They act primarily as a form of insulation for the fowl, keeping it warm in cold weather. They also protect birds from the harmful effects of the sun's rays. Feathers allow birds to fly, and also provide a means of attracting a mate.

Apart from in the downy stage, all feathers, including those of adults, can be categorized into three types: short, downy feathers, long feathers and contour feathers. Additionally, the roosters of some breeds may have long sickle feathers at the tail. All breeds have wing feathers.

Down feathers

Young chicks have very fine down, which is quickly replaced by intermediate chick feathers and then by juvenile feathers. Short, downy feathers are found on the abdomen and provide warmth for the bird.

Long feathers

These feathers resemble hairs; they lack barbules except at the tip.

Contour feathers

These cover the wing and tail. Contour feathers include hackle feathers, such as the long feathers covering the neck and saddle.

▲ *The contour feathers of the Silkie breed have delicate shafts and unusually long barbs. The barbules are elongated and are arranged irregularly, not all in one plane as in normal feathers.*

▲ *Frizzled feathers curl in the opposite direction to standard feathers. One form has an extremely recurved shaft and very narrow feathers. Modified feathers are less recurved but have a normal width vane.*

It is the character and distribution of the contour feathers that create the visual outline of the breed. The contour feather comprises a well-developed central quill or shaft, known as the *rachis*. This has barbs, like small veins, that branch off from

it at an angle. The web of the feather is made up of tiny barbules, which radiate from the barbs. These barbules lock together to create a smooth plane, and allow for flight in birds. The lower part of the quill, which attaches to the bird, lacks barbs and is termed the *calamus*.

▼ *Standard feathers, including the quill, silkie and hackle, all have a quill, shaft, vanes and webs.*

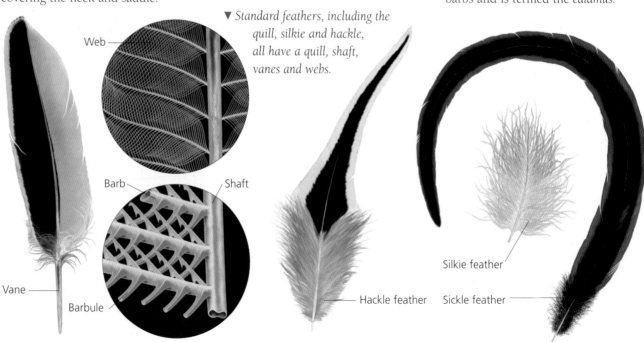

Web

Barb — Shaft

Vane

Barbule

Hackle feather

Silkie feather

Sickle feather

FEATHER PATTERNS

Like feather colours, feather patterns are an enhancement that breeders like to perfect, with points on offer for excellence at exhibition. There are less patterns than colours, but being able to distinguish between some patterns and colours can be difficult for the beginner.

Feathers are the most easily distinguishable features on any bird In poultry, this patterning can show in barring, a feather pattern in which two different colours form bands or bars across the shaft of the feathers, or in mottled feathers which are black feathers with a white tip. There may be other feather colours distributed over its body. Laced feathers have two distinct colours, with one of them forming a clear border around the outer edge of the feather. Gold- and silver-laced feathers are the most common. A double-laced feather is harder to perfect since it has two even bands of concentric lacing around the edge of the feather. Pencilled feathers have a bicoloured concentric band around the feather edge. Like mottled feathers, speckled feathers have a white tip, but with an additional black bar beneath. Spangled feathers have a blotch of a secondary colour at the end of the feathers. Finally, splashed feathers are a dilute form of blue and are not a standardized colour.

▲ *Barred*

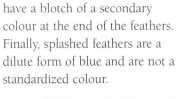

▲ *Mottled*

▲ *Double laced*

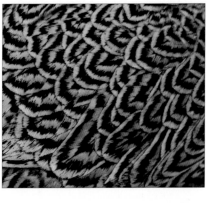

▲ *Pencilled (female partridge varieties)*

▲ *Speckled*

▲ *Laced*

▲ *Spangled*

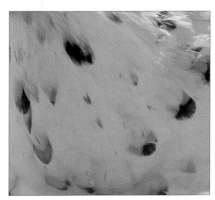

▲ *Splashed*

FEATHER COLOURS

The colour of a bird is a significant visual feature. Breeders who choose to exhibit their prized poultry may spend a lifetime dedicated to perfecting the feather colours of their breed, since breed standards are exacting and marks will be deducted for wrongly placed colours.

New poultry colours are constantly being developed, although it takes time for them to be accepted by the ruling poultry club for each country.

Like the feather patterns, feather colours can vary between roosters and females of the same variety. As exhibition colours evolved over

hundreds of years, there is no logical format to the colours of roosters and hens, and they have to be learned variety by variety.

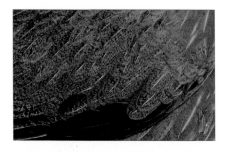

▲ *Birchen (as seen in some Oxford Game)*

▲ *Buff*

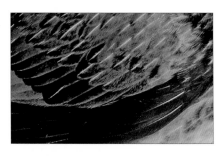

▲ *Furness (female Old English Game)*

▲ *Black*

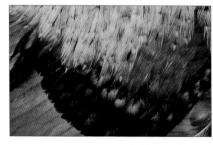

▲ *Crele*

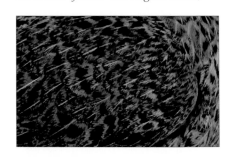

▲ *Ginger (female)*

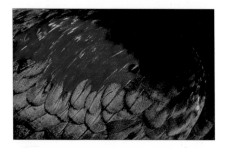

▲ *Black red (male)*

▲ *Cuckoo*

▲ *Gold*

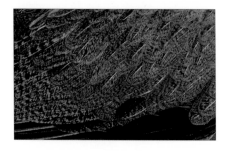

▲ *Brown (Leghorn female)*

▲ *Dark (Indian Game)*

▲ *Jubilee (Indian Game)*

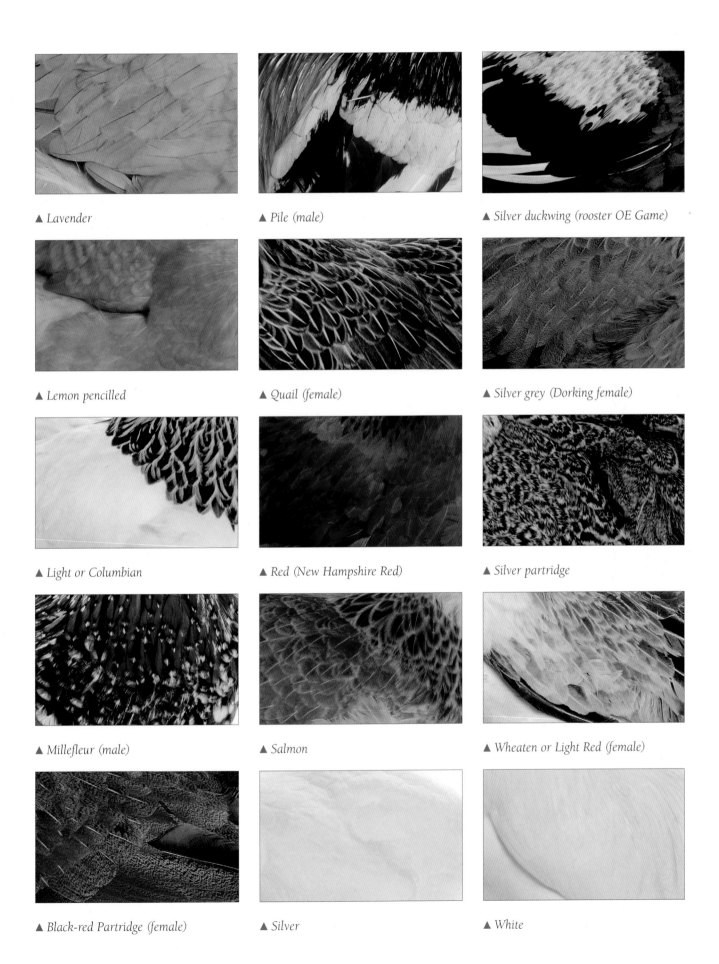

▲ *Lavender*

▲ *Pile (male)*

▲ *Silver duckwing (rooster OE Game)*

▲ *Lemon pencilled*

▲ *Quail (female)*

▲ *Silver grey (Dorking female)*

▲ *Light or Columbian*

▲ *Red (New Hampshire Red)*

▲ *Silver partridge*

▲ *Millefleur (male)*

▲ *Salmon*

▲ *Wheaten or Light Red (female)*

▲ *Black-red Partridge (female)*

▲ *Silver*

▲ *White*

THE LIFE CYCLE OF POULTRY

On average, poultry live between three and five years, with some breeds living longer. They have three distinct life phases: it takes approximately 25 hours for a hen to form an egg. A fertilized egg takes an average of 21 days to hatch. The hatched chick takes six months to mature.

A broody hen will lay a clutch of eggs before she sits on them: up to 12 eggs, with each egg being laid a day apart. Only those eggs fertilized by the rooster will hatch. The hen sits on the eggs in order to maintain the correct temperature for the chicks to develop, turning the eggs every day until they are almost ready to hatch.

The fertilized egg is a capsule of nutrients for the developing embryo. It contains the white, the yolk, an air sac and most importantly a blood spot, which is the beginning of new life. While it is growing in the egg the chick takes its nutrients from the yolk. As soon as the chick hatches, it will take very little time to dry off and stand up.

Birds develop their features quickly. The cute and fluffy chick stage lasts for approximately a month, at the end of which the bird will be developing

▼ *A broody hen rarely leaves her eggs except to take care of her own needs.*

▲ *Running a rooster with the hens is only essential if you want fertilized eggs.*

the characteristics that identify it with its breed. Within six months the bird will have all its adult features.

▼ *The newly hatched chick can walk almost as soon as it breaks out of the shell.*

▲ *A broody hen exhibits specific features and behaviour, such as a raised body temperature and sitting for lengths of time.*

Young roosters

Many young rooster chicks are discarded as soon as they can be sexed, particularly if they are bred for egg production. Some may be reared for meat, or to produce the next generations. Roosters develop quickly, with some light-breed bantams mature enough to sire chicks at four months olds. Most large-breed roosters are at their most virile between six and 18 months old.

The developing hen

Some females may be ready to lay at 18 weeks, although this will vary between breeds; young hens are known as pullets. All birds tend to come into lay earlier during periods of increasing daylight. For instance, productive hybrids that normally start to lay at 18 weeks may start laying tiny eggs as early as 14 weeks, if the birds reach maturity about midway

▲ *Chicks grow and develop quickly. The first true feathers can start to appear in the wings as early as three days old.*

▲ *In this pair of seven-week-old growers, the rooster (right) can be identified by his developing comb and wattles.*

▲ *All birds have an annual moult, during which time they do not lay eggs and start to look decidedly scruffy.*

through spring. Some exhibition-bred pullets may delay laying their first egg until they are well over six months old if they reach maturity in early winter. Productive females will lay eggs until 72 weeks old, depending on the period of their first moult.

▼ *This ten-month-old heavy Sussex breed is in the breeding prime of his life.*

❦ Those in full lay by high summer of year one will often lay right through the winter, moulting in midsummer of the following year.

Ageing hens

Birds have an annual moult, which generally occurs in late summer or early autumn. At this time a bird will lose its old feathers in a specific order working from the head and neck down the body. The result is a bird with a tatty appearance as if in a state of undress. While moulting, birds cease egg production and all energy is directed to providing the bird with a new covering of feathers. While some birds will quickly recover their plumage and soon start laying again, many of those hybrid hens that have already laid close to 300 eggs may be expended, and it is standard commercial practice to dispose of them at this point. Yet given sympathetic treatment in a home environment, they may in fact, continue to lay a similar weight of eggs in the following year.

Some hens, if they live long enough, may continue to produce a dwindling number of eggs for years. Poultry may live for ten years or more.

▼ *A wrinkled and dull face, heavy eyebrows, a sagging underline and an increasing rear width are among the many possible indications of approaching old age in poultry.*

BUYING POULTRY

There are more than a hundred different pure breeds of poultry, including many that you have probably never seen or even heard of, and all have unique characteristics. As well as pure breeds, hybrid poultry are available. Hybrids have been bred for maximum utility value and make up a significant proportion of domestically kept poultry. Being clear about why you want to keep poultry will help you decide whether to keep pure breeds or hybrids. You may like to own hybrid hens if your requirement is for large quantities of eggs or for poultry meat. If an unusual pet appeals, as well as the chance to have a few eggs, then a pure breed may be what you're looking for. Such breeds also bring a rewarding pastime, and those keen enough to breed and rear their own chicks may take pleasure in selecting the best and exhibiting them at a local show. Whatever your reasons for keeping poultry, take care to choose the correct breed for the area in which you live, the amount of space you have available, and the amount of time you wish to devote to poultry keeping. This will ensure that the transition to ownership is as easy as possible. Always purchase your birds from a reputable supplier.

▲ *Hybrid parent stock are nearly always kept in bio-secure surroundings. This should result in disease-free stock.*

◄ *A knowledgeable breeder will be able to point out genetic complexities, in this case, that the black ticking seen in these mature Red Sussex breeding hens is due to their carrying the gene for slate undercolour – an important feature of the variety.*

DECIDING HOW TO BUY

For those new to poultry keeping, beware – the hobby can become addictive. Often, people who buy chickens for the backyard start with just a few birds (three is a good number). They then gradually increase their stock as their confidence grows.

Poultry can be bought at different life stages, including as eggs to hatch, as fully feathered growers and as point-of-lay pullets.

What age to buy?

If you would like to see poultry hatching and be responsible for your poultry from when they are chicks, it is possible to buy fertile eggs from reputable breeders. The advantage of purchasing eggs is that you can question the seller about the antecedents of the parent stock, and how it has been reared. It also means that the poultry is reared according to your own standards after hatching.

The disadvantage is that, for those who want hens only, any one batch of eggs is likely to yield 50 per cent females and 50 per cent males, so unless you want to rear roosters, are able to rehome them, or want the

▼ *Poultry auctions may be a good way of replacing stock if you are an experienced poultry keeper.*

▶ *Experienced auction buyers often take a long look at intended purchases in an attempt to spot possible defects.*

responsibility of culling them, this might not be the most desirable option. There is also no guarantee that all the eggs will hatch, and if they don't it may leave you with less stock than you might like to have. Buying hatching eggs is probably only a viable option for those with some experience of poultry keeping.

Chicks need more intensive rearing than hens, and may need different housing and feed, so unless you are able to provide these, then buying hens at a later life stage may be more appropriate for your needs. It is most common to buy hens as they are approaching their point of lay. Most hens start to lay eggs at around 18 weeks of age. This is the optimum time to purchase hens, since any feed that you buy is converted almost immediately into eggs. Poultry

can be purchased at a younger age, but a reputable breeder is only likely to allow you to have them if you have both the facilities and the knowledge to be able to look after them.

Where to buy?

Breeders may advertise their stock in poultry magazines, on the internet, in a local paper if you live in the country, or, if their reputation is good, by word of mouth. Poultry fairs run by local clubs are an alternative way of purchasing stock, or better still, of gaining an introduction to knowledgeable breeders. If you are looking for one of the rarer breeds,

▼ *As ducks do not suffer from the same endemic respiratory infections as hens, they may make safer auction purchases.*

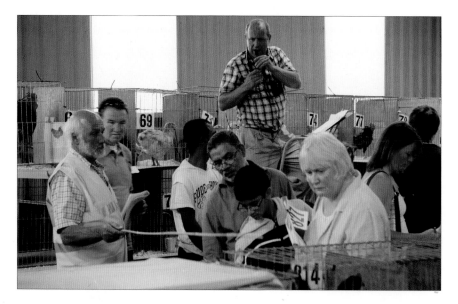

A PRELIMINARY HEALTH CHECK

Check any poultry thoroughly before purchasing it. Look for areas of broken or missing feathers, particularly on the lower back, as this can indicate a degree of overcrowding in the pen, and can lead to later problems with feather pecking. If it is possible to handle the birds, then you always should.

A round, clear eye is a good indicator of health. Any bird that shows any sign of nasal discharge should be avoided. If several birds or pens are affected, it could indicate a contagious infection is present. A clean vent indicates a healthy digestive system. Dried faeces could indicate an infestation of worms, while clusters of lice or lice eggs in this area show that there is an overall health problem. If these are present, the whole purchase is best abandoned.

▶ *A healthy grower of the relatively rare, blue egg-laying, auto-sexing Crested or Cream Legbar breed.*

then you may have to join a breeder's waiting list for stock.

Impulse buying, often from unregulated markets, is an unsatisfactory way to begin poultry keeping. Poultry auctions give little chance of making any real assessment of birds' health or background, especially if you are a beginner. Some of the birds for sale could already have been purchased at auction. For those wanting to keep a few hens at home, poultry auctions are best avoided.

Things to bear in mind

Keeping poultry is a commitment made for the lifespan of the poultry. Whatever the weather, poultry need daily attention, fresh food and water, which makes going away tricky, unless you have friends, neighbours or relatives willing to help out. The birds also need cleaning out and their coop to be maintained. Routine handling must be carried out to check each bird for health problems. Should a bird become unwell, its medication or veterinary care will need to be paid for.

Some breeds are more expensive to keep in food than others. Some like a free-range life, while large breeds will need bigger and more expensive housing units that take longer to clean. You also need a sizeable area in the garden in which to keep them. The longer one keeps poultry, the clearer it becomes that every aspect of their management is interdependent. Take time to think through every aspect of owning and keeping fowl before making a purchase.

Pure breed or hybrid?

If you are clear about why you want to keep poultry, then you will soon know what type of poultry is suitable for your situation. For those whose primary interest is in having fresh eggs, a modern hybrid may best fit your needs. So large is the gap between the numbers of eggs that hybrids lay, compared to the dozen most productive pure breeds, that it is probably best to look at the opportunities for purchasing hybrid fowl first. For those who want a family pet, a hybrid is also suitable, though many pure breeds make perfectly good pets – just choose a breed with a suitable temperament.

▼ *Poultry bought from a breeder can be seen in the surroundings in which it has been reared. A large, airy house and plenty of fresh air provide a good start toward keeping healthy birds.*

CHOOSING HYBRIDS

The hybrid hen, which is now responsible for laying most of the eggs consumed in the developed world, is not a true breed, although hybrids have pure breeds in their distant ancestry. Hybrid hens are the best choice of bird if you are interested in quantities of fresh eggs.

Hybrids were developed in the 1950s in response to the need to supply burgeoning population levels with cheap meat and eggs. Poultry are bred to be efficient producers of large numbers of eggs with the least outlay. The battery system of housing and keeping poultry evolved in response to this demand. Prior to the successful introduction of the hybrid, poultry were reared outdoors, and were prone to disease. Hybrids are now resistant to disease, and are often inoculated to reduce the risk of sickness.

Often people selling or rearing these popular birds will have difficulty in describing their birds' grandparents. In fact, laying fowl sold as hybrids are very like the best of the earlier crosses between high performing in-bred lines of traditional pure breeds.

Egg numbers

All hybrids lay extremely well. They are available in a number of plumage colours, with the various types laying

eggs of a slightly different hue. Nearly all of the brown egg-laying hybrids are incredibly quiet, and batches of these bought directly from a reputable source and observed and handled for a year from point of lay should provide the perfect benchmark to judge the performance of other

◄ Hybrids can be expected to lay between 280 and 300 eggs in their first year.

groups of fowl. The paler brown poultry with nearly white tail feathers are used in battery cages as well as low-density, free-range systems and have proved to be very successful backyard birds.

In performance terms, there is little to distinguish between the main competing hybrid lines supplied to the egg-producing industry. All hybrids are reared within the bio-security of a housed system. All are vaccinated against most of the troublesome respiratory diseases that infect hens, and the salmonella strains that can infect eggs intended for human consumption. These hybrids will usually leave their rearing unit at 14 weeks old and are supplied to farms in large batches.

If you are fortunate, you may be able to share a batch with another customer. The more usual option, however, is to buy from a trader who takes pullets from a hatchery or grower (the point of origin) and has reared them on, ideally in isolation from other indiscriminately purchased fowl. It should be possible to see how they have been reared and to ask about feeding regimes, vaccinations, health issues and on-going care. All hybrids from such a source are expected to have a good health status, but always check.

◄ Those hybrids used by the industry will be bred in small units, and are best purchased as close to your home as possible. All should have good health status.

CHOOSING PURE BREEDS

There are more than a hundred pure breeds of poultry to choose from, all with different characteristics, temperaments and requirements. Pure breeds are generally less productive than hybrids, but many are unusual, with interesting features and attractive feather markings.

Owning a pure breed of poultry is extremely appealing to many people. Pure breeds are less productive than hybrids, though egg numbers vary according to the breed chosen. Pure heavy breeds may lay between 60 and 180 eggs per year; light breeds may lay more. If eggs are a secondary consideration, the pleasure and satisfaction of keeping one of the old and attractive pure breeds will outweigh the egg numbers or the cost of their upkeep. Occasionally, a utility strain of pure breed capable of laying 240 eggs a year may be found. Pure breeds are usually more expensive to keep than hybrids because they eat more food and lay fewer eggs, making the unit cost of eggs more expensive.

With few important exceptions, all birds bred to conform to a breed standard will have visible characteristics that have been influenced by exhibition results. All standard-bred fowl should be capable of breeding similar offspring to

▲ *A blue-mottled Pekin makes an excellent garden companion and broody hen, but is likely to be a poor egg layer.*

themselves, which can, with selective breeding, provide future generations of useful and beautiful fowl.

Pure-bred poultry may also require larger housing and more space to accommodate their size, unless, of course, you choose bantam pure breeds. Many of these miniature fowl are about a quarter of the size of the original breed but replicate them in looks and character. In many circumstances, these make ideal garden fowl. Strains of miniature heavy breeds such as the New Hampshire Red lay plenty of reasonably sized brown eggs. Poultry keepers with the patience to handle and quieten the excitable miniature

▶ *When purchasing a table-type bird (for eating), one would look for both an active fowl and a well-developed breast.*

Mediterranean breeds are likely to be rewarded with quantities of surprisingly large eggs.

With countless beautiful breeds to choose from, it is understandable that many beginners wish to buy pure breeds rather than hybrids.

While vaccination may offer most of the commercially reared hybrids some level of protection, those purchasing and breeding pure-bred stock will generally have to rely on the natural immunity of the birds they have chosen. If the bigger commercial outlets are good at rearing hybrids, the reverse is probably true when it comes to the less common pure breeds. Often, the best stock is found in the hands of hobby breeders. It may be that once you have located a source of your chosen breed, you have to order stock for the coming season and wait for its arrival. Established breeders are often willing to help newcomers on the road to becoming competent poultry keepers.

CHOOSING RARE BREEDS

The term "rare" can be misleading when applied to poultry. In some countries, the term implies that a breed is endangered in some way and that few of its kind exist. In other regions, it merely denotes a breed that is not popular enough to possess its own breed club.

In some countries the term "rare" applies to every breed that does not have its own breed club. This is based on the premise that there are not enough breeders to meet on a regular basis to promote a club for the breed.

The wish to conserve a breed that is ancient, beautiful or rare may be an important factor in the decision to keep specific poultry breeds. Rare breeds are seen less regularly on the show circuit. They may not necessarily be any more expensive to purchase, however, than breeds deemed to be less rare. Many of these breeds remain rare, not because they have fallen out of fashion, but because they are too flighty to be

▲ A red-saddled Yokohama rooster and blue Sumatra pullet enjoy freedom to range. Such an environment helps to promote a healthy constitution.

exhibited easily. Others may be such poor layers that they do not readily reproduce. Alternatively, having been rare for so long, the existing stock may be so inbred that the birds have health issues, and stamina has become a problem. The enthusiast breeder may also be far more interested in the prospective purchaser's ability to keep and maintain the breed.

▼ As the Appenzellar Spitzhauben is a productive and fertile fowl, it need not remain rare, but few people will be able to give it the extensive range that it enjoys; others will find it difficult to handle this extremely active fowl.

LOCAL POULTRY CLUBS

Clubs vary in the way they operate, but are a good starting point in the search for birds, breeders and information. If you are new to poultry keeping, joining a club will provide you with a point of contact. Some clubs organize an annual show, while others see their role as supporting poultry keepers. They may have quarterly or monthly meetings, and arrange guest speakers who will cover all aspects of poultry keeping. The local club secretary will be able to answer most beginners' questions, or may know a member who can.

RETAINING THE INTEGRITY OF THE BREED

Prior to the development of modern egg-laying hybrids in the 1950s, pure breeds were developed for their utility value as well as for exhibition purposes. Utility breeders wanted hens that were productive, laying the maximum yield of eggs for the minimum amount of outlay. Heavy breeds of poultry, which would yield a large carcass, were also developed for the table. Following the introduction of the hybrid hen, many utility strains died out as breeders replaced their pure-breed flocks with the potentially more lucrative hybrids.

Today's pure breeds are predominantly exhibition strains. In order to develop these birds to accurately match the written standard for the breed, breeders

▼ *The White-faced Black Spanish breed is difficult to perfect with its all-white mask-like face.*

have selected and developed their strains on the basis of their visible characteristics, such as shape, leg feathers and plumage patterns, at the expense of the utility value of the breed.

The visual appearance and characteristics of many breeds can easily be recreated, providing the required features exist in other breeds. The Sultan breed, for example, was at one time lost until "remade" by crossing other existing breeds that could donate one or more of its features, such as its head crest or vulture hocks. Extreme care needs to be taken to ensure that, whether utility or exhibition, each breed is maintained to a high standard so that mediocrity does not become the norm. Mediocre birds look like the breed type but do not perform as such.

Because breeders have introduced genetic material from different poultry breeds into the breeding pool of specific

▲ *The Marsh Daisy is an English breed developed in the early 20th century. Fifty years later it was assumed to be extinct, until a flock was discovered. It is now endangered.*

breeds in an attempt to increase the plumage colours, for example, or to improve some other physical characteristic, it is likely that many breeds will lose much of their unique genetic imprint.

At one point, thousands of birds were developed from one highly productive family. The degree of inbreeding needed to fix desirable features within the breed meant that each strain developed its own genetic pattern (genotype). As long as there were thousands of similar flocks, strains of each breed could continue to evolve when crossed with similar genetic lines. Strains kept in huge numbers allowed for some form of reciprocal flock mating so that they could survive as a closed flock.

Huge changes in industrial poultry keeping have seen nearly all of these important flocks virtually disappear. Luckily, some individual breeders have bucked the trend and kept flocks in their families for generations.

REHOMING BATTERY HENS

Battery hens are fowl that have been intensively housed for the purposes of egg-laying by the poultry industry. They no longer have a value to the industry when they reach a point where they are deemed uneconomic to retain. Rehoming battery hens is a moral concern for many.

Intensively farmed poultry has received bad press in recent years. Yet for more than half a century, battery hens have produced eggs and provided meat to feed the world, and will continue to do so in the future.

Historically, poultry was kept along with a range of other livestock on a small-scale home farm. As egg and meat production were given over to intensive farming methods providing sufficient food to feed the world's growing population, the nature of poultry keeping changed. Large-scale, totally enclosed buildings became home to hybrid birds specially bred to produce large quantities of eggs for very little feed. Such housing units can hold a minimum of 10,000 birds, kept in an artificially mantained environment where food is constantly available, and artificial light is provided for 17 hours per day in order to maximize egg production. The intensively farmed hen, guaranteed to lay an egg a day, was condemned to spend its adult life in a deep litter system, unable to express

▲ *Welfare organizations work with farmers to relieve them of stock that are no longer deemed productive. Such birds are found new homes, and make good garden pets.*

its natural instincts and inclination to run, take a dust bath or even stretch. After a time, it was found that hens could be housed in wire "battery" cages suspended above each other. Each poultry house could now accommodate larger numbers of birds in the same space, resulting in a greater yield of eggs.

Such birds are subject to infestations and disease, and often resort to feather pecking and cannibalism to relieve their stress. Revised legislation is due, which will alter the housing conditions for hens, but currently it is legally acceptable to house nine hybrid hens in a cage that measures 1m/1yd square, providing each hen with the floor space of less than an A4 sheet of paper – less than the hen needs to be able to flap its wings. Millions of fowl are still kept in conditions that are now considered inhumane and cruel. Eggs produced by such hens are likely to be those that are the cheapest to purchase.

Consumer power

With growing public awareness and concern for the welfare of the birds, as well as for the food chain, consumers and campaigners have begun to demand more humane treatment for hens. In consequence the market for free-range eggs has increased. Conditions have improved for battery hens; legislation means that farmers of intensively housed birds must now provide cages with perches and dust baths so that hens can take the opportunity to move more freely and take a dust bath. As a result, most new poultry units are now able to describe their hens as free-range, but even the hens kept in these systems will still be considered expendable after laying close to 300 eggs.

▼ *Battery hens are kept in cages with a continual supply of food in front of them. They have little room to move.*

▲ *An intensively farmed hen, with feathers missing but in relatively good physical condition.*

▲ *The same hen after just a few weeks in new surroundings. Ex-battery hens remain productive once rehomed.*

ways that are instinctive to free-range fowl. About 20 per cent of rehomed battery hens will not survive the ordeal of rehoming, despite the fact that they are moving to better conditions. Generally, however, rehomed birds will take very little time to adjust to their new lifestyle, usually just a matter of a few weeks, during which time they quickly grow new feathers and start acting according to their natural instincts.

Productive lifespan

Hens start to lay eggs at approximately 18 weeks old. At this life stage, hybrid hens will routinely lay one egg per day and continue to do so until they reach 72 weeks. Having laid an enormous amount of eggs in their first season, the hens need a recovery period. From this point on they become a burden to the intensive factory production method, since the cost per egg increases as the hens lay fewer but continue to eat the same amount. Such hens are deemed to be beyond their useful life and are treated as scrap by the industry. Most commercial units replace these poultry with a new batch of younger fowl.

Rehoming

Given a short rest period and sensible management ex-battery birds will continue to lay eggs for at least

▶ *Rehomed hens will enjoy rooting in deep straw, especially during the long, dark winter months. All birds are often less productive when daylight is short.*

another year, though not at the same rate. These hens are sometimes sold on to farmers who have adequate, but less costly, housing.

Rehoming battery hens has become a popular and rewarding method of acquiring stock at very little cost, and there are plenty of organizations that specialize in finding new homes for hens that have been rescued from almost certain death. Such hens are likely to be in an unhealthy condition, with feathers missing, and the sight of such birds may be distressing. Many hens are unused to having freedom to roam, and are unable to behave in

HOUSING YOUR POULTRY

Poultry housing must provide shelter from wind, rain, sun and excess heat. It is a place that provides protection from animal predators, yet contains enough room to move and follow their natural behaviour patterns. Fowl have a respiratory system that is intolerant of poor ventilation, therefore the housing should have fresh air freely circulating by adequate ventilation, but at the same time, be draught-free. A roost for the birds to perch on and sleep in comfort at night is essential, as is a nest box in which to lay eggs. Night-time accommodation should be dark, with no windows. The environment should be kept clean, with a fresh supply of drinking water, grit and food, and with an access route to daylight. For many breeds, there should ideally be the opportunity to spend time in an outdoor environment as well as to eat fresh vegetation. Additional access for the owner to inspect the internal house and the birds, as well as to collect the eggs, is essential. Outside the house, the birds require a dust bath in which to clean their feathers of fleas and lice, though many birds will create a space of their own in the garden, if they are able, in which to bathe.

▲ Fowl have a primitive requirement to perch or roost at least 1 metre/3 feet above floor level.

◄ This movable house under trees offers plenty of shade, but the ladder may be too much of an open invitation to the poultry to roost in the trees at night.

CREATING THE IDEAL ENVIRONMENT

Wild jungle fowl, the distant ancestors of today's domestic poultry, would have lived in arid scrublands, roosting at night in trees. Their "run" would have been in an area with a canopy of trees nearby to avoid aerial attack, and with the option to fly to safety to avoid ground predators.

Domesticated poultry have retained their wild homing instincts. From their point of view, the perfect environment is a small, insect-rich patch of land, containing sufficient organic matter to encourage a succession of manure worms that will provide a ready supply of food. An accompanying overgrown hedgerow in which to shelter, as well as forage for a variety of berries, would constitute poultry heaven. A poultry house in the middle of a bare field, with plenty of land in which to roam, represents a free-ranging environment to poultry. When allowed to roam according to their natural instinct, hens produce good-quality eggs and, at the same time, enhance our environment.

▼ *A carefully trimmed windbreak, just far enough from the hen house, provides shelter and allows free movement of the air through the wire pen fronts.*

Choice of site
Careful thought needs to be given to the siting of a permanent poultry house, more than for one that can be moved with the seasons within a large enclosure. Keeping even a few hens is a commitment, and this may be less appealing in the winter months, when

▲ *A house that is positioned for shade under the tree canopy in the summer can be moved further away from the trees and into the light to benefit the birds during the shorter winter days.*

the weather is inclement and daylight hours are limited. For this reason, choosing a site within easy range of the house makes for convenient poultry husbandry.

Remember to consider your neighbours when planning any new poultry house or venture. A rooster crowing early in the morning is not everyone's idea of a perfect alarm call. However, the gentle clucking of hens going about their business may be more appealing, particularly if the neighbours are offered the chance to share some of the eggs.

A well-maintained hedge, like a tree, can shield the poultry house from any prevailing wind. Trees that provide valuable summer shade can also leave smaller enclosures dark and damp in winter, as well as creating a

▲ *Cockerels are likely to crow from dawn to dusk as well as during moonlit nights. House and street lights can also cause unwelcome night-time crowing*

roosting place for wild birds whose droppings have been shown to assist the spread of serious poultry diseases.

It may be possible to site a "lean-to" poultry house or an enclosure against a boundary wall or close-boarded fence. To avoid either scorching summer heat or almost total shade, it will have to be carefully sited, with adequate guttering to prevent dripping water from reaching the covered area.

Daylight and climate

Fowl, particularly laying hens, are more light-sensitive than any other form of livestock. They need plenty of daylight and for this reason early laying houses had large windows and were positioned to capture the maximum hours of autumn and winter daylight.

In a temperate climate, protecting fully feathered fowl from rain and damp is likely to be of greater importance than protecting them

from cold. In a wet climate, a covered area (other than that provided for sleeping) in which to feed and shelter is an essential part of good housing. In high rainfall areas, intensively housed birds kept in static houses will benefit from an entirely covered run. In a hot climate, however,

▼ *A sheltered corner away from the main house is always attractive to poultry of any breed.*

◄ *The garden layout should be planned to provide a clean and pleasant environment for the poultry and their carers.*

providing screening to protect birds from intense heat is imperative.

Many breeds will not cope well with very strong sunlight in summer and will need shelter from it. This latter problem is soon remedied by placing the house close to walls, fencing or vegetation and partially covering a section of it so that the poultry can get out of the sunlight, should they need to. The hen house will need to provide sufficient space and ventilation for larger, fully feathered birds during summer nights. Many birds were once housed in an environment that had netting sides and an overhanging apex roof to assure full ventilation. A fully feathered hen is, in effect, wearing a feather duvet, and a batch of ten growing pullets can generate as much heat as a single-bar electric fire.

▼ *Placing the feed dish under cover can prevent both birds and feed becoming sodden during a rainy day.*

CHOOSING APPROPRIATE HOUSING

Choosing poultry housing that is suitable for the number and type of birds that you intend to keep should be your primary consideration when deciding which type of housing to purchase. Ensuring that you have space to accommodate the house and run is also essential.

There are legal requirements for the amount of space that poultry needs although most poultry housing available to the enthusiastic amateur will exceed such prerequisites. An off-the-shelf system may be a wooden or plastic house, with solid or slatted flooring. The outside should be easy to maintain and tanalized against the weather. The roof should overhang the side walls and be angled so that water drips away from the entrance.

Roofing material is significant, since some types allow mites to live in the surface. When covered with felt close-boarded roofs can provide the perfect breeding ground for mites, which are difficult to treat and remove. A good quality plywood base

▼ Poultry owners planning to move a house on a regular basis should look for a house with wheels or skids for ease of movement. A small garden tractor may be needed to help move larger houses.

to the roof, clad with corrugated sheets, can minimize this problem, and allows for a well-directed spray of crevice treatment should it be needed.

If the floor is a solid wood or plastic, it provides a warm and comfortable surface for the poultry to

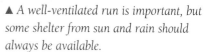

▲ A well-ventilated run is important, but some shelter from sun and rain should always be available.

walk on, though is more labour-intensive when it comes to cleaning. Slatted surfaces allow droppings to fall through the flooring, and may be colder to walk on since air and cold circulates from below. Wire mesh floors may be an uncomfortable surface, and should ideally have a tray beneath, from which the droppings can be collected and removed on a daily basis. Solid floors are easier to clean if done regularly and can then be covered with no more than 1cm/½in of clean wood shavings or high-grade white sawdust. Clean hay should not be used other than to line nest boxes.

Space requirements

For those who have only limited space, it is best to determine how much of that space you have available in a suitable position, and to choose

the breed of bird accordingly. For instance, both large, heavy breeds and active breeds will benefit from an additional covered area in which to exercise. Most of the crested breeds such as the Poland are best housed in a roofed enclosure for most of the year, because of their intolerance of wet crests. Some of the "primitive" light breeds like the Appenzellar Spitzhauben, which require space to roam and to exercise their natural instincts, will be quite at home in a tree – predators permitting.

Miniature versions of the popular heavy breeds such as the Orpington appear to be happy in close confinement. Some strains of true bantams value human contact as well as an extensive run, so ensure that you have comfortable access to their hen house. Large birds clearly require more space than small, and active birds need more than docile fowl. Most standard housing can be modified to also house gigantic breeds, if that is your choice, and if your DIY skills are up to it.

Budget or deluxe?
Since most people keep hens for their eggs, much modern poultry housing is designed for hybrid egg-layers.

▲ *To accommodate large fowl without the run becoming soiled, this combined house and run has to be moved on a daily basis. The run should be partially covered with translucent material in wet weather.*

Certain pure breeds may need more space or differently designed internal features, so bear this in mind when choosing your house. With a huge number of small- to medium-size houses on the market, people thinking of keeping poultry or buying a new poultry house should draw up

a list of requirements that match the breed they wish to keep and the amount of space to hand.

So many types of housing are available that it can be difficult knowing which to choose. Generally, purpose-made poultry housing is the most economical and convenient option. It is unlikely that you could make a basic poultry house as cost-effectively as the cheapest versions on the market. There are any number of types available, catering for all budgets as well as poultry numbers, ranging from deluxe, expensive models through to kit form options. Though "flat-pack" options are convenient, they may be of flimsy construction, and some purchasers question their value for money.

If birds are to be housed in a prominent position in the garden, keeping them in view and a daily reminder of their need for attention, many owners will want the house to be pleasing and complement its setting.

▼ *Modern pressure treatment will add years of use to a wood-clad house, but it is worth finding out if the timber framing has also been treated.*

TYPES OF HOUSING

Many different poultry-house types are available, including semi-intensive systems, combined house and run forms, and free-standing static houses in which an area of land needs to be penned in for a run. Different sizes, to suit various breeds and bird numbers can be purchased.

Keeping small groups of poultry in a garden situation requires well-planned housing. You will also need a management plan that takes into account wet and cold weather as well as short winter days, when poultry barely have time to consume enough food to last them through 18 hours of darkness.

Semi-intensive systems

For first-time poultry owners who want a few hens to provide eggs for the household, a small-scale semi-intensive housing unit may be a good choice. This is a construction where the poultry are locked into an enclosed area at night, protecting the hens from thieves and from foxes. The birds have space to behave

▼ *This semi-intensive house may not be easy to move. There needs to be 20 times the area of the run available in the garden to accommodate moving the house.*

naturally in an area where they are free to move either below or to the side of the sleeping area. Such housing allows for the highest standards of husbandry and welfare for poultry, since it is small, easy to access and to keep clean. Most semi-intensive units are designed for

▲ *Small henhouses, such as the A-framed ark, should ideally be movable, either with wheels attached beneath them or via strong handles, so that the run area beneath or to the side of the house can be moved on to fresh, untainted grass.*

ultra-productive hybrid hens whose small size is appropriate for the space. Many of the smaller units are only large enough to house miniature fowl, while some only have enough room to move for the smallest true bantam. They are inadequate for larger fowl, particularly those profusely feathered examples with feathered legs or feet.

The upstairs-downstairs ark is a triangular house, in which the occupants roost at night in the apex. There is an enclosed part of the housing at the top of the A frame, offering a comfortable and secure sleeping area. The grass-floor area is usually enclosed in wire mesh, offering daylight and access to natural vegetation. Connecting the upper and lower levels are steps or a ramp that

the poultry must climb; an exercise important for the birds' wellbeing. The occupants can be contained within the housing without the addition of a run, provided the natural flooring does not become too muddy. Once it is, the house should ideally be moved to a new patch of land. This housing design has proved so successful that it has assumed a pivotal place in the market. It provides an opportunity to inspect the birds regularly, particularly in the evening when they are roosting, since it is usually designed to allow human access to the roosting area. At the same time it allows easy access to inspect the inside of the house, which is helpful for detecting troublesome infestations of red mite. Designed for productive hybrids, such an ark may also be used for some of the flightier light breeds.

The drawback to this type of housing is that most modestly sized fowl will end up walking to and fro in a very narrow path in the sleeping area of the ark, where they can stand fully upright with ease. In showery weather, the downstairs area will quickly wear to a muddy track.

Unless the food is covered it may also get wet, so that the unfortunate occupants will, on a really wet day, be faced with a choice of going to bed wet or hungry. There is also some potential for stress bullying in small or intensive housing.

Combined house and run

The combined poultry house and fixed run makes the perfect solution for small-scale poultry keepers. Many square poultry houses are designed with a "pop hole", which is basically a trap door that allows the hens access outside. Many square houses without a run integral to the design have the option of attaching a small run to them, so that the poultry can spend time in daylight and have access to vegetation. The run is an enclosed area usually made of wire mesh, so the poultry are free to move but are not free to roam around the garden if there is no one to keep an eye on them. Some designs have a slatted

▼ The type of house where the owner can walk in and spend time looking at the birds on their perches has a distinct advantage over many other versions.

▲ This free-standing house will require two people to move it to a fresh site.

floor cleverly sloped in two directions to give the birds the illusion of going up to roost. Others are set on poles above ground level and have to be accessed by a ramp. An attached run is more useful if it is at least partially covered by fine mesh tarpaulin, to protect the birds from adverse weather conditions.

The availability of a designated run can be useful in the day-to-day management of the flock. If birds can only enjoy the freedom of the garden when a member of the household is on hand to keep an eye on them, and that time is limited, they will also need access to a secure run, even if that space is only small, when the householder is not present.

Free-standing, static and free-range houses

Large houses that hold large numbers of birds, for a small-scale egg business perhaps, include those where the occupants range within an enclosed run that is integral to the structure of the house, or in which a static hen house is placed in a designated area with a larger surrounding area enclosed by fencing. The area between the two provides grass in which the occupants are free to range. In a totally free-range system, it is

▲ *Eggs removed from a large house by a conveyor belt system are kept cleaner and are easier to collect.*

▲ *For those with a small field, a house with a slatted floor may be a good choice. If the housing is moved regularly it will halve the cleaning time. Regularly deposited droppings can help maintain overall soil fertility.*

▼ *These large fowl, kept in a static house and run, will soon make the solid base dirty enough for it to need sweeping clean. Miniature pure breed fowl could also be accommodated here.*

possible to see poultry of varying ages and sexes apparently co-existing happily. Each individual, or sub-group if the flock is large, will find its own space.

Many purpose-built static systems are ideal for hybrids as well as the more productive bantams. The land on which the poultry range is not necessarily of natural materials. This category of housing also includes permanent or semi-permanent

structures containing intensively housed poultry that are rarely allowed to venture beyond its confines. Some sophisticated sheds used to house laying hens have nest boxes that allow the newly laid eggs to roll gently into a collection tray.

Static houses may be the only solution in an urban location where the owner wants to house a large number of birds in a designated space. A lean-to housing design that was once popular among post-war domestic poultry keepers can be adapted to fit a range of situations.

Permanent runs

The base of any permanent run should be slightly higher that the land around it so that water does not flood

▼ *Tiny, true bantams that are kept as pets will, if given lots of attention, live happily in relatively small pens.*

in from the surrounding ground. A solid or concrete surface will require a shallow covering of coir, hemp or even fine wood shavings, and these will need changing on a regular basis. A free-draining base, raised 30cm/12in above ground level, can be topped with 30cm/12in of untreated shredded wood or bark. This does not need regular changing, only an occasional rake over. With much attention from the hens, this lining material will gradually turn into a valuable compost product that can be replaced as it either begins to break down or starts to smell. Poultry runs will benefit from being wholly or partially covered to provide shelter from the weather.

All of the static run systems require more cleaning than movable poultry units. Owners with extensive runs, as required for medium-sized, free-range egg-producing ventures, will have to construct an efficient fence system capable of foiling the most persistent of hungry foxes.

▲ *A small auxiliary house and run can be used for a spare rooster or sick hen.*

Secondary housing

Most poultry keepers are, at some time, likely to require some form of secondary housing in which to isolate ailing or bullied hens. Even owners keeping three or four hens should make some provision for such birds. Nearly all the purpose-built laying houses are built for healthy hens, and have no provision to screen off some of the area for hens that need isolated respite care. A second small-scale,

general-purpose housing unit, with a free-range run that includes a nest box, will be essential for people keeping larger numbers of poultry. Modern plastic housing, which is hygienic and small-scale, would provide an excellent example of a general purpose or isolation unit.

On a simple scale, a poultry sickroom could be a very large box with a mesh top for access or the

▼ *This house has a big enough door to accommodate a large exhibition-standard Sussex, but may not have sufficient ventilation on a hot summer night.*

▼ *These specialist table fowl enjoy searching through this over-long grass for grubs and insects.*

provision of a heat lamp. However, a wire-gated front would give far better human access.

Over the years, the "broody house", usually a small A-framed house, has found a range of uses beyond its original role as a sanctuary for the broody hen and her chicks. The best examples of these had a sliding panel in the roof and removable bars at the front enabling eggs to be carefully placed under a sitting hen, or to give the sort of access needed to tend a sick fowl. In a modified form, when raised off the ground and given a slatted floor, a similar little house could be used to "break" or return a broody hen to laying mode.

Roosters do not need to be kept continually in the breeding pen, so a larger house with a run could be used to give him or his hens a rest from too much sexual activity. A small ark can be used as additional housing to hold a troublesome growing rooster for a few months in the summer until a new owner can be found. It could

▼ Small-scale housing, more usually associated with rabbits and guinea pigs, is also suitable for bantams.

also be used to give one or two exhibition bantam hens or a bird recovering from a health problem access to the best possible show conditioner and tonic – grass.

Housing exhibition birds

The basic principles of housing breeding fowl, or large exhibition fowl, remain the same for hybrids, bantams and standard pure breeds. Protection from the rain and puddles,

▲ Providing plenty of light, a layer of clean straw and a droppings pit under perches covered by strong mesh means that these utility-type Sussex can be kept inside during a snowy spell.

▼ Many exhibitors use the same top-quality, white wood shavings that are used in exhibition pens on the floor of the poultry house. Others use either shredded hemp, or occasionally, wood or paper pellets.

▲ Part of their regular routine may be a period spent on grass, but each of these Belgian bantams will wait patiently to be picked up and taken to their run.

good ventilation and security from predators are paramount. Breeds such as Orpington and Sussex are now far bigger and fluffier than at any

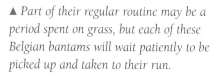

▼ Having been handled since they were one day old, many show birds look for daily contact with their owner.

▲ This wire front of the house (removed) allows good ventilation. Good husbandry and lots of attention means that these bantams are content in a confined area.

previous time. Such large exhibition varieties have become so big that their size limits the options for suitable housing. Instead of modifying large poultry houses, breeders of such fowl have adapted garden sheds and even stables for poultry housing. Some exhibitors, particularly of bantams,

keep their fowl in an enclosed environment for regular inspection and handling. Such breeders may move their birds through a succession of indoor hutches and pens to keep their fowl healthy as they grow. Others will introduce their young stock as early as possible to an outdoor environment.

▼ These bantams may spend time in a grassed run, but still see the surroundings as an alien environment.

BUILDING YOUR OWN CHICKEN HOUSE

There are many reasons for building your own poultry house: to cut the cost of a pre-packaged product; to use good DIY skills alongside easy access to timber; perhaps for the need for a specific design feature within the house; or to accommodate poultry with special requirements.

Before the advent of quality ready-made housing, almost all domestic and small-scale poultry keepers would have made or built their own. While it is unlikely that you will make a house as cheaply as the price of a lightweight flat-pack, there are still instances where making your own may be the best option.

There are gaps in the market for specific types of housing. If the type of housing that you require is not available, then building your own may be the only option. Many features once incorporated into the designs of poultry housing are no longer included today, or modern concepts of how poultry should be kept means that they are available in

▼ The poultry house made from recycled timber will last as long as a shop-bought model if it is well looked after.

less than satisfactory versions. Small broody houses, soundproof rooster pens, and larger housing, tall enough to walk through while still being able to accommodate some of the perching occupants, are a few of the less easily obtainable options.

Additionally, people considering keeping a few hens but who are unsure if poultry keeping is really for them could think in terms of converting a budget garden shed into poultry housing. This conversion should be totally compatible with hen welfare, and if you decide the hobby is not for you, it will still be possible to return the structure to normal garden use. A checklist of the pros and cons, including the costs and type of material used in converting or building your own poultry house, could help you decide whether to buy ready-made housing or build your own.

Thrifty use of materials

The post-war period saw an enormous expansion in domestic poultry keeping. With resources scarce, the majority of poultry houses were homemade, and were nearly always from recycled timber. For those interested in the conservation of a scarce resource, using second-hand materials to make a poultry house is still a viable option.

Parts of the house, or even a small house or broody unit, could be made from new lightweight timber off-cuts if you have access to them. A visit to a reclamation yard may yield opportunistic purchases which may require modification to make them suitable for the planned build.

Bear in mind that many fibreboards are not weatherproof, and all chipboards provide ideal sites for mites, so choosing materials for side cladding and the roof needs careful consideration. It may be possible to treat crevices between boards with mite powder, but not when they are covered by roofing felt; so, while plywood sheets may make an excellent roof, any joints should be treated before being covered with waterproof material.

Aside from cost, the obvious advantage of making your own poultry house is the ability to tailor it to make the best use of the space available. In addition, you will be able to adapt the internal features according to the type of poultry that you wish to house. Many exhibition, large, or fancy poultry breeds have specific requirements not catered for by standard off-the-shelf poultry housing.

Practical considerations

The steps that follow guide you through the stages of making a poultry house or adapting an existing structure, such as a garden shed, so that it is suitable to house poultry. The house shown is a permanent structure, with a trapdoor to allow the poultry access to an enclosed outside run, and also a door to allow human access. An opening is cut into the front external wall of the poultry house, and a nesting box is fitted to the external wall to cover the opening. The nest box has a lid to allow access to collect the eggs from outside.

The house front has a wire mesh-covered "window" to allow light and air into the house. At night, the top of the mesh window can be covered with a drop-down door front, which is held on a hinge. The bottom of the mesh window is covered with removable wooden panels that are held in place with clip-over fasteners.

Internally, the house has a solid floor, a bench, staggered perches on which the poultry roost at night, and easy access for the occupants to the partitioned nesting box area.

This poultry house has been made from reclaimed timber and offcuts salvaged from other projects. It has been clad in shiplap panels, and requires good DIY skills to make a similar structure, or to adapt the plans to suit an existing wooden building. The basic design here assumes that you have or can make a wooden building with four walls, a floor and roof. The building shown has been assembled in a workshop, then dismantled and reassembled in situ.

Choose your final site, ensuring that the ground is level, digging out and filling with scalpings (rock waste) if necessary. The house could stand on treated timber bearers running the length of the building to help preserve the floor joints.

1 This view shows the front exterior wall of the poultry house, with the nesting box area in place, complete with a lid to allow the owner access to collect the eggs and clean out the nesting area. A hole has been cut into the lower right-hand side of the exterior wall near to the nest box area, to allow the poultry access to the house. Above the nesting box is the "window opening", which will be covered with wire mesh and possess removable doors.

2 An internal view of the back wall of the poultry house. The back wall has a bench on which the hens can sit, and staggered perches set above bench height on which the poultry will roost at night. The bench acts as a droppings board. The flooring material is nailed to wooden beams, allowing air to circulate beneath, and a doorway is visible on one side wall.

To make the nest box

Nest boxes can be tailored to suit the occupants of the hen house. Hybrids and most bantams may fit into a 23 x 25cm/9 x 10in space, whereas a large Indian Game bird may need double this space. The four nest boxes added to this poultry house are made of a single length of timber offcut, which is partitioned to make three internal walls. A timber lid, floor, two end walls, and battens to attach the nest box to the exterior house wall are also required. Plastic nest boxes can be obtained for inside the hen house.

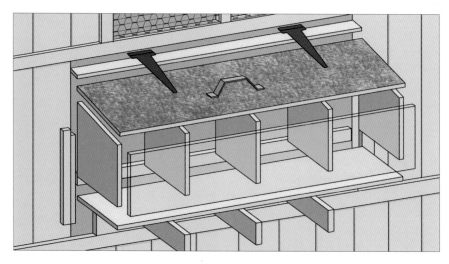

1 Nest boxes have been created by adding three internal walls to the nest area. Battens strengthen the house wall and hold the nest box in place.

2 The nest box area extends from the exterior wall of the house. The lid allows access to collect the eggs without having to enter the house.

3 The lid is attached to the exterior wall of the house and to the partition walls with a length of timber nailed or screwed in place.

4 The rough edges of all timber boards, should be sanded down to avoid owners or birds being harmed by splinters and to make cleaning easier.

5 Nest boxes can be a haven for red mite, and chipboard can provide crevices for them and their eggs, so choose materials carefully.

To make the dropping board and perches

This house has been designed so that the poultry keeper can walk inside and handle the poultry. Such easy access allows the owner to monitor the birds' living conditions and allows him or her to adjust the ventilation as necessary to maintain an optimum living environment for the poultry. The droppings board or bench is set below the perching area. The perches need to be tailored to the size of occupant; the bird grips the perch with the central toe, which is longer than the others. For greater comfort, the front and back edge of the perch should be slightly rounded.

1 The droppings board sits on top of battens which are fastened to the internal walls of the hen house. This helps to keep the floor clear of debris.

2 The board is cut from a single piece of timber. The fewer pieces that make up the house, the fewer places there are for mites to live.

3 The board is fastened to one wall, and is removable to allow deep-cleaning of the house. Line the board with old newspapers, plastic or cardboard for easier regular cleaning.

4 Some large breeds of poultry can be heavy, particularly if a few birds stand on the board at the same time. The space beneath can be used for feeding stations in extreme weather.

5 The perching area is made as a separate unit and is attached to battens fixed to the internal wall. The angle and spacing should allow for the optimum number of birds to perch.

◄ 6 At each end the perches attach to a batten. Right-angle cuts have been made into the batten face to accommodate the perches. Perch ends are a haven for red mite.

► 7 Fit the diagonal battens to the battens on the end walls and hold them in place temporarily with a nail to check the fit. Ensure that the perches are level and have a smooth slightly curved surface for the poultry.

Additional internal features

The roof is a flat surface that fits inside the top of the exterior walls like a box lid. Short battens attached at equal intervals around the internal house walls will support the weight of the roof.

The front of the poultry house has a window for ventilation, a feature that is significant for the wellbeing of the poultry and which is often inadequate in many ready-made or flat-pack poultry houses. The window is securely covered with chicken wire, to keep the birds in and predators out. The wire edges are covered with a thin batten.

1 Roof supports are fixed to the internal walls. Shelf brackets provide additional reinforcement. The roof joists will sit on the supports.

2 Fasten the wire mesh over the window aperture and secure in place with battens, to ensure that sharp edges of wire are not protruding.

External features

The top half of the chicken-wire window is covered by an adjustable shutter, which is attached to the exterior wall of the house with a batten and some hinges. Use a traditional window fitting to prop the window open in daylight and to allow maximum airflow through the house. Two smaller detached doors with handles cover the lower half of the window. These are held in place over the window with clip fastenings at night and in poor weather conditions. Sliding glass windows could also be used. Alternatively, breathable scrim provides ventilation in warm weather.

1 To complete the exterior, cover the nesting box area with roofing felt and add a handle.

2 The adjustable shutter provides additional ventilation in summer and when closed, keeps the house warm.

◄ 3 The trap door is made from a timber off-cut and is attached to a batten, which is secured to the lower edge of the house with hinges. A bolt ensures that the door can be locked to keep the poultry secure at night. This drop-down door acts as a ramp for the poultry to enter and exit the house.

► 4 Finally, paint the exterior of the house with exterior timber paint.

Disassembling and reassembly

For practical purposes and during wet weather, the poultry house is probably best made and assembled in a large covered area. Each section can be temporarily held in place with nails hammered half-way into battens, to ensure that all essential components are present and that the house works at a practical level. The poultry house could also be assembled in situ, depending on the weather; you will need to make sure you have all the components ready. The panels are permanently secured using screws, then the house is clad in weather boarding, treated to prevent mites.

1 Once the exterior wall paint is dry, remove the internal features and each wall panel to disassemble the shed.

2 In situ, the house stands on railway sleepers to keep the floor dry in wet weather.

3 Ensure the floor joists are level. Once the foundations are adequate, the structure will stand securely.

4 The house stands on beams. The underfloor cavity should be blocked off to keep the poultry out.

5 Put the floor in place. The underfloor cavity is an ideal place to position a plastic tray of rat poison.

6 Two people will be needed to lift the component parts of the poultry house into place while they are attached.

7 Check all walls are straight using a level, and that they are secure. The house also needs to be watertight.

8 Cover the roof with roofing felt, nailing it in place according to the manufacturer's instructions.

ADDITIONAL ESSENTIALS

Nesting boxes, perches, feeders and dust baths are essential features of the hen house that can be made or purchased to maintain the wellbeing of the poultry. Lighting will help to secure a regular supply of eggs, particularly during the short days of winter.

Poultry houses must be fitted with nest boxes in which the hens can lay eggs, as well as perches on which the birds can sleep in a darkened area, and feeders in which food, grit and water are supplied. There should also be as much natural light as possible inside runs and feeding areas.

Nest boxes

A nest box is essential for egg-layers. Usually one box shared between three or four hybrid hens in full lay is adequate, but many traditional breeds of large fowl will require larger dimensions than the standard 30 x 35cm/12 x 14in allowed in ready-made houses. The nest box should be filled with sawdust or hay to encourage nesting, and should ideally offer human access from the outside for egg collection. Some provision to stop hens sleeping in them should be built into all nest boxes. A properly constructed nest box will have a partition that denies pullets access while they are being trained to sleep

▼ *Other than in the most secure runs, most poultry keepers will have to close the trapdoor at dusk and open it again in the morning.*

on the perches, otherwise they may get into the undesirable habit of sleeping in the nest boxes.

Perches

All poultry require a sleeping area, which should be a darkened area that does not allow in natural light. Birds

▼ *Birds will soon learn to mimic their tree-living ancestors and climb a ladder in order to roost at night in their sleeping quarters.*

▲ *Feeders should be held at roughly crop height and should be adjusted to allow a feed level of about 1cm/½in.*

obey a natural instinct to settle in for sleep as soon as it starts to become dark outside. If they are not locked into the house early enough, many birds may fly up to a suitable perch

▼ *Birds unable to create a natural dry dust bath will need a bowl or tray of suitable material to dust themselves in.*

▶ *Birds may enjoy a natural bough as a perch in an outside run, but will require one of appropriate width to spend the night on.*

outside the house, which may make finding them difficult, as well as making them vulnerable to animal predators.

For sleeping, all birds require perches, which should be positioned appropriately for the size of bird you wish to house, and should always be above floor level. In most hen houses, the perches are ideally suited for housing hybrids. However, tiny bantams will find the perches provided to be too wide, and a giant Shamo, too narrow. While 25cm/10in of linear perch space may be enough for hybrids, twice this length would not be adequate for a large, feather-footed Brahma. Most fowl may be able to jump or fly 1–1.25m/3–4ft to roost, but an Orpington or Indian Game may need a lower perch.

▼ *Nest boxes should have a fold-down partition to help train pullets not to sleep in them.*

Feeders

The provision of some sort of trough or feeder is essential inside the hen house. As an increasing proportion of laying and growing poultry are now fed "on tap", many people choose a tubular feeder that can be adjusted so that a small amount of feed is always available, while at the same time, spills are kept to an absolute minimum. Wherever possible, feeders should be suspended to about crop height and preferably sited within a covered part of the enclosure.

A constant supply of fresh water is as important as a source of food. Very large poultry units may have an automated supply, but most small-scale poultry keepers will rely on galvanized or plastic founts. These are readily available at most feed barns or pet shops, but most of them rely on the water being delivered via an opening that never seems quite large enough. More experienced users ream this hole to be one or two sizes larger, in order to stop it from being blocked by small bits of chaff. An 8cm/3¼in hole allows free passage of water. Use a translucent container so that you can see when to refill it.

Dust baths

Hens that are free range always seem to find an area dry enough to create their own dust bath, even in wet weather and in the most unlikely soil conditions. Taking a dust bath is the

▼ *A hygienic plastic nest box can be fitted with a rounded base insert that allows the egg to roll to the front for easy collection.*

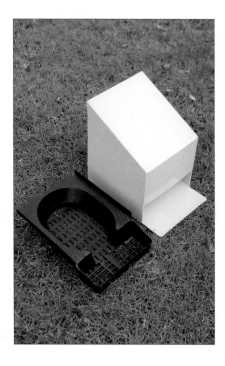

method by which fowl rid themselves of body parasites. Even when they are completely vermin-free, the daily dust bath seems to be an indispensable part of their routine. Hens housed in small runs should have access to a box or bowl of wood ash, fine garden soil or even Fullers Earth.

Interestingly, the very fine dust created by the hen in the dust bath may not be dissimilar to that now used as crevice treatment against red mite.

Lighting (optional)

In the 1880s poultry keepers first noticed that hens kept under the glow of urban gas lights laid greater numbers of eggs than their country cousins. Since then, humans have experimented with providing extra lighting for laying fowl in the hope that they will be tricked into believing it is daylight and lay more eggs.

Today, most industrially reared pullets live under a controlled light regime in order to be most productive. Similarly, both battery- and barnyard-laying hens are usually kept under a regime designed to

▼ *It is control of lighting that accounts for much of the commercial success of hybrid egg-laying poultry.*

obtain maximum output of eggs throughout the year. Traditional breeds, as well as modern hybrids, that live according to natural daylight hours are expected to lay less frequently during the winter, when there are fewer daylight hours. This is because the poultry have difficulty in consuming enough food in daylight hours to sustain themselves properly during up to 17 hours of darkness. For this reason, many small poultry keepers will consider providing electricity to the poultry house, in order to light the house during the dark winter days. A modern time-switch can be set to allow an extra two hours of light per day, which will enable the birds to feed, preen and socialize. This improves the birds' welfare, and also increases the number of winter eggs laid. However, if you keep a rooster and add these extra hours in the morning, you risk receiving complaints from your neighbours about the crowing.

HYGIENE

Practising good hygiene in the hen house and in a static run will keep the environmental impact of keeping poultry to a minimum. All poultry keepers will want to limit smells, flies, noise and particularly vermin, but make sure any rat poison is placed out of reach of other animals.

Keeping too many birds in an uncovered wet run can soon create a foul-smelling, muddy mixture of soil, faeces and spilt feed. This may increase summer fly activity, and attract the interest of visiting rats. Moving the poultry run regularly to allow the hens access to fresh grass can help to limit problems and increase the poultry's wellbeing. Grass that has become soiled or been subject to heavy use by a few hens in a confined area can look unsightly, but will recover. The normal action of grass re-growth and earth-worm activity will quickly disperse a few days' worth of poultry droppings into the soil. Droppings from a static poultry house can be placed on the compost heap and will increase the efficiency of the composting.

If waste feed is kept to an absolute minimum, poultry may attract no more rats than the average garden bird table or compost heap. A precautionary rat-baiting station can pre-empt an unwelcome infestation.

▲ *If not properly cleaned and maintained, a static run can become smelly.*

Pest-free housing

If the air flow in the poultry house is correct and the birds are healthy then any odour will not be that unpleasant. Providing the occupants are free from dietary upsets, even a build up of manure in a droppings pit need not be too noxious. Dust-free cobwebs in the house can indicate air movement rather than draughts. If the birds have clean nostrils and unlaboured breathing the ventilation is appropriate.

▲ *Muddy conditions can be unpleasant for both hens and owners.*

Crevices that could harbour mites need to be kept to an absolute minimum. Having said that, the more accessible the crevices are, the easier it is to coat them with one of the safe, modern, contact preparations. Regular visits to a hen house should mean that you are the first to be aware of any flea, mite or louse infestation. React quickly if there are any problems, since these pests can spread quickly through a flock.

▼ *A tell-tale new rat hole is an early sign of a potential infestation, and will need to be dealt with swiftly.*

▼ *Regular precautionary baiting against rats in a safe location is important. An anti-coagulant poison is a favoured option.*

▼ *In North America the coyote will prey upon poultry and can create havoc in a small backyard.*

HOUSING YOUNG POULTRY

Breeders who rear chicks have a specific set of housing requirements for their stock. Other than those brooded naturally under a mother or foster hen, chicks will need some form of additional heat. Even those brought up by their mother will require protection from predators.

Aside from poultry keepers who hatch and rear chicks under broody hens, most breeders will start rearing their chicks under some form of heat in a cosy shed or outbuilding. This will replace heat which would otherwise be provided by the mother hen.

A cosy coop

As the temperature outside the chick enclosure may rise or fall significantly within a few days or overnight, most chicks require significant insulation. Most brooder rooms are less than perfectly insulated, so it makes sense to erect an insulated igloo around the birds to enclose them, especially if heaters are being used in a given area. Some of the heavier commercial strains grow so quickly that, while requiring supplementary heating, they

▼ *The little apex ark can make a perfect first home for a mother bantam hen and her chicks.*

may also need re-housing. Strains that feather early may be ready to move to an unheated house at three weeks old in the summer, while slow-feathering examples may require an insulated winter home for two months or more.

The difficult transition for the chick comes when it reaches the stage of a just-feathered grower ready to move outdoors. This usually occurs any time from spring to autumn, and requires specialized or adaptable housing if the young are to survive inclement temperatures.

Growers to point of lay

By far the best and most universally popular rearing system used is based on the A-framed ark design. The original, simple Sussex slatted-floor ark used to be the house of choice on most small poultry farms. The slatted floors allow droppings to fall to the ground and stale air to pass upwards

▲ *These newly hatched chicks are housed in an outbuilding, and are retained within a specific area by a hardboard enclosure, which helps to keep the heat in and draughts out.*

and out of the roof vent. With a layer of straw on the floor and the corners insulated with hay contained behind stiff cardboard, this would make a snug home for 40 one-month old chicks. During cold periods, the whole house can be insulated by putting cardboard over the slatted floor. On really cold nights, the young birds could be made cosier by installing a false roof made of wire netting that supports a thick duvet of straw or dust-free hay, or by hanging sacking over the wire pen front.

Stripped of this insulation, the slatted floor, apex roof and sliding wire door of the A-frame ark ensure perfect ventilation when outdoor temperatures rise. On sunny days the solid roof door, which provides human access to see inside the house,

▲ *As growing fowl feather, they may require little extra heat but will quickly outgrow their living space.*

can be replaced with one clad with clear corrugated PVC. The same material can be used to cover any small run used to both shelter and contain its younger occupants. As the birds grow, the ark can house 25 pullets until point of lay.

▼ *Early-feathering chicks are off heat but still kept warm by a false roof and blanket of straw.*

▲ *Growing pullets explore their new straw-littered home and begin to forage as in nature.*

Moved a short distance every day to fresh grass, the droppings fall on the ground to be absorbed back into the soil. Birds reared in this sort of house feather better and easier than in most other types of housing.

▼ *A circle of hardboard within the chicken house restricts the poultry to a small area. Straw is packed in behind to help create warmth for the birds.*

HYGIENE

Chick droppings, that previously dried quickly under the dry atmosphere of a heat lamp can suddenly increase in volume and stickiness as the birds grow and produce greater volumes of waste. In summer, if the waste is left to build up, it may create the sort of warm, damp heat environment in which coccidiosis spores multiply – with potentially disastrous results.

In winter, lower temperatures can soon cause the whole brooding area to become damp and smelly.

Daily cleaning of the housing area can be made easier by covering the floor with sheets of corrugated cardboard. This has the advantage of increasing the insulation in the area, and can simply be rolled up and burned when soiled. The same technique can be employed when growing birds are moved to their more permanent or outdoor quarters.

▼ *Insulation provided by straw will provide slow-feathering breeds with warmth in cold weather.*

SECURITY

With more poultry being lost to foxes than to any other cause, careful consideration needs to be given to ensure the security of the inhabitants of the hen house. The same precautions will help to deter other potential predators, such as cats, dogs, mink, badgers, and even human thieves.

Threats to poultry include wild mammals such as badgers, mink and members of the weasel family, feral or pet cats and dogs, and of course, the wily fox. Especially when driven by hunger or the desire to feed cubs, foxes are intelligent, resourceful and agile. They are quick learners and natural opportunists that will soon take advantage of slack security on the part of the poultry owner, or a temporary lapse in caution. In the USA, poultry are also at risk from coyotes and raccoons. Foxes quickly establish where hens are present, so even though you may not have seen a trace of a fox, this nocturnal animal is guaranteed to know where your stock is kept. Foxes are clever and adaptable; leave the hen house open only once, and the chances are that by morning most of the occupants will have been slaughtered. Foxes don't take just one hen for food. Even if it takes one bird to feed its family, the fox will not leave the house without slaughtering the other birds. And sooner or later, most unfenced hen runs will be subject to a daylight raid, often by a hungry vixen or her growing cubs. If hens are allowed to roam free in the garden, they need constant supervision in order to deter the fox, since the urban fox has lost its wariness of humans.

Apart from the need to keep out the fox, as well as human thieves, free-ranging hens need to be kept from straying too far from home. Rounding up hens that have made a break for freedom might be a novelty at first, but it quickly becomes tiresome, and can be annoying to neighbours, especially if the hens pull up prize plants. Aside from this, the greater the ranging area, the further you may have to look for the eggs. A downside of hens that are free to roam is that they take every opportunity to hide away eggs that may become stained and unsaleable. The answer is to construct a fence

▲ *The increase in interest in pure-bred poultry has been matched by an increase in thefts from exhibitions and breeder's premises. Improving security may deter opportunistic theft.*

around a free-standing house to keep the hens in and the fox out.

Given an hour or so, a fox can quite quickly dig its way under a wire fence, but will usually be defeated by netting that is folded outward at ground level for a few inches before being buried the same distance in the ground.

Outfoxing the predator

Substantial and extensive fence systems are an expensive and long-term investment, so many poultry keepers may look at the alternatives

◀ *Foxes are nearly as agile as cats. They will find it easy to use a taut wire fence as a ladder and climb into the house, whereas a less rigid fence will deter them.*

SHORTENING POULTRY WINGS

Some of the lighter breeds of fowl are capable of flying over fencing, and may need to have the primary feathers on one wing painlessly shortened, a procedure that leaves the birds sufficiently out of balance to deter them from flying. The procedure may have to be repeated after the annual moult, and can be carried out by anyone competent in handling poultry. Use a pair of sharp, clean scissors to clip the primary flight feathers to half their original length.

▼ *Before shortening.*

▼ *After shortening.*

before being convinced that such an outlay is necessary. Electric fence systems can be used to stop predators from burrowing under or scaling a permanent fence. In a modified form, they can be used to keep the predator at a distance from the small run. All electric fence systems rely on a fox or coyote (in the US) having once been given a sharp shock, thereafter treating any similar wires with some deference. The message to the fox can be reinforced by applying some strong-smelling liquid. Cheap scent, timber preservative and human urine have all been tried. The same product can be used on a temporary house to keep a fox away from an isolated sitting hen.

Plastic and wire mesh fence systems can be used effectively to deter predators, even though the bottom of the fence and some of the vertical wires are not electrically charged. There are few reports of

▶ *An electric fence along a perimeter fence may soon deter all the local foxes.*

animals jumping over or burrowing under this sort of fence. However, some hens will either fly over, or worse, get a shock on their way out, and then be reluctant to make the return trip. Some larger poultry units invest in a dual system of traditional perimeter fence reinforced by a single low strand of electrified wire. The way that foxes approach a permanent fence means that an electrified wire positioned 15cm/6in from the fence will deter them from attempting to climb over, or burrow under, the obstruction.

All electric fences rely on an energizer to either transform a small, low-voltage battery supply into a sharp, stinging shock, or mains voltage scaled down to a similar but still harmless level. The efficiency of the system and the distance over which it will be effective is determined by how well the energizer's second wire can be earthed. Even a single electrified wire, if kept in situ can act as a deterrent to a fox in the same way that a similar but smaller output unit, powered by a battery, can be used, to energize a bungee wire system. Some of the more powerful fence energizers may scorch young grass, so any vegetation in close proximity to the wire will need to be regularly trimmed or sprayed.

▼ *Predators make unwelcome visits to poultry houses, but will soon learn to associate a chicken house with an unpleasant experience if a small-voltage electric shock is received.*

ROUTINE CLEANING AND MAINTENANCE

Hygiene and ease of cleaning are obviously priorities when choosing poultry housing. Regular cleaning and maintenance will not only ensure proper hygiene but also prolong the life of housing and runs, making life more pleasant for the occupants.

Poultry and their living environment must be kept as clean as possible so that the eggs they have laid arrive in the kitchen or hatchery in prime condition. In any case, if poultry live close to humans, an unsavoury environment that smells unpleasant will affect their owners too.

The easier a house is to clean, the more often it is likely to be cleaned, so this is important to consider when purchasing a house. A housing system in which the poultry spend a lot of time in a run or a grassed enclosure may take less time to clean than a static house in which the birds spend most of their time indoors. A house that has an integral grass-covered run and can be moved regularly to a new site may be the perfect choice, that is, until wet weather creates quantities of mud that is carried inside by the occupants.

Cleaning the house

Modest numbers of growing chicks in a house soon produce enough damp faeces for their bedding to need changing on a daily basis. Housing with slatted flooring that allows most of the debris to fall between the slats has much to recommend it, but only if the slats are cleaned on a regular basis.

Increased quantities of soya protein in poultry feed is often blamed for poultry droppings becoming sticky and gooey, making the chore of cleaning harder. Domestic pressure washers are useful cleaning tools. If all the poultry are disease-free, then regular household cleaning products will suffice for cleansing poultry housing. However, when cleaning to

▲ *Pressure-washing slatted floors is a routine task between housing batches of growing poultry. Disinfectant may be applied at the point when all organic matter has been removed.*

contain an outbreak of disease, a specialized germicidal preparation should be used.

Many cleaning tasks can be simplified, for instance, cover areas under perches with either small sheets of polythene that can be hosed off, or corrugated cardboard that can be composted. Alternatively, certain areas can be covered with an inert material: wood shavings, absorbent wood pellets, or more readily compostable straw and hemp products.

Keeping eggs clean

Dirt can help germs to penetrate eggshells, so keeping eggs clean is a priority, whether they are for eating or

▲ *This Sussex ark, the universal rearing choice, will give years of useful service if regularly cleaned and preserved.*

hatching; collect eggs regularly. Chicks should ideally hatch germ-free. However, washing dirty eggs has been shown to help germs to penetrate the shell. Approved germicidal products are available to sanitize eggs intended for incubation. As hens rarely foul the nest box, a handful of inert material that is changed on an almost daily basis can go a long way to keeping it and the newly laid eggs perfectly clean.

Maintenance

An annual or bi-annual application of a modern wood treatment will help to prevent rot in woodwork that has not been pressure-treated, but will not control red mite, which live in crevices in the house.

▲ *Spraying crevices to kill red mite must be done on a regular basis to keep the pest at bay.*

▲ *A strong wire grille enables poultry to walk over the top of a droppings pit under the rack of perches.*

▲ *One of the new plastic nest boxes complete with pull-out liner can ease the work of keeping the eggs and nest clean.*

If you discover an infestation of red mite, check to see if they have spread, and re-roof the house if necessary with other materials.

Good husbandry can extend to cultivating and replanting runs with fresh grass if it has become stale or unsightly through overuse, or to provide a crop of fast-growing foliage that may be used to supplement food.

Most small-scale poultry keepers who keep their birds within a confined and shared area will opt for ultimate cleanliness. This means that floors are kept clean and covered with wood products which are inert and slow to break down. Other owners with larger gardens may view poultry droppings as the basis of an active compost system which will ultimately

be used to grow food for the poultry and for their own consumption. Here, a regular cleaning routine will be just as important as in any other system. It is possible to line the floor of commonly used areas under perches with a sheet of cardboard. This can be removed to the compost heap, where it will quickly break down into usable compost.

Changing the bedding

1 Straw or softer hay is the traditional poultry litter used to line the nest boxes, but many owners now prefer wood shavings.

2 Used straw and the accumulated droppings are a valuable part of the garden compost heap. Bales of straw can be bought from suppliers.

3 Rather than using a large quantity of straw or hay, it is better to use a small amount that can be changed as soon as it becomes soiled.

CARING FOR YOUR POULTRY

Good husbandry is imperative to every successful poultry enterprise, whether you have one or two birds in the garden or a small flock from which you sell eggs. Keeping the fowl healthy and their living conditions in good order makes for content hens. Observing and understanding the young bird's natural behaviour, and providing them with an environment that promotes that behaviour, is key to their wellbeing. Hens in good health need less intensive care and attention. They can also add significantly to the garden economy, as well as promoting your own pleasure at spending time in the garden. Not only do hens provide you with eggs, if left to range free they can play a role in the garden's ecosystem. Allowing poultry to eat any crop residue from the vegetable garden increases their dietary range. They, in turn, will provide manure beneficial to the health of the soil. Of all the attributes that make a good poultry keeper, the most significant is the ability to recognize potential problems and nip them in the bud. This means carrying out regular routine inspections of each hen. Learning how to handle them correctly and knowing what to look for will make this task easier.

▲ *A large poultry feeder will allow numerous birds to feed at the same time and should counter any anti-social behaviour.*

◄ *Dark Dorkings enjoy a free-range and natural environment, one that is ideal for most breeds of poultry.*

POULTRY BEHAVIOUR

If you keep a few hens in the back garden you should aim to provide an environment that promotes their natural behaviour. It is essential for a hen's welfare that it is allowed to live according to its instincts, and this is key to any organic or free-range environment.

Should you leave a hen to its own devices in a free-ranging environment, it will spend its time grazing, pecking the ground, scratching in the earth and bathing in the dust. However, unless you are around most of the time to keep predators at bay, most poultry will spend a significant amount of time in a run, and be let out only occasionally to roam in the garden.

Poultry are social birds with a strong social instinct to interact with each other. They naturally live in a small flock, and require the company of other birds, no matter how few. Birds naturally roost together and forage separately. A flock creates the ideal environment to provide each hen with a sense of safety. Within the flock, a pecking order will be

▶ *Some hens habitually choose awkward places to lay their eggs.*

established in which stronger, dominant birds top a hierarchy, and birds with a more passive nature may be bullied. However, birds will not necessarily bully each other unless other factors promote it, such as inadequate space at feeding stations or the introduction of new and unfamiliar birds to the flock.

Ruling the roost

More than one male may be able to co-exist with females in a flock without roosters fighting each other for supremacy, but much depends upon the breed. Males that have been brought up together are more likely to live companionably, but some strains of game breeds are capable of killing even adolescent siblings. Senior males that have a perceived entitlement to remain at the heart of the flock may banish younger roosters

to the periphery. If a batch of young males in a flock starts to become aggressive and establish a pecking order, an older rooster put with them will act as a "policeman". If there are enough hens to go around, all should

▼ *Hens peck for tiny insects and even yeasts to augment their diet. This habit also prevents boredom.*

▼ *He may be small, but being older, this bantam rooster uses this seniority to keep the peace among the much larger adolescent growers.*

live companionably. Since many egg-laying flocks are all female, older female hens may also rule the roost in the same way as do aggressive males. A hen or rooster that becomes too dominant can be separated from the flock by being kept in different housing that is still within view of the flock. A trial reintroduction after a few days will establish whether the bullying behaviour has been circumvented.

Feather pecking

This problem is at its worst during the long daylight hours of summer, when poultry become bored. The dominant birds may turn their attention to a more docile bird that is lower in seniority and peck at it, removing patches of its feathers. A flock of birds may also "attack" newly introduced birds, or peck an unhealthy bird, even occasionally to death. Such aggression may be upsetting to witness and seem barbaric, particularly if you imagined happy birds clucking around your garden. This is a behaviour pattern

that affects egg-laying poultry, and is a serious problem for the poultry industry, particularly where birds are intensively housed.

It is thought that feather pecking occurs because the food that the birds are provided with is either so complete that it frustrates their natural inclination to peck for food, or that it is deficient in minerals and nutrients, resulting in antisocial behaviour. Feather pecking has been seen to lessen if the birds' diet is changed to a high-fibre one that the birds have to keep eating for longer in order to get the nutritional levels that they need, leaving less time for boredom.

Groups of differently coloured hybrids or crossbred layers housed in a small run may also experience problems. The narrow run means that the back of each fowl is always in front of another bird, particularly so if the birds are semi-intensively housed. While the birds may have been reared together and initially cohabited comfortably, on moulting they see that each bird has differing colour feather quills, and inquisitive feather

▲ *A cabbage hung at head height or higher can supply valuable nutrients, and help prevent boredom, bullying and feather pecking.*

picking may begin, which soon progresses to pecking. During the short winter days, there is also competition for trough space, which may create additional problems.

For most of the year, dry mash in the hopper occupies the birds for longer than pellets, thereby reducing the time for them to get into mischief. In a confined space, a cabbage hung at head height rather than thrown on the ground can be of interest to the birds, but may leave some looking for something else to peck.

The problem can be partially resolved by reviewing the housing arrangements. In a small combined house and run system, houses with an upstairs sleeping and nest box area have the advantage of allowing birds to get out of each others' way. This also permits a better view of the birds' behaviour, and the high perch in the sleeping area makes inspecting them for damage easier. Canvas saddles can protect vulnerable breeding hens. However, feather pecking and cannibalism have differing causes, which can be difficult to comprehend.

▼ *Poultry will often be found enjoying a communal sunbathe or dust bath.*

▼ *Feather pecking may have complex causes and triggers.*

HANDLING POULTRY

While behaviour and the readiness of poultry to be handled may vary from breed to breed, it is the way that they are treated when chicks that most affects how poultry view humans, as well as how relaxed they are when they are handled.

Breeds vary significantly in temperament, from quiet and calm heavy breeds to flighty light breeds such as Hamburgs and Anconas. Hybrid strains that have been selected for their calmness in industrial situations may be the quietest and easiest to manage of all poultry. The nature of the breed determines how easy poultry are to handle, and so it follows that those new to poultry keeping would be best advised to choose a breed that doesn't mind, or even enjoys, being handled.

Nearly all the exhibition strains of large and bantam heavy, soft-feather breeds are quiet by nature and easy to handle. It is far easier to manage a flock of reasonably docile fowl than one of active fowl. It is also easier to treat an ailing individual if the bird is used to being handled.

▼ *Game fowl are among the most active, but remain calm when held at the "point of balance" by an experienced handler.*

Not all breeds or strains cope well with being handled. Fanciers keeping ancient populations of poultry breeds that are capable of living in naturally challenging situations should expect their flock to be extremely active and wary of being handled. These are birds that are best observed from a distance. Breeds such as Derbyshire Redcap, for instance, which are

▶ *A younger bird with its thighs gently but firmly held and supported on a forearm can be turned to be examined.*

PICKING UP FOWL

Handling poultry starts with knowing how to catch a hen, pick it up and hold it. Most egg-laying hybrids kept by professional producers are so quiet and tame that they will walk over your feet. Even with such calm creatures it is best to wait until a group of them are relaxing on an easily assessable perch before attempting to hold one, preferably at dusk or in subdued light.

Since airborne attack has always been a major threat to poultry, they are always far more at ease when approached at their level, rather than having a head and shoulders suddenly loom over them, and a pair of hands make a quick grab. With the growing confidence of the handler, the birds will accept being handled and it will soon be easy to examine the fowl in detail.

▲ *Approach the bird quietly when it is settled. Do not loom over it. Gently run your hands over the feathers towards the tail as if stroking a cat. Gently gather the wings around the bird's body.*

▲ *Gather the bird in your hands with one hand high on its thighs and the other thumb in the middle of its back. Gather the far wing around the bird, then gently lift her off the perch, possibly cradling her near side against your chest.*

▲ *Experienced breeders may appear to pick up day-old chicks by the handful, but the beginner would be best to gently gather them in both hands.*

evolved in a form that still enables them to look after themselves in challenging environments, will not welcome a high degree of human contact. Even exhibition breeds of

▼ *Older fowl used to being handled and loved by an owner will actually enjoy human contact.*

flighty birds that are used to expert handling will display a degree of activity in the show pen.

Handling chicks

All farmed birds are affected by the conditions in which they are kept and reared. Chicks, particularly bantams, brought up under a hen that has been handled from an early age will, when handled from one day old, soon learn to feed out of their owner's hand. Chicks hatched in an incubator will soon be accustomed to handling.

▲ *Very small children who love to handle chicks will need to be cautioned about grasping them too tightly, and are best encouraged to allow baby chicks to walk on to an open hand. In the same way, older children are best introduced to poultry by standing still and letting fowl walk around their feet, perhaps initially encouraged by a handful of grain.*

Hybrid fowl that have been selected for their calm behaviour may take months of careful handling before becoming even reasonably tame.

Removing and replacing a hen from a cage

1 A reasonably quiet hen can be gently turned to face an open door and then eased out of its pen.

2 The hen can be returned to the cage after being handled if allowed to walk in rather than being pushed.

FEEDING POULTRY

Like humans, poultry require a nutritionally balanced diet if they are to remain in good health and produce good quality eggs with golden yolks and strong shells. How and what to feed your poultry is a fundamental part of what every poultry keeper needs to know.

In the wild, poultry are sustained by a high-protein insect diet, as well as by the seeds, berries and foliage for which they forage. This comprises a rich source of nutrients that they peck at the ground to locate, or nip from the hedgerows. Wild birds will never consume to excess, and stop eating as soon as they have a full nutritional balance. Poultry only eat in daylight, so they need to satisfy all their food requirements in that time. In the summer, when there are long daylight hours, this is relatively easy since they have plenty of time to feed. In winter, however, some poultry can struggle to access all the nutrients they need to sustain them through short daytime hours and the night.

Vegetation

Grass contains essential nutrients that will vary according to the season as well as how often a run can be moved. Poultry that are free to range

▲ *The brassica family, which includes cabbage, cauliflower, broccoli and turnip, provides valuable nutrition.*

have the opportunity to find a proportion of their own food. Grass is essential to their diet and it is almost always possible to provide, especially where a movable run is employed.

For poultry confined to runs, hang a whole vegetable on a length of strong string and tie it at just above the birds' head height. The birds will

▲ *A balanced diet can be provided in pellet or mash form. Pellets are digested faster and are ideal for winter.*

jump to peck at the vegetable, providing them with a valuable distraction and thus preventing boredom. However, if you provide such a foodstuff and suddenly withdraw it, you will leave a gap in the birds' routine, and it may lead to problems of feather pecking.

Formulated poultry feed

The amount of feed consumed will vary enormously according to the size of bird and the amount of natural material it is able to find. A large fowl may consume 125g/4½oz of feed a day; some large exhibition fowl can eat far more. At the other end of the scale, the smallest Serama may eat less than 25g/1oz a day. While grass and vegetation add much to the diet and general wellbeing of poultry, bulkier supplementary food products

◀ *In the spring, grass can comprise more than 20 per cent protein for the poultry. Its high carotene content helps to create an egg yolk of good quality with a strong yellow colour.*

are necessary in all feeding regimes. Formulated poultry food needs to be kept in hoppers or troughs under cover so that the contents do not get wet. Unless consumed quickly, wet food will inevitably become smelly and unsavoury.

Complete layers' rations, as proprietary feeds are known, are cereal-based and contain between 16 and 18 per cent protein, most of which is derived from soya bean products. These foods are appropriate to give to birds that are about to come into lay or are already laying eggs.

All the complete feeds intended for adult fowl are available either ground into meal or compressed into small pellets. The latter is almost dust free and is less wasteful than meal if spilt.

Mash is also available, a soft meal similar to ground-up pellets, but with a slightly lower nutritional value. This is because mash is usually fed to intensively housed birds and is thus available to eat from a hopper all day long. Since poultry only eat the amount of food that their bodies require, they need to keep eating mash in order to get their essential quota of nutrients. The theory is that if poultry spend more time eating they are less inclined to indulge in other, more antisocial, behaviour. Since intensively housed birds are likely to live in artificial light for 16 or 17 hours per day, they have sufficient time to eat their way through the day and get their full nutrient requirement. Mash is not suitable for birds that are free to roam and are able to forage for their own food, unless they are ex-battery hens used to a diet of mash. In this case, they should be fed higher-quality food mixed with the mash until such time as the mash can be removed.

Birds fed on pellets are able to consume their daily allowance in far less time than those fed on meal or dry mash. This is an advantage during the short winter days, when birds living according to natural daylight hours have less time to take in all the nutrients that they require to keep them going through the dark hours. During the longer, bright summer days, however, birds that eat quickly, particularly those that are semi-intensively housed birds, have time to become bored and start feather pecking and bullying.

POULTRY FEED
Nearly all of the available proprietary laying feeds, meaning feeds for egg-layers, that are available are based on years of research into the nutritional needs of the commercial laying hen, and have been designed to take care of their requirements without the addition of any other feed. All are cereal-based, with the addition of protein.

▲ *Pellets consist of compressed mash. This form is less likely to be blown away or lost when spilled.*

▲ *Mash or meal consists of ground cereals and other nutrients mixed together to provide a complete and balanced diet.*

▲ *Chick crumbs consist of specially formulated feed that has first been made into pellets and then ground to optimum size for chicks to eat.*

▲ *Mixed corn contains whole mixed wheat and broken maize grains. It is high in energy but lacks nutrients.*

▲ *Wheat may be purchased direct from a farm, but lacks the very high energy quotient given by added maize.*

▲ *Grit helps digestion and should be made available to fowl unlikely to access a natural source.*

▲ *Oyster shell assists digestion and can provide calcium, which is necessary to create healthy eggshells.*

▲ Trough and drinking space will need to be increased as the flock grow.

One solution could be to change to mash or a meal formula that takes longer to consume but will lack some nutrients. In the winter, poultry should get the food they need quickly, while in summer, providing feed of a lower nutritional value ensures that they eat for longer and have less opportunity to become bored.

Adding any extra grain to a formulated feed will alter the carefully calculated optimum nutritional value of it and change the ratio of protein to starch of the feed. Birds fed such a low-nutrition diet, may have their diet supplemented with a higher-energy feed containing wheat or maize. This is best fed in the late afternoon in small quantities, as a treat to help bring the birds back to the roost and also to provide them with something to sustain them during the night.

Mixed corn feed consists of whole wheat and a lower proportion of kibbled or very coarsely ground maize. Maize has higher energy levels than wheat and was traditionally used in very cold weather. When added to make up part of a laying hen's diet, it is found to enhance the colour of egg yolk. Some outlets may supply maize in an unmixed form, and farmers sometimes sell wheat at low prices. Feed merchants sell mixed corn feed and may offer maize to those who want to use it as a winter supplement.

Feeding the heavier traditional breeds extra wheat or mixed corn can help to satisfy their large appetites. Some strains of the old ultra-lightweight breeds that travel far in the search of protein-rich insects could also be fed extra grain to compensate for the energy they expend in their search.

Oats are no longer used in balanced feeds. These were once fed to the white-fleshed Sussex breed of table fowl that used to command a premium price at early London

▼ Feed trough height is important and may need adjusting as birds grow.

poultry markets. Oats were also used as a tonic in the feed of slower-developing exhibition breeds; the specific requirements of exhibition fowl may include diets rich in vitamins that enhance leg or feather colour, for example. These are available from specialist suppliers.

Grit and oyster shell

Hens that are free to range over a large area will seldom require extra grit to supplement their diet, since they can collect small stones from the garden environment. Coarse grit ensures a healthy digestive system, particularly when birds are free to consume long grass. It is accepted as good practice to provide grit in a small hopper, along with a separate hopper of oyster shell to maintain a regular supply. Oyster shell contains a source of calcium, which helps to promote strong eggshells. Most balanced mash and pellet feeds contain adequate amounts of this element, so calcium-rich oyster shell in ready supply will only be consumed as and when needed.

Water

Providing water is an essential aspect of poultry management. Fresh water needs to be available all day. It can be supplied through mains-fed systems or movable water founts.

▼ Fowl reared on pasture consume good quality grass, earthworms and insects.

▲ *The bottom half of an egg box makes a useful and disposable feeder for day-old chicks.*

Chick feed

Poultry feed, particularly chick food, is expensive, although it costs no more to keep and rear well-bred and healthy stock than badly bred and ailing ones. It is always worth taking the time and spending a little extra to ensure a healthy foundation for the lifespan of poultry as well as for future generations of useful and productive fowl.

Pullet feed

For traditional laying breeds that do not lay eggs much before 21 weeks, lower-protein "growers" feeds are specifically designed to delay laying until pullets are fully grown. Today's smaller hybrids are usually intensively reared in an environment where controlled lighting rather than food can be used to delay laying until the pullets reach 17 weeks. However, some of the more precocious strains will insist on laying before this age, and it may be necessary to feed them a specially formulated higher-protein "early-lay" formulation, available from feed merchants.

FOOD PROBLEMS

Boiling up household waste that may contain meat residues and giving it to poultry to eat is illegal. Providing poultry with boiled vegetarian kitchen scraps can also be harmful. Today's highly efficient hybrid probably lays 25 per cent more eggs, and weighs and has the capacity to eat 25 per cent less food than the pure-bred fowl of yesteryear. Free-range birds kept will come to little harm when consuming modest amounts of strange bits and pieces while roaming around the garden. However, the same fowl if kept in an enclosed run, will make themselves ill if they consume totally inappropriate food that they are unused to digesting. Feeding unsuitable bulky feed causes stomach upsets and diarrhoea.

Lawn trimmings from mowing and large quantities of earthworms and slugs mingled with the feed of hens that are unused to this type of food can also cause dietary issues. Grazed grass, however, is not a problem, since it is consumed in smaller quantities.

▲ *The divisions in this feeder stop birds scratching the food out.*

▲ *Water dispensers should be kept clean and filled regularly.*

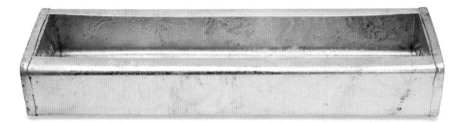

▲ *An open trough has its uses, but allows smaller fowl to use feed as a dust bath.*

▼ *The divisions in this chick feeder stop food being scratched out on to the ground.*

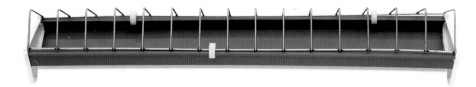

INTRODUCING NEW BIRDS TO A FLOCK

Introducing new birds to an existing flock can often cause welfare problems, and so whenever possible, this is best avoided. The poultry pecking order that has been established will obviously be disturbed by a new arrival to a stable group.

Members of an existing flock are likely to bully a newcomer, so it is probably not worth trying to introduce a single bird to an existing flock. When introducing a small flock to an existing flock, the house to which they are introduced should be large enough to allow space for a netting partition between the groups until they have got used to each other. Even then, the two groups would probably mix better if both could be moved to a new house.

When moving birds into a flock that has an extensive run, a training run can be used for a few days until the newcomers get used to their surroundings, the long-term residents accept the new birds and the flocks get used to sharing their run.

A hen returning to the coop from brooding duties could spend a day in a temporary run before being placed on the perch in the main poultry house at night. The same technique is worth trying when adding a new bird

▲ *Hens that are new to an established poultry house can quickly become victims of bullying by senior hens.*

to an extensive run system. Such a bird may at first be unsure of the new surroundings and have to be encouraged to leave the security of the house. The bird in question would probably benefit from being

▼ *Poultry naturally choose to live in small flocks, and quickly establish a pecking order within that group.*

▲ *A recently mixed group of modern hybrid hens settling down together on a perch.*

removed from the run for a couple of mornings to spend another day or so in an acclimatization pen.

The optimum time to move birds to a new home is in the evening. This also allows you to see if the birds have become used to perching, or if they have been reared on a slatted floor system. Arriving at dusk will allow the birds to move on to a perch just as it is getting dark. At this point, birds will often be reassured by having their tails stroked. If the birds are going to use an outside run, keep them shut in for at least one day. When letting them out for the first time delay their exit until just before dark, so that they have enough time to familiarize themselves with the house entrance without straying too far. If the house has fitted nest boxes, deny the birds night access to these until they have learned to use perches, as once they start sleeping in these it is a difficult habit to break. In a perfect world, new birds would arrive before a weekend, providing you with time to observe their behaviour.

TRANSPORTING POULTRY

Restrictions imposed on the commercial transportation of livestock may have been, in part, responsible for the demise of some specialist pure-bred poultry flocks. More recently it may have led to the growth of poultry auctions.

Birds from specialist breeders were once efficiently transported by rail. Such poultry invariably arrived in good order because of the relatively airy carriages in use at that time. With the demise of this service, birds were sent by road instead, but rarely arrived in such good condition, and so this service was discontinued on welfare grounds. Today, other than the movement of small numbers of one's own birds, a licence and training are required before poultry can be transported more than 40 miles.

Birds that travel in cars, in properly ventilated boxes, in a temperature comfortable for the human occupants, are likely to be healthy on arrival. However, transporting birds in ventilated steel vans on modestly warm days can lead to heat distress. Traffic delays can lead to the death of such birds. In cold weather, poultry

▼ *Assess the weather before moving birds in an open-sided vehicle or trailer.*

need to be packed sufficiently closely together to keep warm, but still have adequate ventilation.

Carrying cases

Dealers may use plastic or wooden poultry crates; exhibitors may favour expensive wicker baskets. Plastic crates allow good air flow in an enclosed and ventilated vehicle, but are unsuitable for an open-sided trailer. A well-ventilated, strong cardboard box can be ideal when moving a few fowl, and is satisfactory in a closed van in cool conditions, but is not suitable on a hot day.

Three or four is the optimum number of birds likely to fit on the back seat of the average car in a carrying case. The box needs to be appropriate to the size of the bird – usually 45cm/15in square for bantams, and sufficiently tall for large fowl. Birds quickly settle in a darkened single or partitioned travelling box. As long as they

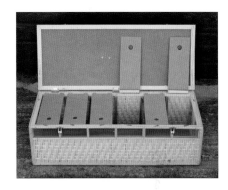

▲ *An exhibitor's bantam show hamper. Hessian lining and wicker construction allows natural ventilation.*

are not cramped and have room to stand, fowl that are used to spending up to ten hours on a perch do not need room to move about in transit. A 5 x 10cm/2 x 4in hole cut into two opposite sides of the box make perfect carrying handholds.

▼ *A show hamper suitably partitioned for two large fowl. Huge, fluffy exhibition fowl will require far larger hampers.*

PESTS AND DISEASES

Livestock health is a major concern for all those who keep poultry, and maintaining that health affects every aspect of their management and breeding. As poultry have the potential to suffer from as wide a range of health problems as any other livestock, these notes offer guidance.

Poultry occasionally suffer from a wider range of less common health problems than other domestic livestock, and this could put off potential keepers, but given the correct care, most fowl are as trouble-free as any other pet or free-range livestock. In many cases, careful observation of poultry can result in many potential problems being spotted at an early stage. This is easiest when birds are either in a large

▼ *A healthy, alert and well-feathered young fowl.*

run or if the owner can walk into the poultry house. Stockmanship is about recognizing the difference between a seriously ill bird and one that is under the weather. Poultry keepers should soon recognize the difference between annual moult and feather pecking, as well as the difference between the usual degree of wear to the back of hens caused by an active male and the damage caused by the male's spurs or toenails, which may need trimming. Local poultry clubs may be able to demonstrate toenail, spur and beak trimming, and give

▲ *A clean, healthy red face, with round, clear eye and nostrils free of clotted mucus, are indications of health and freedom from respiratory troubles.*

advice on what to do to save a visit to the local veterinary practice. Sometimes, fowl considered to be under the weather will perk up after a period under an infrared heat lamp.

To provide a yardstick for good health, it is easier if the first birds that a beginner keeps are as free as possible from inherited illness, as well as from health problems picked up from other fowl. Infections carried by stressed post-auction birds that have had minimal human contact may be severe. Birds used to being washed, handled and prepared for show, on the other hand, will return from show after show in full health.

Potential problems are likely to arise with the addition of new birds to a flock, when health problems that may be introduced by new birds are passed to the flock. Many poultry health problems faced by

non-commercial poultry keepers may be caused by mixing groups of young birds of differing health status. Others will be caused by an unwillingness on the part of the owner to dispose of ailing stock, or, in the case of ex-battery fowl, keeping prematurely aged fowl beyond what would be commercially viable. Observation and commonsense are paramount. Considering fowl as requiring a similar amount of care and attention as family members can also help.

Hybrid pullets born in commercial units will have been bred from disease-free parents. Reared in an enclosed bio-secure environment, they will have been subject to a vaccination program designed to give long-term protection against every disease known to attack commercial poultry. These include many respiratory diseases and salmonella that can make both the poultry, and occasionally those who consume their eggs, ill. Birds reared under less intense conditions rely on their acquired immunity to fight off infections.

▼ *A round, flesh-coloured vent through which the bird's faeces and eggs pass is one of the most important indicators of poultry health.*

In the case of ailments that require care and a degree of nurture, some means of isolating sick birds is essential. An isolation coop is a useful tool for dealing with the sort of problems that often see commercial poultry keepers deciding to dispose of ailing members of their flock.

The poultry tonics now approved for small-scale flock application may be kept on hand for use at times when poultry seem generally unwell.

Marek's disease

Poultry not routinely vaccinated against infection may be left susceptible to Marek's disease, a herpes-like infection that spreads through the respiratory system and can cause paralysis and ultimately the death of infected fowl. Chicks vaccinated against this virulent disease, however, may not pass their immunity on to the next generation. Some of the more attractive breeds

▼ *The high amounts of soya protein in modern poultry rations may produce faeces that are stickier than is ideal. A percentage of firm droppings with a white cap are a good indicator of health. Dietary upsets can cause diarrhoea, but a persistent runny discharge could indicate a worm infection.*

▲ *This soft-feather breed displays healthy feather regrowth following a period of moulting.*

remain susceptible to this painful and usually fatal illness, so owners may need to vaccinate each generation. It is always worth checking if a strain that you are purchasing is susceptible and has been vaccinated. While strains of some breeds are susceptible, others may be completely immune.

Mycoplasma

While many poultry health problems are interrelated, it is respiratory ailments that are likely to cause most concern. Poultry breathe through a series of air sacs and are consequently prone to respiratory trouble.

Chronic respiratory diseases (CRD) are often referred to as mycoplasma. Four main forms of mycoplasma are known, and they can be present singly in many birds without causing disease to exist. However, where combined with other viral and bacterial infections, they can result in outbreaks of sneezing, coughing and nasal discharge. Given poor ventilation in the poultry house or run, hygiene infections can spread rapidly, and while severity and

mycoplasma does not respond to traditional poultry tonics. In fact, there is no licensed vaccine for mycoplasma, although most of the larger hatcheries routinely vaccinate newly hatched chicks against IB.

Although viruses cannot be treated with antibiotics, in order to help birds cope with secondary infections, antibiotics may be routinely prescribed in mycoplasma outbreaks. The overuse of antibiotics is not good practice, however, and many veterinary practitioners may be reluctant to prescribe them. The best treatment is fresh air, clean dry litter and good management. A multi-vitamin preparation can make an effective treatment.

Bumble foot

This ailment is a swelling of the foot that can be caused by a thorn or sharp piece of grit becoming embedded in the soft underpad of the foot or toes. Attempts to lance the area of infection can make the problem worse. Less severe cases may be eased by keeping the bird on soft litter and soaking the foot in warm, salt water. Very heavy breeds may

▲ *An out-of-condition hen that is going into a moult can be misdiagnosed as being sick. Poultry should be carefully monitored during any period of stress, and appropriate action taken.*

causing pneumonia in humans. Prescribed treatments for other ailments break down illness by attacking the cell walls; however, since there are no cell walls,

recovery times may vary, stress can contribute to high losses during some outbreaks of these.

Science has enabled the various strains of mycoplasma to be identified, but exact identification is difficult for the average poultry keeper. Tell-tale signs include runny nostrils and weepy eyes, combined in the early stages of infection with an uncomfortable flick of the head. If combined with infectious bronchitis (IB), which is impossible to identify without a laboratory, it is always likely to be labelled mycoplasma.

Mycoplasma are a genus of bacteria that do not have a cell wall. It is this genus that is also responsible for

▼ *Egg clusters or nits around the vent are often the first indication of this problem, which is easier to treat than an infestation of mites.*

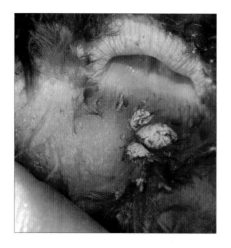

▼ *Bumble foot may be caused by a wound becoming infected, or be the result of jumping off a high perch on to hard ground or stepping on thorns.*

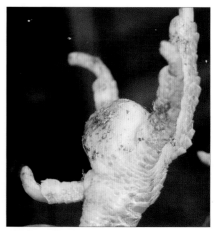

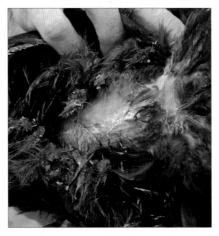

▲ *A prolapsed oviduct is most often a problem in older hens, but can be caused by strain during the laying process.*

▲ *A foul odour and white discharge are the usual indication of vent gleet, which was once thought to be venereal disease, but is usually caused by ulceration of the vent and bowel.*

▲ *Diarrhoea is a condition that may arise from a variety of causes, including a sudden change of diet.*

suffer similar damage after jumping on to hard ground from perches that are too high. Check large, heavy breeds for bumblefoot as part of a routine health inspection.

Prolapsed oviduct

This condition may be prevalent in pullets coming into lay, or in old hens. The failure of the hen's muscles to support the oviduct under the strain of outsize eggs or heavy production, will result in reddish tissue protruding. Even mild cases of this condition can precipitate cannibalism, and so birds should be isolated as soon as possible. Treatment can be simple, but the problem can recur.

Dropped abdomen

A dropped abdomen is caused by muscle failure. Prolific layers and old, overweight birds are among those most often affected by this condition. While there is no treatment for this condition, birds may continue to lay but their eggs will rarely be fertile.

Vent gleet

Ulceration of the vent and lower bowel was at one time thought to be a venereal disease, but it is probably caused by bacteria entering the tissue. Vent gleet smells terrible. Many owners choose to dispose of affected

birds, but, at an early stage, isolation of the infected bird, followed by clipping the matted feathers from around the vent, then washing and treating the area with germicidal ointment that is suitable for humans can be effective if repeated over several days. Veterinary supervision will be required before antibiotics are prescribed in this situation.

Diarrhoea

From time to time, diarrhoea may be a problem for individual birds; however, temporary looseness of the bowels in individual birds should not necessarily be seen as evidence of contagious disease or infection. Diarrhoea may arise from a variety of causes, such as sudden changes in the feed regime or simply the wrong sort of food being provided. Too much airflow in slatted-floor houses can cause abdominal chills, which may trigger diarrhoea. Confined, stuffy houses have the same effect. Infected flocks are treated by a dose of Epsom salts (55g/2oz per 4.5 litres/1 gallon of drinking water). The inclusion of 2 per cent vegetable charcoal in the diet is a reliable treatment in mild cases of dietary upset.

TREATING A PROLAPSED OVIDUCT

Wash the vent with warm disinfectant solution and when clean, gently smear with a proprietary ointment. Gently replace the parts and syringe the vent with cold water to stimulate muscle reaction. A teaspoon of olive oil taken orally for a few days will help to discourage egg production during the recovery period.

▲ *A beak that is too large for an underdeveloped head can indicate an unsatisfactory start in life.*

Parasites

Internal and external parasites are a recurring occasional irritant to both poultry and those who care for them. At times they can escalate to become a serious problem. Poultry have always suffered from parasites, ranging from visible external lice and mites, to the less obvious internal worms, and outbreaks of protozoa, which cause the parasitic diseases coccidiosis and blackhead.

Worms

Domestic fowl are susceptible to infestations of several different types of intestinal worms, with round worms being the most common. While many fowl, particularly free-range birds, will shrug off minor infestations, and routine hygiene will limit outbreaks in intensively housed birds, modern poultry wormers are so safe and effective that most keepers will still opt for the security and peace of mind of an annual or biannual treatment program. Symptoms of worms include ruffled feathers, generally malaise, a bird

▲ *Flowers of sulphur was once used to treat lice and fleas. It can be an effective treatment in the early stages of leg mite. However, a liberal application of petroleum jelly may be just as effective.*

with a messy vent often accompanied by congealed faeces, and clumps of lice eggs. Stunted and uneven growth among young stock can suggest an ongoing problem. Appropriate modern worming treatments are available to eradicate the problem. The gapeworm, a nematode that infests the windpipes and once caused heavy losses in young poultry, can be treated in the same way.

Lice

Lice infestations, like intestinal worms, are often found in or on generally unhealthy fowl. Given access to a large run and a dry dust-bathing area, healthy fowl will rarely suffer from fleas or lice. Lice chew the flesh and feathers and cause irritation that affects the overall health of the fowl, so regular inspections should be made. Lice are light brown, flattish insects, and their tell-tale egg secretions will be found cemented to feather shafts. Lice are easily killed, usually by spraying or dusting with a

readily available proprietary product. Should re-infestations occur, treatment or at least a weekly inspection could become part of the hygiene routine.

Mites

Dealing with the various mites that plague poultry and their housing can be difficult. These are parasites that lives in the hen house rather than on the birds, they needs to be checked for regularly and treated as part of house cleaning and hygiene. The blood-sucking red mite lives in crevices in the house and feeds when the birds are on the perch. Infestations can be confined to perch ends for weeks, only to multiply in days to a point where they will make life unbearable for both occupants and people who have to go into the house. The problem is exacerbated in the summer when the tell-tale piles of dust at perch joints will be visible. These may develop almost overnight into a seething mass of blood-filled

▼ *The effect of scaly leg mite can be long-term disruption of the scales that make up the outer covering of birds' legs and feet. An application of petroleum jelly will help soften the scales, but it may take up to two years for the scales to be replaced with new ones.*

mites. Treatments kill the insects by rapidly lowering the moisture levels of their bodies.

The related northern or plumage mite is spread by direct contact. It can burrow deep into feather follicles, leaving characteristic curled or damaged feathers. Vulnerability seems to vary from breed and strain, but many exhibitors will isolate affected birds and in some cases dust or spray them with proprietary products. The effectiveness of these products varies.

The scaly leg mite can burrow deep into feet and leg scales, and can cause painful and unsightly disruption of the scales. This mite can be eradicated by insect sprays, provided that they can penetrate the area where the mite is, but further treatment will be needed to repair the scale damage. Repeated applications of petroleum jelly are one of the best treatments for the injured area. The jelly works by suffocating the mite and may also encourage re-growth of healthy scales.

Coccidiosis

A protozoan disease, coccidiosis can be a particular problem in young chicks. Its prevention should be considered as part of the rearing regime. It is caused by living micro-scopic organisms (protozoa) called coccidea, different types of which are found in chickens and turkeys. The protozoa undergo a very complex cycle of development inside and outside the birds' bodies. It appears that birds reared outdoors may be more at risk of coccidiosis than those reared in more controlled situations.

Outbreaks will also often occur in groups of chicks being reared in isolation, either under lamps or in brooders. Here, any build-up of damp or dirty litter may, particularly in very hot weather, result in whole batches of young birds becoming ill, and may result in the death of untreated birds.

▲ *Knocks and blisters on the comb resulting from injuries or dried on dirt can usually be treated with petroleum jelly or household germicidal cream.*

Infected chicks present a dejected and ruffled appearance, often accompanied by pathetic cheeping. Bloody droppings are sufficient evidence of the presence of coccidiosis, and treatment is prescribed by a veterinary surgeon. Most treated birds are likely to recover and may acquire resulting immunity. Suitably medicated chick food will give a wide measure of protection until birds gain their own immunity. Some breeders have reported gaining some measure of control over outbreaks by the inclusion of cider vinegar in the drinking water.

Blackhead

Blackhead is a protozoan disease that infects turkeys and can have devastating consequences. It derives its name from the darkening of the head in some, but not all, affected birds. It is an acutely infectious disease common among turkeys, pea-fowl and related species. It has always been a problem in houses that are shared with other classes of poultry,

▲ *An inflamed crop can be an early indication of a crop binding, or sour crop which is frequently caused by birds consuming long grass. Relief is given by pouring a teaspoon of olive oil down the oesophagus. Removal of the obstruction may require the crop to be operated upon.*

since chickens carry, but are not necessarily affected by it. Blackhead is a problem that has increased as commercial production has become more intensive. The industry once relied on a group of powerful drugs for protection to combat the disease, incorporating them into the feed, or keeping them on hand in case of sudden outbreaks. Once it was discovered that residues of these drugs could pose a risk to humans, their use was banned in many countries, and turkey producers were concerned for the future of the industry. However, smaller and organic producers relied on a herbal preventive treatment based on oregano. This product has been so successful, involving only minor adjustments to the way in which turkeys are kept, that many people now question whether the industry has become too reliant on potentially dangerous medications. Turkey owners should be continually vigilant.

EGG PROBLEMS

A regular supply of fresh eggs is one of the main reasons for keeping poultry. Problems can occur with both the eggshells and their contents, however. This section describes some of the most common problems and offers advice on what can be done.

Occasionally, grotesquely misshapen or oversized eggs are laid that are best dismissed as a freak of nature. Sometimes the shell may be covered in blood. This is because the hen will have strained to lay the egg. It does not affect the quality of the content. Double-yoked eggs are comparatively common, the occasional triple-yolk ones less so. They may arise because two or three yolks leave the ovary and pass down the oviduct together or in rapid succession, ending up within the same shell. It is rare that a bird produces one egg inside another. If it does happen, then it is caused by a shock to the oviduct, which has caused one egg to move back up the oviduct until it meets another one coming down.

Eggshells
Shell quality and defects are immediately obvious. Soft-shelled, very thin-shelled eggs, or even shell-less eggs are often wrongly attributed to calcium deficiency. However, all

▲ *Eggs with double yolks are more likely to occur either when pullets are beginning to lay for the first time, or more rarely, when older hens are coming back into lay after a longish rest.*

proprietary poultry feed contains adequate calcium combined with the correct phosphorus ratio and optimum levels of vitamin D to produce eggs with hard shells. The problem is most likely to occur during rapid increases in egg production, when very young, high-

PRODUCING THE PERFECT EGG
The most economically produced and environmentally friendly eggs are known as "low feed miles eggs". These are eggs produced by hens that convert the least possible weight of feed into the greatest weight of eggs, or the hen that consumes the highest percentage of home-grown feed or by a combination of the two.

production hybrids, and occasionally older birds that haven't laid for a while, start coming into lay. Because the ovary is in an extremely active condition, yolks leave it in quick succession and the hens are unable to assimilate enough of the available calcium to provide shells for all of the eggs being produced. The problem usually disappears as the ovary becomes less active.

The reason why some strains of lighter-coloured hybrids start laying nearly white rather than brown eggs

▼ *Crinkle and ripple-shelled eggs are caused by worn and stretched oviducts. Older high-yield hybrids are prone to this.*

▼ *Eggs with rough-textured or "sandpaper" ends can be an indication of a mycoplasma infection.*

▼ *A "faded" eggshell compared with a standard egg, both of which are produced by the same breed.*

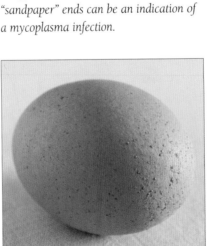

▲ *Soft-shelled eggs are generally laid by young hens coming into lay for the first time, or by older birds.*

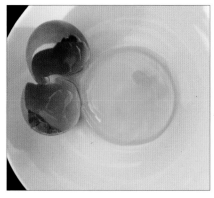

▲ *An egg yolk that fails to form may be produced by a young hen coming into lay.*

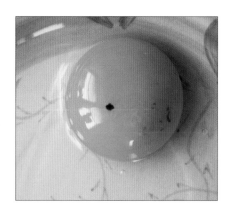

▲ *A blood spot detracts from the appeal of an egg but is harmless and can be removed easily.*

during periods of intense sunlight is barely understood. The problem seems to be caused by ultraviolet light, haemoglobin and a little understood genetic defect that affects some strains with very pale brown feathers that lay brown eggs. Some poultry keepers observe that the problem seems worse during periods of normal summer feather loss. As this is genetic, there is no cure other than restricting access to full sun.

Inside the shell

Poor eggshells detract from both show quality and saleability, but internal defects are likely to concern

▼ *Sometimes an indication of mycoplasma, rough-shelled eggs are attributed to some shock to the hen.*

the consumer far more. Blood spots in both the yolk and the white are relatively common. The former is caused by an intra-follicular haemorrhage while the ovum is still in the follicle. The latter is caused by the rupture of a blood vessel in the oviduct at the time that the yolk is passing through it. Blood spots vary in size. The problem is at its worst when hens are coming into lay. This is the time when egg classes at exhibitions are at their largest too, making the problem appear more prevalent. Eggs with small blood spots may be perfectly edible. The problem usually disappears when the

▼ *Dirty eggs need to be cleaned quickly since the shells are porous and the insides can become contaminated.*

ovary becomes less active, and there is no cure. Meat spots are formed from blood spots that have degenerated after inclusion in the egg, and not, as was at one time thought, due to the inclusion of meat meal in the feed.

The cause of green and other miscoloured yolks is dietary. Hens produce wonderful, yellow yolks when they have access to grass. A slight green tinge may be associated with eating clover and other legumes. Olive and even black-yoked duck eggs are caused by the consumption of ripe acorns or using oak and some other hardwood shaving as litter in the hen house.

▼ *Collapsed yolks can be the result of a dietary disorder, but can also be caused by rough handling after laying.*

BREEDING POULTRY

Once you've had success keeping poultry, the next stage for many owners may be to set up a breeding program to ensure a continuous supply of future generations of fowl. This is particularly the case if you have good stock and wish to have more of it, or if you think you can improve the utility or exhibition value of your chosen breed. For those interested in genetic conservation, the wish to add to the distinguished gene pool of an old or rare breed may be sufficient motivation to begin breeding poultry. In the latter cases, contact with the relevant breed club is essential. For many other poultry owners, including those who have children, the desire to breed poultry is sparked by the simple joy and satisfaction of watching a mother hen fussing over a new brood, or capturing the moment when new life emerges from an incubated egg. While putting a few eggs under a broody hen and hoping for the best can be fun, things do not always go to plan, and plenty of information is included in this chapter on the breeding process and on how to deal with the unexpected.

▲ *The sight of a mother hen and newly hatched chicks will enchant both adults and children.*

◄ *A mother hen nurtures her brood of growing chicks, just as nature intended.*

SETTING UP A BREEDING PROGRAM

To start a breeding program a healthy male and at least one healthy female is required. Most programs involve a male and two or more females; with some light-breed males managing to cope with eight or more females.

The less closely the male is related to the female the more vigour any offspring are likely to have, meaning that the resulting generation should be as free as possible of genetic faults. Provided the male is fertile, male and female birds will mate and a clutch of fertile eggs will result. Breeding poultry produce 50 per cent male and 50 per cent female offspring.

If you are considering breeding poultry, it is quite reasonable to expect that like will beget like. As part of the ethos behind the standardization of a pure breed, the Poultry Club of any country asks for evidence that subsequent generations will "breed true". This means that the offspring will be identical to the parents in terms of visual appearance,

▼ *Poultry selected for breeding will be the birds with the best characteristics in the owner's stock.*

character and temperament. While the emphasis on visual appearance remains the basis of exhibition breeding and selection, most utility selection, for egg and meat production, has always been based on specific genetic properties. Usual commercial practice involves crossing different breeds and strains to produce a generation that not only has hybrid vigour but also encapsulates the desirable qualities of both parent lines. This keeps the breeding stock healthy.

Pure breeds and hybrids
For birds that are not being bred specifically for exhibition, a male bird is usually allowed to run in a breeding pen with a handful of females. Both male and female birds in the pen will exhibit all the desirable traits for the breed. Several male birds may be required for a

▲ *A young red or genetically gold male saved for use in a quality table fowl breeding program.*

largish flock of females, with the result that it will not be possible to determine the exact male parent of the offspring.

Exhibition breeds
If you wish to breed birds for exhibition, always begin with the best stock that you have or can buy.

BIRDS THAT DON'T MAKE THE GRADE
Other than keeping males for breeding or for fattening for the table, most males will need to be disposed of as young as possible. Similarly, birds that do not exhibit sufficient characteristics to match the breed standard should be discarded.

It takes longer to build good stock from average birds than to breed a few undesirable traits out of quality stock. As most pure breeds descend from relatively few ancestors, breeding to type (creating offspring that match the parents) may result in having to breed poultry with parents that are distantly related. In fact, inbreeding is essential for pure breed lines, and it is common to cross offspring back to their parents or with their siblings. The result is that hybrid vigour is lost, but desirable traits are retained. Hybrid vigour can be reinstated by breeding unrelated birds from the same breed, but there is no guarantee that undesirable traits from the new birds' heritage will not resurface in the next generation. For exhibition, pure breeds are selectively bred, meaning that individual birds are chosen to breed for specific traits. The lineage is clearly traceable with exhibition birds, and each is tagged to aid identification.

Double mating

Generally applied to exhibition birds, the term double mating is used to describe the practice of selecting one breeding group to breed exhibition birds of one sex, and a second group

▲ *A Blue Cochin mother and father produce Black, Blue and dilute blue, or Splashed blue chicks.*

to breed the other sex. For example, many of the Mediterranean exhibition-class breeds have large single combs. In the exhibition male the comb is expected to stand boldly upright, while the female comb is expected to fold gracefully over to one side. In order to stand upright the tall male comb needs a wide strong base. In order to flop gracefully to one side the female comb needs to be relatively slim. Some breeders will make up a "cock breeder" group headed by a male with the required tall upright comb, along with hens that have a shorter, stronger comb than would be the exhibition ideal. The intention is to produce offspring with the desirable tall, upright combs that have a strong base. Similarly, "pullet breeder" groups consist of hens with fine, floppy exhibition combs, headed by a male with a large but less substantial comb than would be the exhibition ideal, in order to produce a large floppy comb.

GREGOR MENDEL

The 19th-century scientist, Gregor Mendel, found that by crossing two tall pea plants, the offspring (the F1 generation) were equally tall. When the F1 generation were crossed, however, only 50 per cent of the offspring (the F2 generation) had the combined characteristics of both parents, while 25 per cent had the characteristics of one parent, and 25 per cent had characteristics identical to the other.

The principles of this theory are used, for example, by breeders of the Blue Andalusian breed. In order to produce a Blue bird, a White male is crossed with a Black female. However, if the Blue offspring are mated, 50 per cent of the next generation will be Blue, 25 per cent per cent Black and 25 per cent pale

diluted blues or "Splashed". When Black and Splashed birds are bred together, 100 per cent of the resulting chicks feather with a blue-grey hue.

The Frizzle breed has broad backward-curving feathers. Pairing two Frizzles will produce offspring in which 50 per cent are identical to the parents, 25 per cent will have narrow, over-frizzled feathers, and 25 per cent regular, straight feathers. Although 100 per cent of the chicks are Frizzles, at least superficially, only half of the offspring breed true. Birds that do not breed true are discarded from any future breeding pool.

Many desirable exhibition-standard birds can only be achieved by pairings that will produce a given percentage of offspring that are different to the desired breed standard.

AUTO-SEXED AND SEX-LINKED BREEDS

The offspring of auto-sexed and sex-linked breeds can be identified as male and female by the colour of their down when they are one day old. The advantage for the egg-producing industry is that unproductive male birds can be discarded, keeping resources focused on the valuable hens.

In order to produce auto-sexed and sex-linked offspring, specific pure breeds must be used in the breeding programs.

Sex-linked breeding

Birds bred to produce chicks in which the offspring are easily distinguished by the colour of their down are planned crosses. Only certain pure breeds, when crossed with other specific pure breeds, produce offspring that can be sexed on hatching. As well as being able to identify male and female offspring, which is economically advantageous for the poultry industry, the offspring will be hardy and have a greater utility value than the breeds' parents. The crossing of two specific breeds will always result in crossbred offspring. The next generation

▼ A typical sex-linked pairing is a genetically gold male such as a Rhode Island Red, crossed with a genetically silver female such as a Light Sussex.

produced by these first crosses, like hybrids, can be sexed at one day old. The first generation of crosses can be used for breeding, but the colour, and to some extent the type (shape) of resulting generations will not be predictable. It is also impossible to distinguish whether the offspring is male or female at a day old, unlike in auto-sexing breeds.

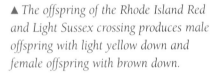

▲ The offspring of the Rhode Island Red and Light Sussex crossing produces male offspring with light yellow down and female offspring with brown down.

Auto-sexing breeds

In 1920, on the basis of research by renowned geneticists Professor Punnett and his associate Michael Pease, a Barred Plymouth Rock was crossed with a Gold Campine to create offspring with a completely new type of plumage pattern known as Barring. The result of the cross was the Cambar breed, now known as an auto-sexing breed.

Auto-sexing is a method of identifying the sex of young birds at one day old so that unwanted male birds may be culled, thus reducing food and housing costs for those birds. Of those poultry breeds that are auto-sexing, it is the colour of the chicks' down that indicates whether the chick is male or female. The down may be light for one sex and dark for the other, or one sex may be identified by clear spots or barring.

▶ *These chicks are one day old and have been bred so that males and females can be identified easily by the significant difference in down colour.*

Additionally, with an auto-sexed pairing, the resultant offspring is always a pure breed, meaning that if the new Cambar offspring are mated, the third and subsequent generations will always breed true to the Cambar breed.

An understanding of auto-sexing breeds was a significant commercial development prior to the arrival of the hybrid lines. This research showed that science could be used to modify poultry breeds and for the first time, birds could be bred to produce chicks that were effectively colour-coded on hatching, with the colour of the down indicating which were male and which were female. Breeders soon found that even when Barred males were mated with females of other breeds, it was still possible to tell the sex of the offspring upon hatching. Later it was found that other barred breeds could pass that characteristic on to other auto-sexing breeds.

The group of breeds whose names

end in "-bar" are auto-sexing varieties of a parent breed that has had barring added to its genes in such a way that generation after generation of their offspring can be feather-sexed by their colour at one day old.

The other half of the breed's descriptive name, such as "Wel" in Welbar, for example, is from one parent of the new breed, the pure breed Welsummer, in this case. Other auto-sexing breeds or varieties follow the same formula, the first part of the name denoting the parent breed, with "bar" added to show this modification. However, it should be pointed out that in spite of their

▼ *The Cream, or Crested, Legbar was created using Araucana rather than Leghorn. Its name is derived from the down colour of the chicks, but breaks the rules governing the naming of the other auto-sexing breeds or variants.*

AUTO-SEXED BREEDS OR VARIANTS
Auto-sexing breeds or variants have been made by using either Cambar or Plymouth Rock fowl as one half of the breeding program. The format for naming the offspring runs as follows:
Rhodebar is an auto-sexing Rhode.
Legbar is an auto-sexing Leghorn.
Hambar is an auto-sexing Hamburg.
Welbar is an auto-sexing Welsummer.
Wybar is an auto-sexing Wyandotte.
Redbar is an auto-sexing New Hampshire Red.
Barnebar is an auto-sexing Barnevelder.

adopted names, many hybrid fowl that have the suffix "bar" do not auto-sex.

Another development is that bantam versions of many auto-sexing breeds have been created using the same formula, and, like other auto-sexing breeds, other than the barring factor they are expected to be otherwise the same as their original unbarred parent breed. Their essential characteristics will be expected to exactly replicate those of that parent.

▼ *The natural barring found in the newly created Suffolk Chequers would provide a basic feather pattern for any auto-sexing project.*

CLASSIC GOLD AND SILVER SEX-LINKED PAIRINGS
Rhode Island Red x Light Sussex
Buff Rock x White Wyandotte
Brown Leghorn x Light Sussex
Brown Leghorn x White Wyandotte
Buff Leghorn x Light Sussex
Buff Leghorn x White Wyandotte
Welsummer x White Wyandotte
Indian Game x Light Sussex
Indian Game x Faverolles

SEX-LINKED PAIRINGS RELYING ON HEAD SPOT SIZE
Black Leghorn x Barred Rock
Rhode Island Red x Barred Rock

Crossing two barred breeds

The barring of the plumage in auto-sexing breeds is finer and more sharply defined than that of the Pencilled pure breeds. The auto-sexed Barred Rock, which has black down with a white head patch, was crossed with a pure breed (Barred) Gold Campine, which has mottled brown down with a light head patch, to determine the offspring's plumage.

As the chicks hatched, only those that showed the light head patch and brown down (of the Gold Campine), which combined the dominant sex-linked barring with the recessive pure breed Campine barring did not auto-sex. These birds were heterozygous (impure) for sex-linked barring. The second generation, however, when mated, gave a combination with homozygous (pure) sex-linked barring, and an entirely new down type appeared. This new down was strikingly paler. The light head patch had spread over the neck

and back, blurring the sharp, spotty pattern of the Campine down. These chicks were males. This new breed was named Cambar to reflect its parentage.

The barring factor was so complete that given a proper understanding of the genetic formula, a breeder could increase the content of the original pure breed to the point that it was at least 90 per cent pure for that breed.

This finding opened the way to create a range of auto-sexing forms of both well-known commercial breeds.

As light breeds, Leghorns are among the best layers. A new-found ability to eliminate the males, which have no table value, at hatching meant that the Gold Legbar variety had for a while considerable commercial

▼ *The Wybar bantam was created from a Barred and Silver-laced Wyandotte.*

value. The obscure Araucana was used to create the Crested or Cream Legbar for what was potentially the best producer of blue eggs. Its descendants still have a commercial role to this day.

Such pioneering work was only possible because small-scale hobby breeders refined their exhibition breeds to have the purity of feather pattern which was expected in a standardized breed.

Welbar

The Welbar is a British bird created in the 1940s from Gold Barred Plymouth Rock hens crossed with Silver Welsummer males. The "Wel" in the name refers to the Welsummer male's genetic input.

This utility breed was primarily bred to lay plenty of dark brown eggs, and the feather colour of the breed remains of secondary value. The male is gold with black barring. Hens are paler versions of the same colour. Just one variety exists now, although two were developed. The silver variety would be easy to recreate, however.

The Welbar has the broad carcass of all egg-laying breeds, with a long and deep breast. This is an attractive and upright bird that holds its tail

▲ *The Welbar bantam is a Welsummer bantam with an added barring factor that enables feather sexing of its day-old chicks.*

▼ *A large version of the German auto-sexing Bielefelder breed.*

aloft. It has a neat habit with soft, silky plumage, and the yellow legs should be clear of feathering.

Wybar

Like the Welbar, the Wybar uses Barred Plymouth Rock in its composition, this time crossed with Silver-laced Wyandotte. It is a British fowl developed in 1950 to be a dual-purpose bird with exhibition qualities. It is

likely that it also has Light Sussex added to its genetic pool, though the bird predominantly takes its mother's characteristics. It has a pea comb, silver-laced coloration, yellow legs and beak. The basic formula can still be used to create new varieties, including bantams. Wybar fanciers have created a small fowl that enables breeders to eliminate unwanted male chicks at hatching.

Bielefelder

A German breed created out of a broadly barred form of Plymouth Rock and Rhode Island and New Hampshire Reds, the Bielefelder is an attractive heavy breed with chicks that can be sexed at one day old by down colour. This is a relatively new

breed developed in the 1970s. Bielefelder are available in just one colourway, with males being paler versions of the hens. It was bred as an egg-laying breed that was tolerant of cold.

Suffolk Chequers

Not yet standardized, the Suffolk Chequers has been created very much in the form of earlier Plymouth Rocks in which broader feathers enabled their pure-bred offspring to be feather-sexed at one day old.

Rhodebar

The Rhodebar was created in Britain in the 1900s. It was produced by crossing Barred Plymouth Rock males, an auto-sexing breed, with Rhode Island Red hens. The result was originally called a Redbar but later renamed Rhodebar. The breed was created as an egg producer, with hens laying up to 200 brown-tinted eggs in their first season. Adult Rhodebars look similar to Rhode Island Reds, but have a black tip to the tail. Day-old male chicks are yellow, while females have dark stripes or barring down their backs.

◄ *Suffolk Chequers is a new breed in the UK and is yet to be approved by the Poultry Club of Great Britain.*

► *The Rhodebar has a large, deep, broad body and a long back. The single comb, earlobes and wattles are red, and the tail has a black tip.*

REARING CHICKS UNDER A BROODY HEN

Many hen breeds have a tendency to broodiness. This is an inclination to sit on the eggs, to allow them to hatch, and then to nurture a young brood of chicks. Hens will do this regardless of whether they have mated with a rooster.

Some breeds are more prone to broodiness than others, and may become broody at any time of year. Other fowl are most likely to be broody and reach the peak laying period when the daylight hours lengthen in spring. Broodiness is not always a welcome characteristic and retrieving eggs, particularly unfertilized eggs, from under a broody hen can be difficult.

The broody hen

A hen that is broody during the autumn and winter, when daylight hours are shortest, produces chicks that inevitably get off to a slower start than their artificially incubated counterparts. Some breeds have had the brooding instinct bred out of them, particularly breeds that are

▼ *The enclosed apex ark makes a cosy place for a hen to incubate a clutch of eggs, but a rapidly growing brood can quickly outgrow the space.*

▲ *A broody hen has a raised body temperature. She will stay on the nest at night and tuck every available egg under her protective skirt of feathers.*

egg-layers. Broody hens can alter the balance of the pecking order, and other birds in the flock may become aggressive towards a broody hen.

If you have a cockerel running with the hens, unless you want chicks, collect the eggs every day. A hen will lay roughly one egg per day and will sit on them only when she has her full clutch. A clutch could be up to 12 eggs. The hen waits for a full clutch before she sits on them so that the chicks hatch at the same time. A hen that sits on her eggs and does not move for several hours may be broody. She may also be disinclined to leave the nesting box, and may start nesting. A broody hen's body becomes hotter than usual, and she may remove feathers from her chest area so that the eggs benefit from the increased body heat. The hen will sit on her eggs, spreading her wings over

▲ *Large fowl chicks may quickly outgrow a surrogate bantam's capacity to nurture in cold weather, but these chicks will soon be sufficiently feathered to keep warm.*

them for 21 days, only leaving them once a day to tend to her own needs. Each day she will turn the eggs to ensure the embryos develop evenly.

Broody hens need continual assessment to ensure that they are not neglecting their own health. Not all hens that have sat tightly on their eggs can be relied upon to be trouble-free mothers.

Some breeders think that chicks hatched under a hen in their natural environment have a healthier start in life than those reared in arguably more sterile conditions under the continual warmth of an infrared heat lamp. Hens that hatch and rear their own chicks may be naturally stronger. Without human intervention only the fittest survive; this hardiness is often a desirable trait in specific breeds. Chicks brought up by hens often display very different characteristics

Housing for mother and chicks

A mother hen carefully brooding her family of chicks is an appealing sight. Her natural maternal instincts are best served by simple but specialized housing. Left to her own devices, a mother hen may drag her chicks too far in the search for food. The broody coop, which was used when much of the industry still relied on natural methods, provides a safe, dry home for the mother hen, while allowing chicks access to fresh air and their own chick feeders. While they are suitably confined with their mother, chicks may choose not to venture too far, at least for a few days. Cats and other threats will not be able to get too close while the chicks are kept within a small, safe enclosure.

A well-designed coop allows easy access to the hen through a sliding roof panel or removable front rails. These rails confine the hen and chicks to the coop, but allow enough space for them to live comfortably. Confining the hen after hatching, while allowing the chicks plenty of room to exercise in the protected run, ensures the hen does not take the chicks too far. If day-old chicks are free to roam it can result in loss.

▲ *Big breeds like Cochins and Brahmas are natural broodies that can cover a lot of eggs, but their large size and feathered feet make some hens clumsy mothers.*

from those hatched in an incubator, where the first glimpse of another living creature may be the person that handles it and on whom it is dependent for food and water. Chicks hatched under hens rely on the hen to call them back to the coop. They have the additional security of being able to hide under their mother's feathers. If they are not regularly handled during this period, they may grow up with a natural suspicion of humans. Yet chicks brooded under the tamest bantam hens, which have also been bred and reared in tiny pens, often at head and shoulder level with the sort of breeder who constantly checks on their progress, can soon be found walking up an outstretched forearm in order to get a better look at the benefactor who comes several times a day to tend to their every need.

Discouraging broodiness

Stopping a hen from broody behaviour is possible and is most easily done as soon as the behaviour commences. Hens allowed to be persistently broody can, after some weeks, become debilitated. Putting the hen in a coop that has a wire mesh base, which is set upon bricks at its edges, makes an uncomfortable surface for the hen, so that she will stand rather than attempt to nest. The cold air circulating from below also helps to cool her body temperature. A few days spent on draughty slats should cure a broody hen and is a short-term solution that a battery hen endures all its life.

Another method is to fill the nest box in the coop with an obstacle that the hen is unable to displace. This will encourage the hen to move on.

▶ *A mother hen will call her chicks to bring them home. She will scold and issue alarm calls on the approach of unfamiliar or potentially threatening humans or animals.*

HATCHING USING AN INCUBATOR

Artificial incubation is a method to bring fertile eggs safely from point of lay to hatching without including the hen in the process. This procedure was initially developed to increase the volume of eggs hatched by breeds that were less likely to go broody.

The process of artificial incubation mimics the natural function of the broody hen sitting on her eggs, keeping them warm and turning them regularly until the point of hatching.

Artificial brooding methods

The industry has relied increasingly on artificial incubation since the 1930s. The early "brooders", or incubators, sought to mimic the dark and cosy warmth provided by the hen. Early "foster mothers", as they were known, relied on paraffin to generate the heat and consisted of an enclosed oil lamp under an insulated canopy, surrounded by a felt skirt. It provided similar insulation to the sitting hen's feathers. The eggs were turned by hand.

Fertile eggs could be hatched earlier in the year than had previously been possible. A lack of daylight, however, meant the newly hatched chicks spent longer staying close to

▲ *The incubation process extends the laying season beyond that in which hens naturally hatch and brood chicks.*

▲ *Incubators are available in a range of sizes, from mini seven-egg models to designs housing thousands of eggs.*

the warm glow of their brooder lamp than they did eating and drinking, and so some early batches failed to benefit from the head start that their early hatching should have offered. Apart from being a bit smaller than those chicks bred naturally at a more usual time of year few of those chicks in fact came to harm, provided a reasonable room temperature could be maintained. Sunlight was thought important to the chicks' development and as this was readily available in the form of vitamin D it was included with cod liver oil in the chicks' feed.

Contemporary methods

The advent of reliable miniature appliances, like the tiny seven-egg incubator, has enabled eggs to be

◄ *The tiny low-voltage incubator enables schools and other organizations to safely demonstrate the miracle of hatching to groups of young children.*

hatched at home. Ideally, a small group of eggs laid within a day or so of each other will be put in the incubator at the same time. Being genetically similar, they should hatch within an hour or so of each other. Incubators are available in different sizes.

The incubation process from point of lay to hatching can take up to 21 days, with some chicks hatching at 18 days and others taking a few days longer. Any eggs that have not hatched after this time should be discarded, since retaining them can lead to disease. Modern incubators are run digitally, and enable egg temperature to be controlled to within a fraction of the optimum temperature of 37.5°C. Even the smallest machines now available for home use have efficient self-turning systems, which means that poor hatches, particularly those resulting in excessive numbers of chicks dead in the shell, should practically be

Hatching

1 Hatching starts with the chick pecking, or "pipping", a tiny hole in the eggshell around the air sac.

2 The first tiny holes appear at the point of the enlarged air space in the blunt end of the egg.

3 The chick may not do much more for an hour, or it may quickly peck its way around the edge of the air cavity.

4 The chick pauses to take its first breath of open air. Then with one heave it can be almost free of the shell.

5 Some chicks take a little longer to break free of the egg shell, but one should never be tempted to help speed up the process.

6 As the chick emerges it is possible to observe the "egg tooth" on top of the upper mandible that the chick has used to hammer through the shell.

eliminated. Breeders planning larger hatching operations could look at a bigger incubator system, one in which the eggs are removed for the last two or three days of the incubation period to a separate hatching compartment, or better still, to a completely different device known as a "hatcher".

If the embryo is not to drown during the latter stages of development, the egg will need to lose moisture during incubation. If turned properly, a healthy developing embryo should hatch into a healthy, fluffy chick even without perfect conditions. After all, hens that sit on eggs are not always able to provide ideal conditions themselves.

Even the smallest incubators are fitted with some method of controlling moisture and humidity, with 60°C being the optimum temperature. The incubator should remain closed during hatching in order to retain moisture levels. Experienced breeders may have

▶ *Empty egg shells with a few unhatched eggs are indications of a reasonable hatch in a conventional incubator.*

▲ *A few hours old, and this healthy batch of Legbar chicks are nicely dried and ready for transfer to a brooder unit.*

differing opinions about the moisture levels. Some of the more successful breeders, when using modern fan-assisted incubators, add little extra water during the early stages of incubation, only increasing moisture during the hatching period. Slow, late or difficult hatches, particularly those where nearly all of the emerging chicks have difficulty getting out of the shell and appear to be dry and sticky, are often wrongly blamed on lack of moisture. The viscous excess fluid on the chicks dries like glue

▼ *By comparing the internal view of the egg to a candling chart, it is possible to see if the egg is fertile or not.*

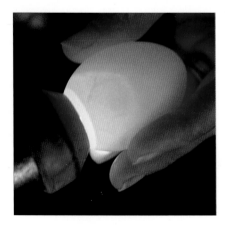

when in contact with air that enters the shell as the chick "pips" or begins to break out.

The incubation period will vary between breeds and last longer when eggs have been stored before being placed in the incubator. Hatching may start as early as the 18th day when a chip appears along the line of the air space. Turning should cease during the last 24 hours, which are technically in the hatching period.

Candling

This is a method by which the embryo developing inside the egg can be checked. Traditionally, a candle would have been used rather than the more high-tech gadgetry used today. Nowadays, a strong electric light source is used to illuminate the contents of the egg. An egg is "candled" by holding it in front of the light source. It is easy to candle eggs from an incubator using a modestly priced candling device. Eggs being incubated by a broody hen are less accessible, because the hen will only leave her eggs once a day to look after her own needs. Attempting to take eggs from under a broody hen will cause upset to the hen and is best avoided.

By day five of the incubation period, a good lamp will illuminate the beginnings of the vascular system within a fertile, white-shelled egg. By day six, even with a less powerful lamp, it will be possible to see changes happening within a fertile white or tinted egg. Examination between days seven and ten will reveal the most noticeable feature of a fertile egg – a clear, definite line between the air sac and the rest of the egg. When this is sharp and distinct the egg almost certainly contains a live embryo. Next to this is a spidery form, a few veins near the line between the air sac and the rest of the egg. It may be possible to observe this

spider-like form moving, a sure sign of a live embryo. An infertile egg will remain clear.

Sometimes there will be a less distinct boundary line accompanied by a dark blob that only moves as the egg is turned. In this case, whichever way you turn the egg, the blob moves in the opposite direction. This is usually a sign of a broken yolk. Those new to egg testing may wish to leave these a little longer to see if they develop. However, a broken yolk usually represents a failed egg that has the potential to spread spores and

▼ *From top to bottom and left to right: a clear, infertile egg at 7 days, a fertile egg at 7 days, an egg with broken yolk at 7 days, an egg containing excess moisture at 14 days, an egg with insufficient moisture at 14 days; the air sac content of the egg as it should appear at each annotated day.*

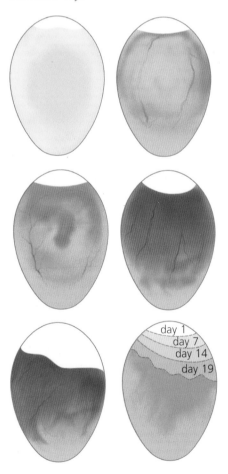

day 1
day 7
day 14
day 19

disease in the incubator. It should be removed as early as possible.

Viewing through the plastic dome of a modern incubator allows adjustments to be made to moisture levels. Some poultry keepers rely on weighing eggs at set stages of incubation to monitor moisture loss, but this takes little account of variations in incubation moisture levels. Eggs that have been stored for more than a week before putting in the incubator will have lost some moisture. Really fresh, disease-free eggs remain the most important prerequisite of a healthy hatch.

Hatching

A hatching unit is only necessary if you hatch enough chicks to justify the purchase, otherwise the eggs can remain in the incubator. A hatching unit is a warm, still-air environment like an incubator. The hatching dust, debris and waste from newly hatched chicks can contain diseases that have incubated along with the eggs. Using a hatcher ensures that hatching chicks can be isolated from eggs still being incubated. This makes cleaning the incubator easier, and helps to control egg-borne diseases.

The freshness of the eggs placed in the incubator, and the identity of the breed that laid them, determine the optimum time to transfer eggs from incubator to hatcher. There is an obvious advantage in incubating eggs laid by similar breeds at the same time. Hatching can occur between days 18 and 21. During this stage the eggs do not need to be turned, and should ideally be moved to a purpose-made hatching unit. If the incubator manufacturer's instructions are followed, any hatching problems are likely to be caused by egg storage or by health problems in the parents. Most chicks are dry and strong enough to be removed to a brooder unit 24

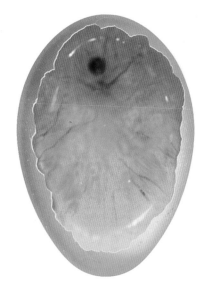

▲ *Day one embryo growth inside the egg.*

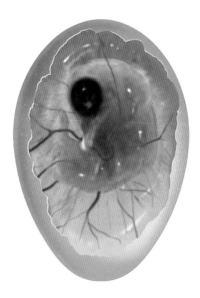

▲ *Day seven embryo growth.*

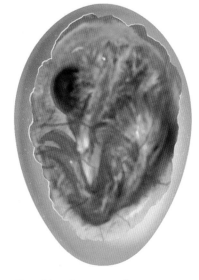

▲ *Day 14 embryo growth.*

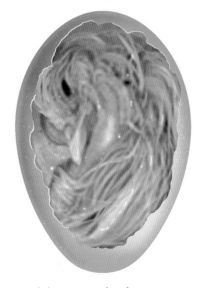

▲ *Final day prior to hatching.*

▲ *Only by candling eggs regularly will you know what to expect inside the egg.*

hours after hatching. During their time in the hatcher unit, hatched chicks live off the egg yolk and it is not necessary to provide them with food. Commercial operators often clear unhatched eggs from the hatchers on the 22nd day, but hobby breeders may often wait longer in the hope of rescuing a last precious emerging life.

Traditionally, the point of hatching was the time when commercial operators boosted the moisture content of the incubator in order to increase chick size. As dry air can toughen the shell membrane, making it harder for

the chicks to hatch, the hatcher should be opened as little as possible during this period. In order to hatch, the chick requires freedom to move within the egg. This means that the air space has to be large enough and there has to be sufficient moisture to prevent the egg membranes from drying out. If moisture has been properly controlled during incubation, difficult hatches are unlikely. The temptation to give chicks a helping hand should be avoided.

The brooding unit

Day-old chicks have a natural resilience, and, given the right sort of warmth and food, are surprisingly easy to look after. As they grow, their housing and management should be tailored to reflect breed feather growth and for a wide range of external conditions.

For days 1 to 28, chicks can be contained inside a brooder unit. This is simply an indoor space warmed by the heat of a reflective infrared lamp. Infrared lamps vary in output from 100–300 watts. Most other lamps do not heat space effectively. Glass reflector lamps break easily; ceramic versions emit dull lighting; while clay-based lamps are extremely durable. The reflected directional heat from the lamps can cause draughts at floor/chick level, so it is necessary to surround the area holding the chicks with a draught-proof hardboard barrier forming an area that can expand in size as the chicks grow. Surrounding the chicks ensures that the entire brooding area can be heated and the heat lamp kept at a reasonable temperature.

Lamp height and resulting temperature are best judged by observing chick behaviour. If the lamp height is correct, the chicks, when not eating and drinking, will be dispersed across the floor area. If the lamp is positioned too high, so that not enough heat reaches the floor area, the chicks will huddle together to keep warm. At this point it may be necessary to deploy an extra lamp. If the lamp is too low, making the area beneath it too hot, the chicks will not sleep directly under it and will constantly reposition themselves away from the heat source. However, as the infrared rays may damage the vitamin content of the chick feed, feeding troughs should be placed outside of their immediate beam.

▲ *Chicks are moved from the hatcher to the brooder, where they will stay until they are sufficiently feathered.*

While a shallow cardboard lid may suffice for feed for the first few days, a quickly growing family will require larger feed troughs. Disposable, but clean cardboard, covered by a shallow layer of clean white wood shavings, provide perfect insulation from a cold, solid floor.

▶ *Clean water founts need to be within easy reach but feed and feeders should be positioned outside of the direct beam of an infrared lamp.*

The growing chick

1 At 30 minutes old, this little chick is still wet, but will soon be a ball of fluffy chick down.

2 At only 5 days old, the first true feathers appear on a young female from a heavy breed.

3 At 7 days old, a Sussex chick like this one will begin to look like a young table rooster.

4 At 9 days old, the chick will be relaxed enough in its surroundings to sit and take a rest.

5 At 12 days old, this chick is beginning to show the typical heavy breed bone development.

6 At 13 days old, the chick's wing feathers are showing definite signs of strong development.

7 At 16 days old, this young female Sussex chick shows significant feather development.

8 At 19 days old, this Sussex shows untidy feather development often associated with males of the breed.

9 At 29 days old the same male is beginning to look like a smart young man.

EXHIBITING POULTRY

Regional and national poultry shows provide an opportunity to see practically every breed of poultry available under one roof. Among the cacophony of noise, smell of ammonia, excitement and general hubbub will be some of the best examples of breed type that you are ever likely to encounter. Showing poultry is a serious business, with exhibitors travelling considerable distances to a national or regional show with their prize fowl for the chance to win a coveted rosette. This is an old-fashioned sport, in which prize money is minimal and the competition is all about the skill of producing a bird that fulfils the exacting criteria of the written standard. For those exhibiting, such events provide the chance to show your best birds and make your mark as a breeder of quality poultry.

Large-scale annual poultry shows are not just for exhibitors, however; those with a specific interest in a particular breed will find most breed clubs take a stand at such exhibitions, providing the perfect venue to discuss the merits and finer points of your chosen breed with the experts.

▲ *Eggs are exhibited in different classes at poultry shows, and judged according to set standards.*

◄ *Regional shows offer the opportunity to exhibit poultry and other livestock, and are a great way to introduce breeds to the public.*

THE BREED STANDARD

The concept of pure-bred fowl being developed to a recognizable standard dates back to the craze for poultry which spread throughout Britain and America in the mid-19th century. At this time, fowl from Asia arrived on the poultry scene with much fanfare and media hysteria.

The first national exhibitions of poultry began in the 1850s. These were events where breeders from far and wide brought the best examples of their breeds to be shown and compared with others of the same breed, as well as with other breeds. It was the exhibition scene, rather than the poultry industry (still in its infancy at this time) that determined what characteristics constituted a breed profile. With new birds from foreign lands being shown, poultry judges began to propose and compile written breed standards for the newly imported fowl, as well as for the local types for which appearance and attributes were well known and understood. The standards determined the accepted colours, weight, dimensions, character and visual appearance to which each breed must aspire to be considered a pure breed of distinction.

Prior to this date, poultry breeds were developed for their utility qualities. The best birds were either the most productive, or produced a heavy carcass with visually appealing white meat that was saleable at a high price. Each breeder would have been aware of the requirements for the breed, and would have endeavoured to reach that standard with their breeding fowl. At this time, the standard was an acknowledged set of requirements rather than specific written details. Soon the Cochins and Brahmas, which were Asiatic imports, were being bred to meet the written standard.

Written standards can be complicated. For instance, the visual characteristics must take into account variations in comb shape or feather type. In some breeds, such as the Dorking, for example, it is possible to find complex rules that permit some

colours to be bred and shown with single combs, and others to be shown with rose combs, or both.

It is likely that in the need to be specific, the standards may have over-emphasized the size and fluffy feathering of these Asiatic breeds to the detriment of their utility potential – a trend that persists in many breeds to this day. Later breeds like the Rhode Island Red and Sussex were bred and judged to standards that put the utility considerations of the breed first.

These standards are accepted in each country by an accredited body. In Britain this is the Poultry Club. Similar clubs and societies exist in other countries worldwide to set the standard for acceptable colours and characteristics for each breed. There are differences between countries in the standards for each breed. Colours and even breeds that are known and

▼ *The Silver-laced Wyandotte was originally selected on the basis of the attractive and ornamental lacing seen on this example. Such lacing is difficult to perfect and is a challenge for breeders.*

▼ *The White Wyandotte broke many early laying records, but as exhibition strains of Whites were selected for excessive feather and fluff, these strains became poor layers.*

▼ *The large fowl that arrived from Northern China in the 1850s introduced many new traits to breeding stock, including an excess of foot feather and fluff as in the Cochin breed.*

▲ *The Suffolk Chequers bantam has yet to be accepted as a standardized breed.*

Early standards

Though written standards were officially logged from the mid-19th century, breeders and enthusiasts prior to that date would have had agreed acceptable standards for their breeds. Much of the indigenous poultry of Northern Britain, Northern and Central Europe, Turkey and the Eastern Mediterranean countries had distinct feather and colour patterns which had long been selected to conform to very precise local "standard" patterns. Nearly all of these consisted of combinations of black spangling or pencil markings on a gold or silver ground colour. Bolton Greys, Manchesters, Moss Pheasants, Yorkshire Hornets and Mooneyes are regional breeds that would have been exhibited locally long before the first organized shows. Today there are more breeds than ever, and with new breeds being created and imported, the trend looks set to continue. All need to be exhibited to an agreed written standard.

▲ *More than 200 years ago, Sebright breeders found that they could get perfectly laced male tail feathers by selectively breeding for female-type feathers: 70 years later this characteristic became part of the breed standard.*

Manmade breeds

The first poultry shows changed the whole perception of poultry. New breeds were made and selected to meet specific requirements of markets and commerce. Later, when the value

▼ *When Langshans were first imported from Northern China they would have looked like the earliest Cochins.*

of selective breeding was fully understood, commercial strains of many breeds were developed that became the basis of modern hybrids.

Most of the old standard breeds have, for a time at least, played their part in economic poultry development. Selection on the basis of features such as excessive fluff and feather has diminished the usefulness of many exhibition strains of previously important utility breeds. However, it is largely thanks to poultry exhibiting that most of the breeds of the last 150 years are still with us. Breed standards remain the means used to define a breed.

While many of the original standards were written with the breeds' utility in mind, it is now more than 40 years since standard pure breeds played a major role in either egg or poultry meat production. As a result, commercial interests no longer influence the way that breed standards have been interpreted. Those flocks of pure breeds that once supplied the industry with breeding fowl to produce meat or eggs in quantity have been almost entirely replaced by hybrid-breeder flocks.

▼ *The Cochin group of fowl introduced Buff coloration to the western world.*

recognized in some countries are not accepted in others. It may often take years for a breed to be accepted.

THE POULTRY SHOW

Enter the world of the poultry show and you will find yourself in a large hall filled with row upon row of wire cages containing every breed of poultry imaginable. Exhibition birds are organized according to similar criteria throughout the world.

Show criteria are the same whether you are visiting a small-scale local show or a huge national exhibition. Exhibits of each breed are positioned next to each other so that like can be compared with like. Large and bantam versions of the same breed are judged separately, and may be located in different places within the exhibition hall. All breeds that belong to the same class appear in close proximity to each other so that the best of each breed within a class can be compared to other winners. Visit any of the large poultry shows and you are sure to find examples of local or rare breeds.

Poultry are divided by class, which is defined by the world geographical region responsible for selection and development of the breed. Sometimes this can be confusing, for example,

▼ *Trained show entrants know how to display themselves to advantage. Many are happy to stand to attention and move to the pen front when being viewed.*

the Hamburg breed hails from the Netherlands but is classified as English, because English breeders were responsible for developing the breed that exists today. The confusion arises because the breed's name suggests it should be of German origin, but it is, in fact, named after the port through which it passed on its way to England. The classes that exist are Asian, American,

◄ *Poultry are exhibited locally at agricultural shows during the summer months. Local poultry clubs often take an interest in such shows, and this can be a good opportunity to locate breeders and even buy birds.*

Mediterranean, European, English and Rare, the latter being the only class not defined by region. The occasional appearance of breeds that are not well represented in their homeland has become a regular feature of rare breed classes at major shows; rare breed categories include minority breeds. The same categories exist in the bantam classes. Turkeys and waterfowl are also judged according to breed. Some breeds and varieties that are recognized in some countries are not acknowledged in others.

▼ *Eggs that are exhibited at poultry shows are often of interest to the public. Judging the contents class means looking for the same qualities as the discerning cook.*

EXHIBITING POULTRY

While only a small percentage of people who keep and breed pure-bred poultry are likely to become regular exhibitors, a visit to a well-run show can add much to our understanding and appreciation of those breeds and the standards to which they are expected to adhere.

With thousands of entries, the great national shows are a wonderful window into the world of poultry breeds and the numbers of breeds and varieties that are available.

For the competitively minded, the opportunity to exhibit prized fowl and collect a winning rosette or trophy on the show circuit may be the most important reason to keep poultry. Others will find that showing poultry and attending shows is enjoyable and adds much to an interesting hobby. Poultry exhibiting is likely to attract different people for very different reasons and there are plenty of other reasons to exhibit and attend poultry shows.

For those interested in the conservation of rare breeds, poultry shows are essential. Without the persistence of a few breeders, many

▼ *The best of each class is removed to winner's row to be judged against one another. The supreme champion for each show will be decided here.*

▲ *Shows are the best place to see good examples of each breed type. The trained eye will be able to detect differences between exhibits of the same breed.*

breeds, particularly those with less utility merit and therefore less obvious reasons for keeping them, would have ceased to exist. The fact that these breeders have made the effort to gain recognition for their

breeds by showing them in rare breed classes means that the poultry world has a richer heritage to draw on in the future. The exhibiting of good examples of specific breeds helps to generate interest from new breeders

▼ *Birds that are used to being both confined and handled will suffer less stress than those taken direct from a poultry run to a crowded show.*

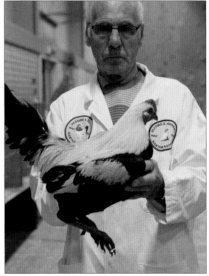

interested in continuing to preserve this heritage. Endangered regional breeds such as England's Derbyshire Redcap may be shown locally in order to maintain local interest for strains genetically adapted to a specific environment. Conservation of these important old breeds is in the hands of a few small-scale breeders, hobbyists and the specialized societies that support them, their exhibition classes presenting the results of centuries of careful selection.

Breeders who keep birds with specific or unusual colour markings, patterns or lacing that are difficult to perfect may only breed a near-perfect example every few years. As a result, the chance of seeing perfect examples of such breed coloration are few and far between. A breeder may exhibit a perfect specimen mainly so that he or she can show it to his or her peers, if only to discuss how it compares with previously shown breed examples.

▼ *Having first gained an overall impression of a bird's shape and type, a judge goes on to examine it critically in greater detail.*

▲ *Staging any show can involve a lot of paperwork. Making sure that every entry receives the correct prize card and award often relies on the efforts of a small group of volunteers.*

Beginners unfamiliar with the visual appearance of different breeds may find that few of the exhibits are labelled, though most classes are. This can be frustrating, but show genuine interest in any exhibit, or ask about any breed, and you are likely to find yourself with your own show guide or an introduction to a local breeder.

Local shows

With a more relaxed and slower pace than national shows, local shows may provide a better introduction to poultry exhibiting, as well as to local exhibitors and poultry keepers who are in the best position to help the beginner. Would-be exhibitors can see how others carry birds to shows and put them in pens.

Due to the internet and an increasing number of quality poultry magazines, it is easy to find details of breeders and dealers, but there is nowhere better than the local poultry

show to find those breeders with the best breeds in the area. Local breeders may have surplus breeding stock for sale, or in some cases may be willing to sell reliable hatching eggs from healthy stock that you can incubate and hatch if you have the facilities. Such breeders may also accept requests to breed a few extra birds that they would be willing to sell. Above all, the local show is the place to see the best examples of poultry breeds that do well locally. It is a chance to make contact with like-minded people, catch up with old friends and support the efforts of those who have helped to organize the show.

There will be fine examples of many different breeds on display. However, the breeds that are kept locally will obviously be greatest in number. This may be because a good breeder has successfully sold his or her birds into the local community, or in areas that experience extreme temperatures, it may be because certain breeds survive better in the environment than others.

New or would-be exhibitors who have bought stock from a breeder who has the long-term interests of that breed in mind will be actively encouraged to enter a local or regional show. They are likely to have the benefit of the original breeder's expertise to guide them through the preparatory steps necessary to exhibit their fowl competitively. Over a cup of tea or coffee, important local contacts can be made at the show, and it should also be possible to learn about other activities such as open days, poultry courses and discussion groups that the local club organizes. It is how well a club looks after its newcomers as well as existing members that boosts and retains membership, and encourages new members to take up exhibiting.

Agricultural shows

Poultry are often shown at agricultural shows, which are held outdoors in the summer months. Unfortunately, this coincides with that period of time when most adult fowl are losing their feathers, beginning to moult or showing signs of breeding-pen activity, so one cannot expect to find many good examples on show.

Judging

As most judging at local shows does not commence until mid-morning, an early visit to the show hall provides a good opportunity to watch the hustle and bustle of "penning", and the hurried cosmetic touches that are made to the poultry. Old hands may well help juveniles or absolute beginners prepare their birds for exhibition.

Watching the judges and stewards get the exhibits out of their pens is not only a good way to learn how to handle fowl, but also provides those considering exhibiting poultry with an idea of the amount of handling their birds need in order to be calm when held by unfamiliar hands. Teaching the birds to stand and remain quiet is essential, and many

▲ *New judges can learn much while deliberating with more experienced judges.*

exhibitors have plenty of tricks for training their birds. Experienced exhibitors may select their birds for exhibition from a young age, and start to train them as soon as they show promise of fulfilling the criteria for the written standard. Others will leave their poultry to grow up as part of a small flock in a healthy outdoor environment, and then select the best to train for the show pen.

Whatever the nature of the breed, the more excitable types must be accustomed to being handled and confined prior to showing. At exhibition, birds are placed in small cages, in which they may have to stay for up to 36 hours. Some breeders place their birds in training pens, visiting to give a tidbit of food, and then when the bird is totally relaxed, they will gently pick it up a few times and replace it in the pen in the same way that the judge will handle it. At exhibition, thus familiarized with being handled, birds will come to the pen front to see if the hand that picks it up has food to offer.

As most shows allow "open" judging, meaning the public can view the judging process, it is possible to get some idea of the finer points of exhibition judging. You may see a judge or steward looking for broken or missing wing feathers, incorrect skin coloration and even the discovery of a poultry flea or mite.

While those with a specialist knowledge of a single breed may be asked to judge that breed, all experts engaged to judge general classes will have passed practical and written tests on a group of breeds.

By mid-afternoon, most of the prize cards for the best of breed will be in place. The best breeds in each class are compared and the best class champions are moved to their place in the champions' row. It is from these that the best bird in the show will be decided. Every show will have unexpected results – perhaps a juvenile beating the experienced exhibitor, or a first-time exhibitor winning a major award.

▼ *A knowledgeable judge will be able to tell much about the overall condition of a bird in his hand.*

PREPARING FOR THE SHOW

Weeks before the show, preparation begins. Owners train their birds to cope with the restricted show pens and stand to attention. Ultimately, the bird has to present the best characteristics of the breed and measure up as closely as possible to the written standard.

The first requirements of a show bird are fitness and health. If a bird is not in the best of health, then there is no point in showing it. A whole range of specialist poultry feed is available that may help to condition show birds.

Some dedicated exhibitors start work on the showing posture of their birds as chicks. Birds need to be used to being handled, and at ease with being confined to a small show pen for the duration of the show. A show training room set up at home, composed of pens not much larger than show pens, will help accustom young birds to being confined before being exhibited at their first show.

Breeders of true bantams may generally keep their tiny charges in pens not much larger than those used at exhibition. These fowl should be accustomed to being handled by a dedicated breeder, who devotes time and attention to them.

Breeds like the Orpington, which are docile, require little show-pen training, but they do need to be sufficiently alert and attentive when viewed to come to the pen front. Indeed, some of the heavier breeds, such as the large Buff Orpington, can be almost too immobile to be really attractive. Judges of active breeds such as the Egyptian Fayoumi accept that agility is a breed type, but the birds still need to be accustomed to being handled. A little hard-boiled egg, mixed with chick feed and offered to the bird from the hand, will get it used to being in close contact with humans. With the expectation of a food treat, small birds may walk straight on to the judge's hand as the show pen is opened.

Washing poultry

To be seen at their best, most soft feather poultry will benefit from being washed with specially formulated poultry shampoo prior to being exhibited. White varieties and those breeds with very fluffy feathers will certainly need washing before a show. It was once thought that cleaning black fowl "washed out" their lustre and natural beetle-green top colour, but this is no longer believed to be the case.

Washing and drying poultry

1 Use a small bath or sink filled with warm water for bathing. If the water feels warm to your bare elbow, then the temperature will be acceptable to the bird. The bird should be carefully but firmly submerged, leaving just its head out of the water.

2 Holding the bird firmly, gently pour water over it to wet it thoroughly. Keep the water tepid and keep hold of the bird. Birds unused to such treatment may try to break free. For this reason, a small bath is a good choice, leaving no room for flapping.

3 Use a damp, soft, small sponge to gently cleanse the comb and wattles.

4 Add a squirt of shampoo to the bird's back.

5 Thoroughly massage the shampoo into the fluffy feathers and carefully rub it into the wing feathers using a small sponge. Rinse thoroughly with tepid water.

6 Wrap the bird in a warm towel to remove excess water. Wet poultry feathers can hold a lot of water. Pat gently dry, but do not rub or you may damage the feather structure.

7 Use paper towels to rub down the bird and remove the excess moisture before blow-drying. Pat dry in the direction of the feathers.

8 Blow dry the bird using a medium heat setting on a hair dryer, starting with the area around the heart and lungs. Check the bird is not too hot.

▼ *White-feathered birds will almost certainly need to be washed at the last minute to ensure that they are in pristine condition when they are shown at exhibition.*

9 A bird that is used to being handled will move to accommodate drying.

Clipping the beak

1 The tips of beaks, like toenails, are usually kept in trim by running about and pecking feed from hard surfaces. Birds kept in a protected pre-exhibition environment may need the upper mandible to be trimmed.

2 Trim away any horny toenail-type material carefully with nail clippers. The bird will feel no pain, but like many other simple poultry procedures, this is best done by an experienced poultry keeper.

However, specialist shampoos are now available to enhance nearly every feather colour. These shampoos can be purchased at all major poultry shows, as well as from some feed barns. Specially formulated shampoos are kinder to the feather structure of the bird than washing-up liquid or

▼ *"Closed" leg rings can only be bought from national poultry clubs and must be fitted while the bird is young and small enough for the ring to be slipped over its closed foot. The ring indicates the original breeder and the year that it was hatched. This can deter thieves from swapping birds in show pens.*

standard hair shampoo. The feather web has interlocking characteristics and so most feathers retain their normal structure.

Since showing poultry is a competitive business, many fanciers develop their own formula for shampoo, which is tailored to their particular breed's show requirements. Most poultry clubs hold demonstrations on how to wash and prepare birds for show. Drying the fowl properly is as important as washing it, and will be easier if the whole drying room can be kept at a minimum 20°C. It is at this point, provided the bird is tame and accustomed to handling, that most fowl appear to enjoy the washing and drying process. By the time the fluffy areas between the legs and under the tail are dry, many birds will start changing position to dry those areas that are still wet. Some exhibitors

▶ *Exhibition birds that are used to being handled and preened for exhibition will become familiar with the "unnatural" environment of washing and drying.*

leave their fowl to finish drying in a warm room once the initial wetness has been removed from the feathers. Others wrap their bantams in kitchen paper for up to 15 minutes, and then leave them to slowly dry and "fluff up" in a warm room.

Final preparation

Birds kept in conditions other than free range will occasionally require their toenails trimming and may suffer from an overgrown beak. These are both regarded as serious exhibition faults if shown on an exhibition bird. Dry and dead skin on combs, face and wattles can be carefully removed with a toothbrush or soft nail brush a day or two before the show. The final preparations can be left until the morning of the show. Most of this last-minute preparation involves ensuring that mouth, face and comb are scrupulously clean. You may see exhibitors using "secret" lotions to brighten red areas of the face, or wiping baby oil off the kid glove-textured lobes and applying a dusting of fine powder. Some will simply use a smear of petroleum jelly on the face feathers, other will use different products with a slightly astringent quality. Whatever is used should be washed off carefully after the show. In fact, it is these last-minute preparations that add to the excitement and drama of show day for many exhibitors.

White birds that are inclined to look tan or yellow, and buff birds that look bleached, will have to be shaded from too much direct sunlight. The large white lobes of breeds like Spanish and Minorca may become chapped or blistered by cold winds when in the open. Another form of blistering may occur when males are being prepared for show and confined to smaller pens. As this has long been thought to be linked to overeating and a change in energy levels, earlier exhibitors used to add a measure of bran to the pre-show diet. Other than

a quick dust with baby powder to dry them, there is no last-minute fix for these blisters, which were probably caused by knocks.

Leg mites should be treated as a matter of routine, but even birds kept in reasonably clean conditions will have some dirt that has found its way under the edges of the leg scales. To remove this, exhibitors first soak the legs and then carefully clean under each scale with a cocktail stick. Others have found this dirt easier to dislodge after a few hours' soaking in industrial hand cleaner. Combs and

wattles that have become dirty and discoloured will benefit from a thin coating of petroleum jelly that should then be wiped clean. Most fanciers will have their own secret dressing recipe.

Having bred a good bird and then spent days or weeks on pre-show preparation, every exhibitor will want to give every one of their exhibits the final show touches. For many exhibitors, the pre-show preparation is often a means of relieving their own pre-show tensions. However, many well-prepared exhibits are spoilt by evidence of the bird's breakfast.

Final show touches

1 Cleaning and putting a spot of comb dressing on a flat single comb is relatively easy, but reaching every nook of the intricate Sebright comb will take time, patience and the assistance of a cotton bud.

2 A final wipe of the beak and wattles makes a pristine impression. It is surprising how often a judge will find an otherwise beautifully prepared exhibit spoilt by the remains of the bird's hurried breakfast.

3 Nearly every exhibitor will have a favourite comb preparation, varying from petroleum jelly to baby oil, with some containing just the right proportion of astringent. Wash the preparation off after the show.

4 Dust the bird's muffs and beard with an artist's paintbrush to ensure they are in pristine condition.

5 Scales on the legs and feet may benefit from a rub with baby oil. Remove dirt at the same time.

6 A quick check for dirt under the toenails is an essential part of last-minute show preparation.

EXHIBITING EGGS

Eggs are often shown at the same shows as poultry and the classes are every bit as competitive. Viewing the trays of specimens on show is a good opportunity to see the assortment of differently coloured eggs as well as the varying sizes that different poultry breeds lay.

Not everyone who is a member of a local poultry club will have bred the poultry they own, and for that reason they may see little point in exhibiting their prized pets, leaving that opportunity for the serious breeders. For some owners, the task of washing and preening their poultry to exhibition standard fails to hold appeal. For those interested in the utility aspects of poultry keeping, however, the opportunity to show and compare quality eggs may have appeal.

Egg classification will usually include single eggs, threes, and less commonly six or even a dozen eggs. For the classes of multiples, all the eggs shown are expected to be the same size, shape, texture and appearance so these classes provide a great challenge. Often exhibited at the same show as poultry, a long trestle table containing plates of eggs are judged with equal seriousness to the birds. Washing is not allowed.

There are exacting rules that define the appearance of a winning egg.

▲ *Eggs are judged on their contents as well as exterior appearance.*

Bantams, pullets and large breeds all lay slightly differently shaped eggs; however, judges accommodate this and the weight of the egg has to be appropriate for the breed.

Egg judges and exhibitors are enthusiastic, and many are willing to share their knowledge to help beginners. Unusually, the mid-brown or tinted eggs laid by hybrid hens can compete with pure-breed eggs.

▲ *The "three brown eggs" class includes all shades from light to mid-dark brown and can include hybrid eggs.*

▲ *The "dark brown egg" class results in strong competition between owners of the Welsummer and Marans breeds.*

▼ *Bantam and miniature fowl weights have increased, but the standards for their egg weights have remained constant.*

▲ *The class for "eggs of three distinct colours" requires finding similarly shaped and sized eggs laid by different breeds.*

▲ *At a few days old, white eggs may display tell-tale grey spots, so the "white egg class" is not always well supported.*

▲ *Judges may sometimes move a plate of eggs to a more appropriate colour class.*

THE PERFECT EGG

In external appearance, the prize egg has to have good shape, which means that it has an even dome at the widest end, or, as one leading egg judge defined it: "one that sat perfectly in an egg cup". Eggs should be longer than they are wide, and the top should be broader than the bottom. The whole should be curved, and taper to a narrow bottom, which should not be pointed.

The shell texture has to be smooth, without lines, bulges, blemishes and rough edges. The shells should be clean, though unwashed, and should be freshly laid. Stained shells are not permitted. Eggs can be shiny or matt; the colour has to be even. Speckling and mottling should be even. Egg colours can be white, cream, brown, mottled or speckled, olive, blue, green and plum.

Inside the egg, the air sac should be visible, with the membrane attached to the shell. The air sac should be to one side of the domed end of the egg. The yolk has to be uniform, bright, golden yellow, and unblemished. It should be rounded, standing proud of the albumen, and there should be no sign of embryo development. The albumen has to be clear and blemish-free, with two distinct layers; the thicker albumen closer to the yolk must be distinct from the thinner albumen.

Stale eggs are disqualified. Those with a bloom that suggests absolute freshness are well-placed. The judge will gently shake an egg that he suspects of being stale and will often tap a shell with his fingernail and listen for a tinny ring that indicates a sound shell.

Egg colours

Dark brown eggs were partly responsible for the 1850s poultry craze, since they had never been seen before. A really dark brown shell has remained as the mark of exterior egg quality. The public assumption that brown eggs are healthier than white is completely unfounded, however.

▼ *Unlike the bantam egg weights, the standard weight for large fowl eggs takes a more logical approach. Size is not necessarily a deciding factor, but should be appropriate to the breed and species.*

Even in today's competitive egg classes it is the darkest eggs that attract the attention. While one perfect egg in the single egg class can and often does win the "best egg or eggs" award, three perfectly matched eggs will score higher than a single exhibit. Similarly, six identically coloured, perfectly matched eggs of any colour will always be high on the priority list for the award of "the best eggs in show".

Newer hybrids are now being marketed on the basis of their dark eggs, though few yet lay the quality egg of long-established strains such as the Welsummer and Marans. White eggs must be perfectly clean, but as their nearly translucent shells are inclined to quickly show grey "age" spots, they are among the hardest to exhibit to perfection. Blue eggs that are still seen as a novelty are not always full-sized. Olive eggs, or those with a green tinge, are produced by fowl created by crosses between blue and very

dark egg-laying fowl. Their appearance at shows can enliven mixed or novelty egg classes.

▼ *The egg classes always interest visitors to summer agricultural or poultry shows. Often there is a class for children for the best decorated egg.*

KEEPING OTHER DOMESTIC FOWL

This chapter includes domesticated ducks, guinea fowl, geese and turkeys – birds bred to provide meat and eggs for human consumption. These birds are traditionally associated with a farmyard or backyard setting, more so than hens. Many of these birds are large and require plenty of space and, for ducks and geese, a body of water.

Often poultry keepers begin with hens and graduate to keeping other types of poultry or domestic waterfowl. Few poultry keepers have the space to allow different species to integrate, though it is possible for those who work on a small scale.

In terms of welfare, housing, health and economic considerations, separate management regimes for each poultry type are generally the norm, particularly on farms, which have to adhere to rigorous guidelines regarding health and welfare. Many breeds of ducks and geese can make fabulous pets, and if you have the space and time available to look after them, they can be very rewarding to keep. Being larger birds, turkeys are most likely to be reared for a special occasion feast than as a pet.

▲ *Swiss Crollwitzer turkeys are more strikingly marked than the older Pied variety that they have largely superseded.*

◄ *Ducks kept on farms and holdings have always been kept for eggs or meat.*

KEEPING DUCKS

Most domestic ducks are larger than their wild counterparts, and are the result of selective breeding. Like their ancestors, they are mostly aquatic birds. The adult female is known as a duck and the adult male as a drake.

Nearly all the pure breeds of duck were selected, bred and developed from the end of the 19th century for either meat or egg production. Today, people keep ducks for the same reasons that they keep chickens, for meat, eggs and also to exhibit, as well as for purely ornamental purposes. Lighter breeds would historically have laid more eggs than the heavier breeds, which were generally kept for their table properties.

Duck meat

Most of the world's commercial duck meat is now produced by ducks descended from Aylesbury and Pekin bloodlines. Aylesbury and Pekin ducks and the Aylesbury-Pekin cross have been developed to make good table birds. Aylesbury have pure white flesh and feet, a feature that has been

▼ *Muscovy and Pekin crosses are often reared in close confinement. These free-range ducks are enjoying their daily dip.*

▲ *Duck eggs can be much larger than hens' eggs, and are highly prized by cooks.*

highly prized in the Western world, since it was thought to be the sign of high-quality meat. Pekin have yellow skin, legs and beaks, and their commercial crosses also have yellow legs, beak and skin. However, Rouen and Muscovy ducks, which have dark, richer-tasting flesh, are also bred for meat. The Rouen is slow to grow and mature from the duckling stage. The slow-growing Muscovy can

be crossed with other heavy, fast-growing table breeds to produce an infertile hybrid generation that have huge, superbly flavoured carcasses. Pekin ducks are often intensely fattened and at 14 weeks they are slaughtered in the industry for meat. Keeping ducks for meat beyond this point does not make commercial economic sense, since the meat will not improve in taste and the bird will continue to cost more in feed.

People who keep birds for meat either keep a few birds for themselves, or may run small-scale businesses with a relatively fast turnover of the product. Birds reared for meat can be bred from existing

DUCK DOWN

Soft duck down is one of the best insulating materials, and is generally used in duvets and clothing. It has a high thermal content. Warm air becomes trapped between the fibres helping to provide heat and insulation. Down feathers are those closest to the bird's body, generally beneath the outer layer of plumage. The best-known source of down is from the wild Eider duck.

▲ Ducks will cause considerably less damage to your garden than hens.

stock. If you have the facilities to hatch ducklings, eggs can be purchased from reputable suppliers, or they can be bought as day-old chicks from hatcheries. Some pure breeds (such as the female lines of modern Aylesbury-Pekin crosses) that used to be kept for meat production have been selected to lay 200 or more eggs in the year-long breeding season.

Duck eggs

Breeds such as the Indian Runner and the Khaki Campbell are the most productive egg-layers. If you want eggs, then these are the breeds to choose. Utility strains of Indian Runner ducks can lay 250 eggs per year, while commerical Khaki Campbell ducks can lay up to 300 eggs in the same timeframe. No other pure breed of duck can convert food into eggs at the same production rate as the Khaki Campbell.

The lighter utility strains of ducks may come into lay at 18 weeks and may, with careful management, continue to lay well for up to two years. At this point, they no longer

convert feed to eggs at an economic ratio. Some breeders retain older ducks for breeding, and these may live on for many years as family pets.

Duck eggs are usually larger than hen eggs, weighing about 75g/3oz or more. Shell colour can vary from shades of pale green-blue to white. They have a slightly higher fat content and oilier texture than hen's

▼ Few strains of Khaki Campbell lay as well as those previously kept on commercial duck farms.

eggs and are richer in flavour, which makes them ideal for baking. Duck eggs are often laid in muddy places so they should be cleaned and thoroughly cooked. They are available from speciality food shops.

Ornament and pet

Ducks can live for up to 15 years depending upon breed, making them quite a long-lived pet. Many ducks have striking plumage as well as appealing characters that make them interesting garden companions. In many breeds ducks and drakes have very different feather patterns. Drakes generally have far brighter and more flamboyant plumage than ducks, but lose much of it for a few months each year as they go into a post-breeding summer moult. During this period drakes temporarily revert to the muted shades normally associated with the female members of the family.

If you have a large pond, or live near open water, then keeping pure breeds of ducks can be an appealing and rewarding pastime. Many breeders are happy for their pure breeds to live alongside wild ducks.

CARING FOR DUCKS

Ducks are relatively easy creatures to provide for. As aquatic birds they need a body of water, although how much depends upon the breed of bird. Some require water for exercise, washing and preening, while other breeds will not mate and breed without an expanse of water.

Ducks require a clean, dry shelter, particularly from extreme weather conditions, in which to preen and rest, as well as protection from predators and a ready supply of food.

Buying ducks

Pure duck breeds can be bought as eggs to hatch at home, as day-old ducklings or as young adults. Ducklings require different housing and feed than adults, and may also require heat for the first seven weeks of life. Unless you are able to provide such facilities, buying young adult birds from a reputable breeder may be the best choice for stock, especially for beginners. Buying eggs to hatch is a possibility for those with facilities. Check local press, or contact your local poultry waterfowl club for breeders of the type of bird in which you are interested. Before you buy,

▲ *Ducks may enjoy the security of a nesting place on stilts, but to be foxproof it must be surrounded by water.*

however, ensure that you have the right sort of housing and a sufficient area of water for the type of duck that you are going to keep.

▲ *While most ducks lay eggs first thing in the morning in nest boxes within their overnight houses, separate outdoor nesting places can be provided.*

Housing ducks

The amount of land and water required to keep and breed ducks varies according to breed type. Most ducks spend their time outdoors. Would-be owners with running water or a pond will be able to choose from a wide range of breeds, while others may be restricted in their choice of breed by the amount of land and water that they have available. Breeders of small ducks will be able to keep a family of pet ducks or exhibition Call ducks with as little water as a baby bath on raised decking, in addition to a small area of land on which to exercise. Such a restricted living space, however, will need to be accompanied by the highest welfare standards. Breeders of the large and stately Aylesbury will need to provide a considerable body of water for the birds to mate and breed for any measure of success.

Handling a duck

1 Pet ducks may get used to being handled, and will accept being gathered and held in one hand or arm without fuss.

2 Those unused to handling ducks should pick up the duck by firmly grasping its wings together – an experienced breeder will demonstrate.

Unlike hens which perch at night, ducks sleep and lay their eggs at floor level. Their housing needs to be designed with a door that allows human access to change the bedding and clean the nest boxes at regular intervals. The housing should be located on a raised, well-drained area. The flooring should be covered with straw or hay, rather than wood shavings, which can cause digestive problems if the birds eat it. Ducks lay nearly all of their eggs early in the day. In order to prevent eggs being laid in water, some breeders do not let their birds out of the housing until after 9am.

Feeding ducks

Ducks can be messy feeders. Their drinking and communal bathing habits result in spilled water, and dabbling in the mud may not make them the most appealing housemates for other poultry. Ducks eat grasses, aquatic plants, fish, insects and other small water-dwelling creatures, and their beaks are adapted to pull up food from beneath ground level. Ducks have different nutritional requirements at different ages. Formulated adult feeds that are made of predominantly wheat and soya are available as a supplement to the foraging diet. They contain many other essential minerals and trace elements. When natural feed is plentiful, very little food supplement

Cleaning out a duck pond

1 Call or other small ducks can be kept in a small garden. With care and good management, these pets can live on a small pond or even a baby bath, although this will need cleaning on a regular basis.

2 Algae soon builds up on the surface of artificial ponds. This is best removed with a soft brush before it can build around the edge of the pond or bath.

3 After a rinse, the water can be replaced. As ducks splash water everywhere, some owners may place the bath on decking.

4 Pet ducks will soon learn to interact with their owner, and may start to ask noisily for more water to top up a half-filled bath.

is required, but during short, cold, winter days, or when highly productive ducks are in full lay, they need to be given larger quantities of supplements. Ducks kept on ponds and open water may ignore clean drinking water, but those kept in less natural situations should always have a fresh supply.

◄ *Heavy rain turned this duck run into a temporary swimming pool.*

Changing bathing water

Ducks are undoubtedly messy creatures, and any bathing water set down for them will not stay clean for long. Although they prefer a large pond or bath, using a smaller, lightweight bath will ensure that regular changing of the water is a less onerous task and therefore is less likely to be neglected. A pair of ducks will be happy in a bath that is about 70cm/28in in diameter.

BREEDING DUCKS

All breeds of domestic ducks descend from the wild mallard and will readily interbreed with wild birds. Anyone wishing to breed pure-bred ducks that conform to the breed standard may have to keep their birds in separate pens that are covered with nets to prevent crossbreeding with wild males.

Breeders prepared to go to the trouble of breeding their own ducks will have a breed standard or other criteria, such as egg numbers or meat quality, in mind when buying or selecting an adult breeding group.

While one light-breed drake may readily mate with several ducks, very heavy exhibition drakes of breeds such as Rouen and Aylesbury, that find it easier to mate on water, may be able to cope with no more than three or four females. An excess of drakes can make life unpleasant for the ducks that share their space.

Hatching the eggs

Fertile eggs intended for hatching should be collected first thing in the morning, as soon as possible after they are laid, and carefully stored and

▼ *These little Call ducks are now popular as garden pets.*

turned until they can be put under a suitable broody duck or placed in an incubator. While some domestic ducks make good mothers, many small-scale breeders rely on foster mothers, including broody hens or a purpose-bred crossbreed bantam hen willing to sit on the eggs for 28 days (33–35 days in the case of Muscovy ducks). Larger quantites of eggs may be better hatched in an incubator, with the newly hatched ducklings being reared with the aid of an artificial brooder. The advent of very reliable, moisture-controlled small incubators means it is now far easier to hatch ducklings artificially, leaving the ducks occupied with laying eggs.

Sexing the ducklings

Luckily, vent-sexing chicks is easy, and given a little tuition, most breeders will learn how to gently press the vent area to reveal emerging organs.

▲ *Muscovy ducks that are willing to sit for a full 30 days can make satisfactory surrogate mothers for other breeds.*

Young and adolescent female ducks soon develop a characteristic, loud quack, while the drakes only manage a quieter, almost hoarse or hollow, note. Drakes also develop characteristic curled feathers immediately in front of their tails.

Rearing ducklings

Ducklings can be reared by three methods: under the mother duck; under a foster mother, which may be a hen or another duck breed; or in an incubator. Small clutches of ducklings can be raised effectively with a mother duck or mother substitute. Ducklings do not require heat for as long as chicks, and may soon spend less time with their mother. Since ducklings may not need artificial heat provided by the breeder for too long, vigilance is essential. As with chicks, an infra-red heat lamp within a draught-free enclosure allows growing ducklings the option of sitting under the lamp, or moving to the periphery

▲ *A "mother hen" brooder with an overhead electric element may be preferable to an infra-red unit. With its scrim curtain hung to mimic the mother's feathers, these day-old ducklings will soon learn to spend much of the time when they are not feeding or drinking under its secure warmth.*

SEXING DUCKS
Hold the duck firmly on its back and very gently press the vent area with your thumb to expose the genitals.

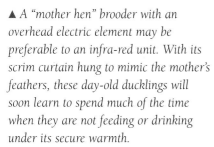

▲ *Male*   ▼ *Female*

if they become too hot. Carefully observe this behaviour and adjust the lamp height as appropriate to ensure healthy ducklings. Red-tinted or dull-heat emitting lamps are available, and are preferred by many breeders who think that the alternative of 24 hours of bright white light creates an unnatural lighting pattern for the young birds. Lamps can be turned off for short periods during daylight hours, when the ducklings spend little or no time under the heat source.

▲ *In this self-coloured variety the drake's curly tail feather helps to differentiate it from the duck, which has flat tail feathers.*

Feeding ducklings
Like adult ducks, ducklings can be messy feeders, and from an early age like to mix food and water into porridge, which they then treat as mud to be rolled in. To combat this, many breeders keep a supply of dry mash or crumbs at some distance from their source of clean water. Some breeders use special duckling feed, but care should be taken to avoid feed containing specialist chick anti-coccidiosis medication. Ducklings being fattened for the table will be fed, first on duckling feed and then on a lower-protein fattening mash.

◄ *Not all broody hens will be willing to sit for the extra week that it takes to hatch ducklings, but are likely to be far more amenable to being moved to a suitable broody coop. Using a hen or an incubator can extend the breeding season beyond the late spring and early summer months when ducks are more often inclined to sit. Ducks will lay and sit in a place of their own choosing, and then bring up a family on their own terms.*

KEEPING GEESE

Like ducks, geese belong to the order Anseriformes. Both species have webbed feet and are developed for an aquatic way of life. They have a strong bill adapted to pecking for food. Male birds are ganders, females are geese and the young are known as goslings.

Geese may have been kept and domesticated by humans long before they kept poultry. Archaeological excavations of Saxon settlements have uncovered bones of geese that had a sufficiently large stature to have rendered flight difficult. As a result, it seems that at this point in their history geese could be considered domesticated, since they would have relied on human shelter to protect them from predators.

Large white geese have been selectively bred, primarily for meat, in northern Europe, including Holland and Germany, for centuries. The Bremen or Embden geese from Germany were notably large. It is likely that strains of domestic geese would have developed in the same

▼ *Once a Christmas goose was commonplace. Popular goose fairs or markets were established in September to sell purpose-bred geese, which were fattened by the buyer ready for Christmas.*

way as other poultry, with different breeders selecting the best in terms of size and shape for meat, or egg-laying capacity, and then using those birds to supply the next generation in the hope that the desired characteristics would be present in the progeny.

Today geese are kept for much the same reasons as other poultry: for meat and eggs; to breed and sell the young or eggs for hatching; for ornamental value; to exhibit at shows; as attractive pets whose antics are entertaining to watch; to keep large swathes of pastureland neatly kept; and, uniquely among fowl, as a deterrent to burglars. Geese are territorial and easily alarmed when faced with the unfamiliar. These are large and strong animals, and will hiss in an aggressive manner if disturbed.

Goose meat – a seasonal treat

European pure-bred stock provided the genetic material needed to create the crossbred, fast-maturing goose

WALKING GEESE TO MARKET

Geese were traditionally walked to market at the end of August or the beginning of September depending upon the time of the harvest. The bird's feet were protected by driving them through a sticky, tar-like solution and then through sawdust before each day's journey. Drovers guided the birds to their destination, which could take several days and cover 30–40 miles. Many were sold along the way. After the harvest, the birds feasted on the stubble in the fields until late autumn, when they were fattened for Christmas.

that was historically commercially bred to supply meat for the Christmas market. The goose lost favour with the introduction of relatively cheaper turkey meat in the early to mid-20th century. Now considered a luxury meat, the goose is increasing once more in popularity.

Unlike other domesticated poultry and animals, the goose has defied the instigators of intensive rearing methods. Geese are not prolific layers and they are one of the few remaining sources of seasonal food. This large,

▲ *Goose eggs are available from specialist butchers and delicatessens.*

fatty bird traditionally survived by pecking about and foraging for any available food. Found on humble farms because it was economical to keep and a good source of meat or fat, a special bird would be fattened for Christmas. It is the traditional celebration bird and has always been seen as a treat: a bird for both the poor and the rich.

Goose fat had all manner of additional uses for country people, including rubbing into the chest to ward off colds, as well as for cooking.

Goose eggs

A gander is not required to produce, only to make fertile, eggs. Weighing in at about 200g/7oz each, goose eggs are twice the size of hens' eggs. The shell is chalky white and very hard. Goose eggs need washing and thorough cooking to kill any harmful bacteria that may be on the shells. In flavour, they are milder than ducks' eggs but stronger than hens' eggs.

Ornament, exhibition and pet

Most breeders are interested in selecting strains of pure-bred geese for utility properties, but others will find that breed characteristics are the appeal of keeping geese. Pure-bred and exhibition geese may be more

▲ *Geese are an effective deterrent to burglars and will hiss and show aggressive behaviour if unfamiliar people or animals appear on their territory.*

expensive than some other forms of poultry, but, with specialist breed clubs and regional poultry clubs as contact points, reliable breeding stock can usually be found. The increasing

▼ *Geese love to preen, and in doing so add tranquillity to the poultry yard.*

numbers of European breeds now being kept reflects regional interest in local breeds. Some of these are small and compact breeds that are useful for owners with large gardens or small paddocks. Many will want to keep geese, if not as pets, then as loyal companions that interact with their owners and friends more readily than any other domestic fowl.

Exhibition forms of the larger, slow-maturing birds may still have a place in future breeding programs.

CARING FOR GEESE

Geese are long-lived birds, with some breeds thriving for 20 years or more, so investing in an ornamental bird for your garden is a long-term commitment. Geese bought and reared for their meat have a short lifespan, since it is not economically viable to keep them beyond 23 weeks.

Geese can be aggressive, and may adopt an intimidating attitude to strangers. They are also protective of their brooding spouse, goslings and nest, though they will generally settle down to become companionable, if noisy, garden neighbours. Pure-breed geese have a variety of characteristics. Lightweight Chinese geese are alert, with loud voices that make them good watchdogs, while the far heavier and more statuesque Toulouse will provide a more placid companion.

Buying geese
When it comes to purchasing stock, people wishing to keeping pure breeds should choose stock from an established breeder. Breeding groups, comprising of a gander and two to four geese, will need time to get used to each other and to their surroundings. This means that the best time to purchase them is in autumn or early winter so they have time together before spring.

▲ *Some geese have been known to challenge a fox; nonetheless, all geese will need to be securely housed at night. They require a big door as they will sometimes have to be herded in at dusk. Geese love a clean bed of straw that they will soon get messy, so to assist in cleaning a low house, a removable roof can sometimes be fitted.*

▼ *A plentiful supply of fresh, clean drinking water must be provided for geese, along with enough to spare for them to bathe their heads and necks at all times.*

▲ *Geese are good grazers, and when grass is both plentiful and nutritious they will live and fatten off good grass. During very dry weather and the winter months they require extra cereals, changing to a proprietary ration complete with minerals and other nutrients during and just before the breeding season.*

Housing geese
Nearly all geese are vulnerable to attack by predators at night and should be housed in a secure pen or similar fox-proof run. These adaptable birds can be kept in any type of shed or building as long as it is secure. Rather than perching, geese spend the night at floor level, so a wide door-way will be useful when persuading them to retire. Smaller units are easiest to clean if they have human access to remove soiled bedding.

Geese love water, but it is not necessary to provide a pond for swimming. They will enjoy a small tub, which should be adequate for bathing; geese do not have to spend as much time on the water as many of us think. Make sure fresh water for drinking is provided every day.

Feeding geese

Geese eat a totally vegetarian diet that for much of the year consists of grass. Good quality, well-managed grass and clover can provide a high proportion of the total nutritional needs of adult and growing geese. However, remember that geese eat huge quantities of grass, and much of it after the main grass-growing season is over, leaving large areas of soil exposed. The resulting exodus from their bodies also means that paths may be covered in pea-green goo.

A regular feed of proprietary goose feed will help to ensure healthy goslings that hatched early will be able to take advantage of any later flush of spring grass.

Baby and young goslings, particularly those being intensively brooded, need four or five feeds a day of damp, crumbly mash. This should be a specialist waterfowl formula rather than chick feed, which may contain unsuitable additives.

Fattening the goose

Goslings hatched in spring were traditionally fattened on grass and finished on gleanings from fields in time for Michaelmas (29 September). Such birds were known as "green

geese" and were prized for their tender flesh. Nowadays most of the larger flocks of geese used to supply the specialist Christmas market will have been supplied as goslings produced from specialist breeders. Such goslings are generally from breeders using advanced strains of

▼ *Geese that are to be sold for their meat are fattened on grain ready for market.*

▲ *Geese can add much to the domestic scene if you have time and inclination to care for them.*

good laying geese mated to heavy, quick-growing ganders. These young birds are started on specialist gosling mash or crumbs, then feed on the succulent, high-protein grass of spring and early summer. The later drier, higher-fibre grass may make up much of the maintenance diet of adult geese, but growing goslings and young fattening geese will quickly require this to be supplemented by a grain-based mix.

Fattening geese require unstressful conditions. They may be left on grass in a restricted space, so that they conserve their energy. Some owners use electric fencing to pen their geese. If open ground becomes waterlogged the geese may be moved to a yard, and transferred to a house at night. These sociable birds may go off their feed if some of their number are removed early. Avoid changes to their regime that may unsettle them.

BREEDING GEESE

The gander is best put in a breeding pen known as a "set" with the chosen geese in the autumn. Together they will bond as a group. If the bond is broken or changed it can take weeks or even months to re-form into a fertile breeding group.

Like swans, geese are known to mate for life, and if kept to be ornamental, they will seek out the same partners each year. It is customary to make up domestic geese breeding groups as early as possible before the start of the breeding season. Even then, these groups may not bond if they can see or hear an earlier mate.

A gander is in his prime at around six years of age. Heavier breeds, such as Toulouse, may be penned with three females to one male, while with light and agile breeds such as Chinese ganders for example, one male may cope with five or more geese. The breeding season continues until early spring. Geese can be expected to come into lay in late winter, but this depends on factors such as age, breed and the amount and quality of feed available. Good breeding results will depend on supplementary feeding.

Broody geese

Geese can make excellent broodies and mothers, successfully sitting, hatching and then brooding their offspring, but some may choose not to sit on their eggs, or they may wander off after the first gosling hatches, taking no further interest in unhatched eggs. Since geese only need shelter from the weather and security from predators, any outbuilding or shed will suffice as a nesting area. A broody goose should be removed from the communal laying area to a large broody coop, or be partitioned off. She will collect her eggs in a nesting site, and generally sit when there is a clutch of five. The eggs may often be found carefully covered with straw or litter.

▲ *Goslings need protection from predators.*

Eggs should be removed daily into controlled storage, and can be replaced with a single large ceramic egg, to placate the female. The freshest eggs are returned to the nest as soon as the goose goes broody. The incubation period is approximately 31 days, with all the eggs hatching within a day of each other.

Since goslings are best hatched early in the year so that they make best use of the most nutritious grass, many breeders use large broody hens as foster mothers or incubators. Others will use an incubator capable of handling larger eggs.

Breeders willing to start with domestic stock could try hatching their own goslings, if they find a reliable source of hatching eggs and a hen willing to sit for the necessary 28–30 days. If successful, it could be easier to get to know and make friends with these youngsters than those hatched under an often aggressive mother goose.

Caring for the young

Goslings require less heat than chicks, and by day 10, if an incubator is used, or day 14 if a broody hen is used, they may be off-heat and spending less time with the "mother".

▼ *A goose will often create a nesting place of her own choosing, in a slight depression in the ground, loosely covered and lined by feathers, straw and other litter.*

KEEPING GUINEA FOWL

Until recently, guinea fowl were rarely seen as part of serious poultry keeping. There was a general acceptance that they lived an almost feral existence, slept in trees, laid a few dozen small eggs in the spring, and were mainly useful in alerting their owners to visitors or intruders.

Today, growing numbers of these birds are being reared commercially for their gamey meat and small but delicious eggs. While chickens, ducks and turkeys have been selected and managed for centuries, guinea fowl have been left to fend for themselves and have nearly always been allowed to breed indiscriminately.

Guinea fowl meat

Continental poultry keepers have treated guinea fowl more seriously. The French have an interest in the game-like qualities of the meat. In recent years, they have made enormous strides in improving both growth rates and laying capacity, to the point where the end product can compete at the top end of the specialist poultry meat market. These advanced strains of guinea fowl rear as well as any other poultry, feather early and are often independent

▶ *Some traditional strains of guinea fowl can be the bullyboys of the farmyard.*

▼ *These "improved" 18-week-old female guinea fowls are perfectly at home in a fenced run. However, they are unlikely to be at ease with being handled in the same way as other poultry types.*

▲ *Guinea fowl eggs are roughly half the size of hen's eggs and weigh about 25g/1oz each. They are light brown and very uniform in colour.*

earlier than chicks. Having been reared in an enclosed situation, they adapt to being housed and shut away at night like other poultry.

Guinea fowl can provide a delicious alternative to several game species and can be expected to weigh 1.5kg/3lbs at 71 days. Guinea fowl

eggs are also sold commercially. They have a very hard shell and rich, golden yolks.

Breeding guinea fowl

Guinea fowl make poor mothers. As a result, most breeding schemes put guinea fowl eggs under broody foster hens to ensure the breed's survival. Females come into lay at around 16 weeks and can lay a reasonable number of smallish eggs.

Breeders happy with the almost-feral habits of guinea fowl may be able to supply fertile eggs to the industry, providing the owner can find where the eggs have been hidden! Breeders wanting to keep any of the newer, advanced table strains of guinea fowl should initially buy in day-old poults from a specialist breeder of continental-type strains. These young birds will quickly adapt to a more regulated form of poultry management, and may be reared on either turkey or normal chick and poultry growers' rations.

KEEPING TURKEYS

No other member of the poultry family interacts with its owners quite like a turkey. These are large, friendly and docile creatures that add interest to a larger garden and can add variety to a domestic poultry fowl collection, in much the same way as they did to traditional farmyards.

Turkeys may be a much rarer sight and sound in the neighbourhood than garden hens and roosters, but people keep them for much the same reasons. Turkeys are large birds, with several species available. As a breed, turkeys can make unusual pets, and like chickens, there are rare varieties, each with their own distinctive characteristics from which to choose. Like chicken fanciers, there are turkey fanciers, who select and breed turkeys for conservation and exhibition purposes. However, being larger and with a greater risk of breaking feathers, not to mention being unwieldy to transport, turkeys are much less prominent at poultry exhibitions than other types of fowl.

For some people, the opportunity to rear the bird that they will eat at Christmas or Thanksgiving may be appealing. Birds can be bought in as young, known as poults, at one day old, and may be reared in the garden in much the same way as chickens. Provided the source of origin is reputable, you will have the security of knowing how the bird has been reared and on what it has fed, helping to allay concerns about animal welfare and any contamination of the food chain. However, turkeys are classed as livestock by some local authorities and permission may be required in order to keep them.

Male turkeys, known as stags or toms, make a wide range of vocal noises, particularly gobbling, so if you live in close proximity to neighbours, it may be sensible to discuss your ideas with them before going ahead and making a purchase. Keeping your neighbours' goodwill is always preferable. Since all fowl require care and attention for 365 days of the year, asking your neighbours to help provide emergency cover, should you need it, will be easier if they have no objections to the fowl in the first place. In many countries, turkeys have to be slaughtered by a qualified butcher, so if you are keeping a bird in order to eat it, ensure that you know how far you may have to travel with it in order to have it prepared for the oven. Turkeys can also be large and expensive pets to feed.

Turkey eggs

Turkeys have never been bred for egg production in the way that hens have, but some strains, notably the Buff turkey breed, are good egg-layers. Turkey eggs are rarely seen for sale, since relatively few are produced when compared to the numbers of hen and duck eggs laid.

Turkey meat

The original wild, native American, bronze-coloured turkeys would have had boat-shaped bodies, and be well flavoured, but by modern standards, the meat would be regarded as tough. Today, turkey is farmed commercially to supply meat for human consumption as a cheap source of protein. Since turkeys are closely associated with the commercial meat trade, their shape and size have been directly affected by market demand.

▼ *The American Bronze turkey is farmed for its meat. The various forms of this breed have added size and their distinctive character to farmyards for hundreds of years.*

▼ *Turkey eggs can be used for cooking and baking in much the same way as a hen's eggs, though they are never produced on the scale of hybrid hens reared specifically for this purpose.*

▲ Good management and an attention to detail helps ensure that turkeys being reared in groups on straw remain both healthy and contented.

In order to produce birds that will develop a large quantity of meat for very little feed, and which sell at an economic price, breeders have consistently, over time, selectively bred from fowl that display the most desirable characteristics.

Several strains or varieties of Bronze or Black turkeys evolved between the 1850s and 1950s to meet market demand. The American Bronze has Mexican ancestry; the wild bird was taken to Spain when Mexico became Spain's territory. The breed was taken back to America by migrants from Europe centuries later. These European-bred turkeys were crossed with American wild turkeys to produce larger birds that became known as the Bronze. The new breed was first standardized as the Cambridge or Standard Bronze. Early crossing of the new breed with giant American birds produced a new type known as the American Mammoth or Broad-Breasted Bronze, which

weighed up to 18.4kg/40lbs. This larger type could not mate naturally, and only survived via artificial insemination in order to produce fertile eggs. These breeds were developed to such an exaggerated size that most were only suitable for intensive indoor production. However, the arrival and development of these fast-growing strains enabled the industry to implement intensive or factory farming methods, with the

product often sold frozen and far more cheaply than any other similarly produced broiler poultry meat.

Trade and consumer preference for birds with a large carcass and white breast meat led to the demise of utility flocks of the old pure breeds, which could not compete on the same scale as intensively produced meat. By the 1980s, consumer preferences began to change, and over the following decades the discerning diner began to demand turkey meat with more flavour, while animal welfare campaigners demanded that birds be reared in more humane circumstances.

Small-scale pure-breed farming

Norfolk Black and American Bronze pure-breed turkeys that remained in the hands of traditional, small-scale farmers and breeders throughout the decades of mass production were to

▼ Traditional free-range Bronze turkeys being fattened will find some of their own feed. Spending time investigating every part of the run in the pursuit of food can help prevent boredom, which can lead to feather pecking and aggression.

become the basis of the growth in farming traditional breeds. These breeds, having taken longer to mature to a less exaggerated size, are considered better quality, with superior meat flavour. In addition, they are reared in a more humane way than those under the intense factory farming system.

These breeds are also being developed to meet the same market requirements, competing with intensively farmed products by appealing to consumer conscience. A growing demand for quality Christmas turkeys may see a return to medium-sized flocks being reared on less specialized farms.

Small-scale turkey farmers vary considerably in the scope of their interest, and each will have a management regime that reflects their commercial requirements.

Since turkeys lay eggs less reliably and in much smaller quantities than hens, in order to ensure a regular supply of birds to grow on farmers may buy in poults at one day old,

▼ *A free-range turkey farm provides good conditions for its stock.*

▲ *Turkey-keeping will require a higher standard of stockmanship and management skills than nearly any other form of poultry keeping.*

supplementing rather than relying on breeding their own turkeys. Poults are best purchased as two mixed batches of different types, each timed to finish at different weights, sourcing them from a specialist breeder who will advise on optimum age and weight as well as growth rate of available stock.

Turkey franchises

Many medium-sized producers run franchises. Working within a franchise arrangement may not suit every producer, since the end product still sells to a smaller, though growing, niche market. Producing a top-quality turkey meat requires the most selective breeding, feeding and free-range production. There must be close co-operation with the breeders who supply the franchise to ensure the poults arrive at the right time to meet the required weights.

A franchise will ensure that the smallest hens of the batch reach 1.7kg/3½lbs (oven-ready weight) at 10 weeks and that the biggest stags finish at 11.8kg/26lbs (oven-ready weight) at 24 weeks. The turkeys are killed, processed and dry-plucked a short distance from the rearing farm.

Intensive turkey farming

Much large-scale turkey production is based on a factory system that sees birds intensively housed throughout their lives. As they reach optimum weight, they are killed and kept frozen until they are marketed.

Most of the available day-old, usually white poults that form the basis of the industry will have been selectively bred for a monocropping system. The larger hatcheries will often keep flocks of laying females that are artificially inseminated from heavier males. As it is not viable to maintain this type of breeding setup to produce poults all year round, most small-scale producers will find themselves competing to purchase poults during the same summer period. Poults can be reared under broody hens, but most producers will opt for the heat lamp system used for day-old and growing chicks. While turkey poults require marginally higher brooding temperatures during their early life, as they mature to

become fully feathered, many will require less shelter during their remaining lifespan.

Conservation of old turkey breeds

Within this specialized market, smaller producers and exhibition breeders have adopted differing breeding and management practices to those of industrial producers.

The purest strains of the old breeds of turkeys are selected to finish growing at a specific weight, with some slow-maturing Bronze males increasing to a huge size at eight months old. The females mature at a younger age and to lower weights. At the other end of the size scale are lighter breeds, such as the Beltsville White, that mature as plump tiny birds at less than 16 weeks old. Examples of the old pure breeds are still occasionally seen at poultry shows. The fact that these breeds have survived means that they may still have a role to play in the future of commercial poultry production.

Enthusiastic conservationists often farm the large Bronze and White varieties as well as breeds such as the Norfolk Black, steering a path between over-developed dimple-breasted types while still providing a rounded, full-flavoured product. Most of these producers rely on bought-in chicks or poults.

Buying and caring for turkeys

People who favour rearing pure-breed turkeys will purchase poults or eggs from a specialist breeder. If you intend keeping turkeys they will need an adequate space in which to roam.

◄ *Turkeys will relish left-overs, overripe fruit, and fruit and vegetable peelings.*

A breeding pair will require 8sq m/ 90sq ft of space as a minimum. A 2m/6.5ft-high fence should be sufficient to prevent the birds from escaping. It is not advisable to allow turkeys to roam free in the garden as they will destroy plant growth and blooms. Turkeys are naturally curious birds, so make sure that the penned area is free from all potential hazards that could harm them. Turkeys kept outside will find their own grit to aid digestion. Be sure to provide those kept indoors with sand or fine gravel.

Feeding turkeys

Grass makes up a small proportion of a free-range turkey's diet. The majority of the feed regime consists of grain, vegetable protein, pulses and dried grass. This diet will provide essential minerals and trace elements without recourse to drugs, genetically modified feed or animal protein. This ensures that the meat is well flavoured.

▼ *Narragansett turkey.*

▼ *Beltsville white turkey.*

▼ *Norfolk Black turkey.*

Housing turkeys

Growing up to 1m/3ft tall, turkeys need considerable space in which to live. The housing provided must be appropriate for the size and number of birds, with adequate ventilation, light and space, and access to a fenced-off run in which the birds can exercise. Some breeds have little interest in going outdoors, and ensuring the roost is large enough is important. Other breeds prefer to roost outdoors in all weathers, so covering the run so that the turkeys cannot fly out is essential. In spite of their large size, the slow and clumsy turkey is vulnerable to attacks by foxes, so a large house with a wide door incorporated into a really secure run is a key requirement.

Intensively reared birds are housed in barns with low light levels for the duration of their lives. The typical fast-growing, medium-weight turkey may be as content when kept in a well lit, straw-covered barn as it would be in an open environment.

▼ *Heavier and less mobile turkeys being fattened for market may pick each other's breast feathers. A good stockman will isolate offenders at an early stage.*

▲ *A hangar-type structure can keep the birds dry, allow free movement of air and provide enough height to allow for perches for the turkeys.*

Free-range birds are free to wander in pastures and woodland, and to sleep at night in open-sided pole barns, which keep out wild birds and any infections or disease that they may spread.

However well kept they are, older birds are given to boredom and may start pulling a few feathers from other birds in the flock. If allowed to continue unchecked, such behaviour may even lead to cannibalism, so an isolation pen will be essential.

If you keep other types of poultry, it may be sensible to keep turkeys in a separate enclosure. This is because other types of poultry may carry diseases such as blackhead, a condition that young and growing turkeys are particularly vulnerable to.

Housing poults

As turkeys object to radical changes in their environment, and any growth is likely to be checked by moving them, a well-planned housing scheme should be in place from the outset, particularly if you are buying in poults. Baby turkeys need more heat than other chicks, although, once feathered, they can manage with rather rudimentary housing.

Young poults are very inquisitive and inclined to wander into corners.

When reared under heat lamps, they are best enclosed within a circular hardboard ring that can be expanded until they are about seven to ten weeks old. After that time a well-lit, airy, straw-littered barn is usually adequate.

▼ *Young poults are quick to feather and far more likely to roam or otherwise get into trouble than other young poultry.*

BREEDING TURKEYS

Pure-breed turkeys with slim bodies may be bred without human intervention. Large commercial breeds usually require assistance in the form of artificial insemination. Adult turkeys breeding in a farmyard on smallholding are now a rare sight.

People who keep turkeys may be happy to let the flock make its own breeding arrangements. However, this strategy often results in there being years when insufficient replacement stock is produced to maintain the group's numbers. Many turkey breeds have been bred to such a size that the larger males are, at best, clumsy breeding partners. Most commercial turkeys are artificially inseminated, since the selective breeding of some breeds for large quantities of breast meat means that many can no longer mate, and without human intervention the breed would die out. Artificial insemination allows very large males to breed with small hens that lay well and are cheaper to keep. It also means that more hens can be fertilized.

Many pure breeds, maintained by enthusiasts, often have a slimmer body better adapted to everyday farmyard life than breeds fattened for the meat industry. These smaller birds can breed as nature intended.

Conservation breeders who have maintained a gene pool of breeding birds often adopt whichever methods produces sufficient poults to allow the selection of good-quality offspring for future breeding and distribution to other enthusiasts. Turkey exhibitors within this group may place greater emphasis on feather colour and markings than meat quantity and quality, and may take greater efforts to maintain selected examples in pristine condition.

Incubating the eggs
Some females may successfully incubate their own eggs for the required 28 days, but care must be

▲ *Bred to have large quantities of breast meat, turkey stags, with their huge dimple breast, will be front-heavy and may fall off the female during mating.*

taken that the hen leaves the nest once a day to tend to her own needs. Providing the hen with an isolated coop in which to nurture her eggs and tend the hatched young has proved a successful method of keeping the hen focused in raising the young poults. An incubator is used on larger-scale farming operations, where closer control over the hatching can be exercised.

Rearing the poults
Young turkeys are generally thought of as delicate, and from day one need feeding a slightly higher-protein diet than other day-old poultry. The standard baby turkey crumb will contain all the protein, trace elements and micro-nutrients required for normal early development. Being susceptible to change, growing turkeys move on to grower food, preferably made by the same manufacturer, gradually.

Unlike the traditional breeds, modern turkey strains are designed to finish at several different weights, sometimes at a relatively young age, and so require a specifically designed feed regime. To prevent blackhead, some breeders now include organic products such as oregano in the feed, as well as segregating young turkeys from other fowl.

▼ *Young turkey poults are monitored carefully from a young age.*

A DIRECTORY OF FOUNDATION BREEDS

Foundation breeds are pure breeds of poultry. They are generally old breeds with distinct characteristics and visibly identifiable features. Pure breeds are recognized officially by a poultry club. Each country has its own poultry club, which holds the written standard for each breed type. Each country's poultry club is supported by members who breed poultry to the accepted standard. Between them, these members are responsible for maintaining and safeguarding the bloodlines and breeding stock of each pure breed and ensuring that they conform to the breed standard. Members are usually passionate about their chosen breed, and each strives to produce the best poultry by selecting specific features and attributes found in individual birds, and using those birds to produce the next generation. Each pure breed must produce offspring that is a replica of its parent. Foundation breeds form the genetic basis of many of today's modern hybrid poultry.

▲ *The Sussex hen is an important foundation breed.*

◄ *Swiss Appenzellar Spitzhauben and Sumatra game are both early breeds that developed in isolation. Each will thrive in very free-range situations.*

WHAT IS A FOUNDATION BREED?

A foundation breed is considered by many poultry breeders to be any breed of poultry that has been used in the creation of another breed. Often these are old breeds of poultry that have been developed and selected over time for their significant desirable features.

For the purposes of this book the foundation breeds are characterized by geographical region – British, European, Mediterranean and Asian. These are categories that exist in show classes at exhibition, with the latter category being subdivided into soft-feathered Asian birds, and game and hard-feathered Asian birds. All of the ancient fowl groups from each of these regions provided humans with the genetic material required to create the breeds of today.

Poultry breeds differ significantly in character, appearance, egg-laying capacity and quality of meat. Even within a local area, the same general type of poultry will fare differently in the hands of different poultry keepers and farmers. Breeds of poultry were developed in response to market demand by exploiting the natural qualities of the poultry and selecting

the best birds of each generation that displayed desirable qualities from which to breed. Many of these went on to become foundation breeds.

The heavy-boned Asian fowl added significantly to the gene pool of the later economically important standardized breeds. Crosses between

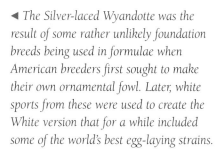

◄ The Silver-laced Wyandotte was the result of some rather unlikely foundation breeds being used in formulae when American breeders first sought to make their own ornamental fowl. Later, white sports from these were used to create the White version that for a while included some of the world's best egg-laying strains.

very different Asiatic fowl produced the Asian soft-feathered Brahma breed. This in turn provided genetic material for the British Dorking-type fowl, which was then selected to create the British Sussex breed as well as a whole range of innovative American breeds and hybrid strains.

British foundation breeds

In Britain, there seems to have been significant investment in developing breed type, at first by breeders keen to take advantage of the high prices people were willing to pay for poultry with white breast meat. With the introduction of huge Asiatic birds, genetic material from Asian birds was used to develop larger table fowl with more meat on the carcass than previously recorded. The Dorking breed was one such, bred for market using genetic material from Asian birds, which added bulk to its size. Fanciers in Britain also spent considerable time and effort developing strong, light and agile birds for cockfighting.

◄ The Speckled Sussex, like the Jubilee Orpington, first developed as a table fowl out of crosses between local strains and Dark Brahmas. Their descendants developed into one of our most spectacular exhibition breeds.

▶ *Early crosses between completely unrelated heavy-boned Asiatic fowl gave the world one of its best known breeds, the Brahma. This in turn would be part of many of the world's later economically important breeds.*

European and Mediterranean foundation breeds

In past times, poultry fanciers selected and developed breeds of poultry from Europe and the Mediterranean for their ornamental value. Crests, muffs, beards, feathered feet, five toes and vulture hocks were seen as desirable traits that added distinction and character to different breeds. These breeds offered meat and eggs but were also valued for their appearance by fanciers, who were motivated by competitive exhibitions to produce the best of each type.

Early forms of European fowl were probably descended from jungle fowl and fowl from Western Asia. Nearly all ancient European breeds are lightweight and have fabulous egg-laying qualities. Mediterranean foundation breeds differ from other European breeds in their upright stance and wing carriage, which they

share with many domesticated Asian breeds. Some types were also selected and developed for their head points. Their origins are uncertain, but heavier Leghorn-type fowl almost certainly display the influence of Asiatic stock.

Asian foundation breeds

Asian soft-feathered breeds are massive birds that have been selectively bred for their size. However they probably no longer closely resemble the first domesticated Asian birds imported to Europe in the 19th century, an action which greatly influenced the development of many modern breeds. The hard-feathered breeds of India and South-east Asia have also influenced the development of many modern poultry breeds outside the region.

▲ *Table-type New Hampshire has similar coloration to the Rhode Island Red which probably results from both having some Red or Cinnamon Malay in their founding ancestry.*

HOW TO USE THE DIRECTORY
Each poultry breed listed in the following chapters of the book is accompanied by an account of breed history and interesting qualities. Each has an Essential Characteristics panel, which contains a number of features. The desirable weight of standard and bantam versions (where applicable) are given. The panel also lists the environment in which the breed thrives, the breed's temperament, and the number of eggs a good specimen of a utility breed might produce. NB There is considerable variation in egg numbers produced by different strains of a breed. In many cases, exhibition strains lay very few eggs, since other characteristics are deemed more important to the breeder. Weights given for bantams are often exceeded by show winners. The general rule is that if no bantam weight has been agreed, most individuals will be expected to weigh between 20 and 25 per cent of the large version.

▼ *Utility-type Rhode Island Red rooster (below) running with Light Sussex hens (right) would have made up much of the early British laying flock.*

BRITISH FOUNDATION BREEDS

In Britain, the selection of birds for cockfighting historically influenced the types of fowl that were bred, as well as those physical features that were considered desirable traits in fighting birds. Generally, such birds have a lightweight appearance and flighty nature.

Later, with the introduction of heavy-boned Asiatic breeds, heavy poultry breeds were developed to meet a growing demand for table fowl. It is likely that many native British foundation breeds were influenced in their breeding by Asiatic fowl. Such birds naturally grow bigger than lightweight fowl. Prior to the introduction of hybrid lines to the poultry industry, many British pure breeds were also selected for their white flesh and plump breast meat, which was highly saleable.

The foundation breeds that appear in the following pages have all been developed by British breeders for specific character traits. Many are widely known all over the world. Others have retained their regional popularity and remain contained within a small geographical area. Such birds are in the hands of a few breeders. All of these fowl are considered heritage breeds, with some being rare and highly prized.

Hamburg/Hamburgh

Hamburgs are known to belong to an ancient group of fowl that are thought to have been dispersed along the routes of Viking conquests or Nordic traders. Contrary to its name, the Hamburg breed is thought to have originated in the Netherlands rather than Germany, though it may have passed through the port of Hamburg on its way to Great Britain. The breed, as we know it today, was refined by British poultry fanciers in the mid-19th century, at a time when the first poultry craze was sweeping the country. The standard for the breed was set at this time.

It is because British breeders refined the breed that the Hamburg is listed as a British breed.

In appearance, Hamburgs have a light bone structure and almost pheasant-like carriage. They are a soft-feather breed and a prolific layer of white eggs. Neither large or bantam versions lay a big egg, although both are capable of converting a given weight of poultry feed into as great a weight of eggs as any traditional breed. All, or nearly all, have a rose comb, white lobes and slate-coloured

> **ESSENTIAL CHARACTERISTICS**
> **Size:** Large male 2.5kg/5lbs. Bantam male 680–794g/24–28oz. Large female 1.8kg/4lbs. Bantam female 624–737g/22–26oz.
> **Varieties:** Black, Gold-pencilled, Gold-spangled, Silver-pencilled, Silver-spangled, White.
> **Temperament:** Flighty, active.
> **Environment:** Happiest given free range.
> **Egg yield:** One of the best layers of small to medium, white to tinted eggs.

legs. Typically, they have either a gold or silver ground colour with some form of black pencilling or spangling. Prior to the breed standard being established, local strains in northern England were selected for breeding refinement on the basis of the precision of their feather

▶ The Hamburg breed has a shared ancestry with much of the poultry indigenous to Northern Europe and the Eastern Mediterranean. Regional populations of the Hamburg breed were developed with different traits. This is a bantam Silver-pencilled rooster.

▶ A standard Black female Hamburg.

patterns. Strains known locally as Bolton Greys and Bays were selected for the quality of their pencilling, which took the form of a series of fine straight lines across the feather. Similarly, Lancashire Moonies, another strain, were selected for their precise spangling to each feather end. Other regional British strains included varying forms of Redcaps and Pheasant Fowl, which were known locally as Corals, Creels and Chitterpats.

Regional Mediterranean populations, in contrast to British birds, often have either broken barring or spangling on the feathers. Because of the similarity of many of these local populations, organizers of the first shows chose to categorize all of them as Hamburgs. This decision later caused countless complications for those charged with providing a written standard of the breed. Gold and silver varieties, for example, may have different markings to those with a different ground colour. However, such a wide definition of the breed has proved advantageous for its conservation, as it ensures that other bloodlines have not been used in its make-up and that the breed retains genetic vigour. As it is difficult,

▼ A large Gold-pencilled male. The Hamburg is a hardy breed that can cope with cold weather.

thanks to their exacting colour standards, to make use of any out-cross, the genotype preserved within many Hamburgs remains virtually identical to that of fowl that existed a century ago.

Because breeders pursue precise feather marking, many Hamburg bantams are permitted to creep up beyond the standard bantam weight. Most of the large versions fall just short of their standard weight. Black bantams have never been standardized in Britain, as the Rosecomb bantam breed is thought to be too similar in appearance to warrant a separate classification. Breeding exhibition-quality examples or show winners without the help of someone knowledgeable may prove difficult, and breeding stock of the large versions may be hard to find, but the bantam versions are generally plentiful.

These birds are flightly by nature and, given their desire to range, will need to be surrounded by high fencing. They are active foragers, lively and alert, and do not do well in confinement. Their temperament makes them perfectly suited to barnyards, though they can make appealing garden companions.

▶ The Hamburg also shares its ancestry with some of the early English game strains. Being reared in a harsh climate helped to produce a breed with an in-built toughness that was invaluable to breeders. This is a bantam Silver-spangled female.

▶ A large Silver-pencilled male.

Old English Pheasant Fowl

This is a distinct regional breed from Yorkshire, Lancashire and the farms of Cumberland. It is an old breed, named in 1914, and has the Hamburg in its lineage. Unlike the fanciers and exhibitors who selected the colours and feather patterns of the Hamburg breed to conform to exacting standards, farmers and commercial poultry keepers selected their fowl on the basis of vigour, egg-laying ability and quality of meat. The result is the Old English Pheasant Fowl, once known as the Yorkshire Pheasant. Good examples are still seen in the rare breed classes at exhibitions. For much of the 20th century there was enough support for the breed to make it a commercially viable alternative to the main poultry breeds. As a farm bird from Northern England, it is known to be tolerant of cold, and is still highly regarded as a dual-purpose bird. The hen is a good egg-layer and the male is kept for its meat.

The basis of the breed's colour standard is a simple black crescent at the end of gold or silver feathers. It is a graceful bird with pheasant-like characteristics.

It has a rose comb, white earlobes, and slate-coloured legs and feet.

◀ *An Old English Pheasant Fowl is a forager by nature.*

ESSENTIAL CHARACTERISTICS

Size: Large male 2.7–2.9kg/6–7lbs.
Large female 2–2.7kg/4½–6lbs.
Bantam male 794g/28oz.
Bantam female 737g/26oz.
Varieties: Gold, Silver.
Temperament: Active and alert but can be quieter than the related Hamburg strains. Hardy.
Environment: Suits a free-range environment.
Egg yield: A good number of white eggs per year.

Derbyshire Redcap

True to its name, the Derbyshire Redcap originated in the county of Derbyshire, and was recorded as early as 1848, though the breed had to wait for national recognition. The breed's most distinguishing feature is its comb, which is made up of fleshy protrusions that cover the head. The comb can be up to 7.5cm/3in long and points backward. Initially, emphasis was placed on the size of the comb, which may have detracted from the overall usefulness of some strains of the breed. However, the standard defines the quality, rather than size, as being the breed's most important feature. The fact that it has red, rather than white, earlobes sets the breed apart from its closest relatives. The bird is a light breed with soft feathers, and has a single body colour which varies from orange to brown. Its tail plumage is black and its legs and feet are slate.

This bird has an active nature, making it suited to a free-range environment. It was originally kept as a dual-purpose bird.

▶ *This Derbyshire Redcap rooster has black plumage.*

ESSENTIAL CHARACTERISTICS

Size: Large male 3.4kg/7½lbs. Large female 2.7kg/6lbs. Many large fowl do not reach this weight. Bantams weigh 20–25 per cent of large fowl.
Varieties: Black.
Temperament: Active. A keen forager.
Environment: Free range. Needs a large amount of space.
Egg yield: 150–200 large white eggs per year.

Dorking

Named for the town of Dorking in Surrey, this is an ancient breed of poultry with Italian ancestry, thought to have originated at the time of the Roman Empire. The breed is prized for its five toes, an unusual feature in poultry. Five-toed poultry were recorded by one Roman author, and so there is an assumption that the breed was taken to the Dorking region by Roman legionaries. The early Dorkings depicted in art are slim, game-like fowl with five toes.

This is an important breed with a significant place in poultry history. The breed was highly prized in the mid-19th century, when white flesh was thought to indicate delicacy of flavour. By the 1860s, the Sussex breed had replaced the Dorking breed as the poultry of choice for the London markets. At this point, the French used the Dorking to help create the Houdan and Faverolles breeds that were sold through the Paris poultry market. The Dorking breed remained popular until the mid-20th century, when farmers began to change their flocks to hybrids.

During the mid-19th century, the Dorking standard, breed type and colours were stabilized and settled in a form that can still be seen among the best examples at major shows today. Standardized in five colours, Silver-grey, Dark, Red, Cuckoo and White, the breed also has single and rose combs, though not necessarily in each of the standard colours. The white variety is often found to be smaller than birds in other colours. The rare Cuckoo variety is always expected to have a rose comb, while the Red variety and the common Silver-grey, by contrast, should have only a single comb. The Dark variety, with its enigmatic

▼ This is a Silver-grey pullet, smaller and slimmer than the hen.

coloration, which seems to owe much to the old Kent and Surrey regional strains of fowl, may have a single or rose comb. The breed has a square frame, short, clean legs and five toes. It is a large breed, with males weighing up to 4.1kg/9lbs, and so requires a large poultry house and plenty of space. The standard for weight varies considerably between countries, and the British standard contains the heaviest weight, though not all birds attain this. This is a hardy breed, although the five toes and the male's large comb may need protecting in winter. The female is an average egg-layer, but interestingly, this breed is the only one with red earlobes to lay a white egg. The breed also has a red comb and wattles, and white legs. It can cope well with confinement, and is shy and docile by nature, making it the perfect companion in a garden. For flavoursome meat and eggs this breed must be fed good-quality feed. Bantam versions of the old single original breeds have proven difficult to perfect and are becoming rarer.

ESSENTIAL CHARACTERISTICS

Size: Large male 4.1kg/9lbs. Large female 3.2kg/7lbs. Bantam male 1.1–1.3kg/40–48oz. Bantam female 0.9–1.1kg/32–40oz.
Varieties: Coloured, Silver-grey, White.
Temperament: Calm and docile.
Environment: May require some protection from cold.
Egg yield: 150 large cream eggs per year.

◀ Anyone interested in studying the character and evolution of British foundation poultry breeds could well find a starting point in the Dorking breed. This is a large Silver-grey hen.

Sussex

The breed we know today as the Sussex developed from the indigenous fowl of the south of England – birds once recorded as Kent and Surrey breeds. For much of the 19th century the old breed had an almost unchallenged reputation for its quality poultry meat, which was sold to the important London markets, quickly surpassing the Dorking breed as the poultry of choice for the table.

This early market required very large-framed birds. South-east England had long been home to a population of large-bodied, white-fleshed fowl, and thus many breeders would have used this stock for the basis of their breeding pens. Soon, adventurous breeders began introducing the newly imported Asian Cochin poultry into the breeding pens in order to produce larger fowl. The Sussex that were later standardized as a pure and distinct breed, separate from the Kent and

ESSENTIAL CHARACTERISTICS

Size: Large male 4.1kg/9lbs. Large female 3.2kg/7lbs. Bantam male 1.1kg/40oz. Bantam female 794g/28oz.
Varieties: Brown, Buff, Light, Red, Silver, Speckled, White.
Temperament: Alert and docile.
Environment: Free-range or confinement.
Egg yield: 200–260 eggs per year.

Surrey breed, are made up of regional indigenous fowl crossed with Asiatic imports. Three varieties of Sussex were originally recorded – Speckled, Brown and Red – although eight are now standardized. During the whole of the pre-standardized period, the poultry would have been scrutinized by poultry dealers and consumers. Such a high level of scrutiny probably resulted in all varieties of Sussex being

▲ *A large Speckled Sussex hen.*

true enough to their English roots for the breed to be considered one of the poultry world's foundation breeds. The Sussex breed that we know today dates from around 1900, though it existed and has been husbanded commercially for at least 50 years prior to that date. In 1902, the exhibition standard for the breed was established. Like most of the 20th century's successful breeds, the Sussex has proven capable of development to meet the demands of changing times and circumstances.

As a growing middle class wanted a more reasonably priced table fowl, the Light variety was developed in order to lay the extra egg numbers needed to produce chicks for fattening for market. The Sussex

▶ *Evidence suggests that it took more than half a century of judicial crossings between local poultry populations and heavy-boned Asiatic breeds to produce the Sussex breed that we know today.*

◀ *A Light Sussex hen.*

FATTENING FOR MARKET

Historically, in order to produce birds for market, male birds were surgically caponized. After a period of captivity, if the birds had not reached the size and weight required for market, they were force fed with a mixture of locally grown ground oats, imported condensed milk and even tallow – a practice regarded as cruel today.

▼ A bantam Silver Sussex rooster.

▲ A prize-winning large Speckled Sussex rooster.

breed were selected for their white legs and flesh. When the variety was later selected as an egg-laying fowl, it consistently produced enough eggs to be considered as a utility fowl; it became one of the world's best heavy-breed egg-layers.

Today most strains of the large versions, including the later Silver and Buff varieties, are now kept as exhibition fowl. Meanwhile, the bantam Light variety has become one of the most popular and successful exhibition breeds of all time. The breed owes much of its popularity to the fact that the Silver hens, when crossed with Gold males, produced sex-linked chicks, meaning that the sex of the chick can be determined by colour on hatching. This provides an important economic motive for keeping the breed.

In appearance the Sussex is a large and graceful bird, with a broad, flat back and a stocky appearance. Its tail should be held aloft at a 45-degree angle. It has red earlobes and dark orange or red eyes, but white skin and legs. It has a docile nature and can adapt well to different surroundings. Today it retains its dual-purpose capacity. While some strains of old table-type Lights can lay more than 200 eggs, and a few Whites may lay more than 250 eggs per year, some exhibition strains of Lights are poor layers.

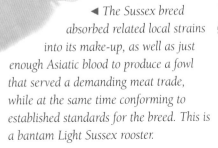

◄ The Sussex breed absorbed related local strains into its make-up, as well as just enough Asiatic blood to produce a fowl that served a demanding meat trade, while at the same time conforming to established standards for the breed. This is a bantam Light Sussex rooster.

◄ A bantam Brown Sussex rooster.

Scots Grey

The tall Scots Grey breed is at least 200 years old and is possibly older, since identifiable related populations are known to have been kept as far back as the 16th century.

Appropriately named, this breed hails from the crofts and farms of Scotland. It also has a dark grey base colour, a coloration that could suggest some early connection with the pencilled grey fowl of Northern England. In appearance, the Scots Grey is a tall, upright bird with long legs, a trait that was selected at a time when exhibition classes for game birds were dominated by tall examples. The breed has white skin, a single comb and red earlobes. The very full tail is essential for the standard of perfection and a significant part of the breed's character. This feature suggests that grey game may also be part of its genetic composition. This is a naturally active breed that prefers a free-range, foraging life. The inter-war years saw the breed find favour among farmers

▼ A large Scots Grey hen is found in only one colourway. It is suitable for those looking for an active fowl capable of adapting to a challenging environment.

looking for an all-round fowl that would lay a reasonable number of white eggs without the need for large quantities of purchased food. Today it is still classed as a dual-purpose bird, although the Scots Grey is also an endangered species and is largely kept for exhibition purposes. Large and bantam versions are available. The breed has retained a loyal following in Scotland.

ESSENTIAL CHARACTERISTICS
Size: Large male 4.1–5kg/9–11lbs.
Large female 3.4–4.1kg/7–9lbs.
Bantam male 623–680g/22–24oz.
Bantam female 510–567g/18–20oz.
Varieties: Barred, Cuckoo.
Temperament: Active.
Environment: Free range.
Egg yield: May lay more than 200 large white eggs per year.

Scots Dumpy

The Scots Dumpy, as its name suggests, sits low to the ground on very short legs. It has a boat-like appearance, with a broad and flat body. Its appearance is that of a heavy bird. This breed has a single comb, with red eyes and earlobes. It was kept originally as a dual-purpose bird, laying 180 eggs per year. Because the bird did not exercise much, the meat was highly regarded as it was probably wrongly thought to have less tough leg meat. Its shortened legs ensure that the bird waddles from side to side, no doubt an attractive and appealing characteristic to farmers keen to have birds that would not roam far. Its docile nature also ensured that flocks could be caught

▼ A Scots Dumpy bantam pullet, in one of the new, but as yet non-standardized, colours.

▼ For years Cuckoo was the most popular colour in large and bantam Scots Dumpy birds.

ESSENTIAL CHARACTERISTICS
Size: Bantam male 794g/28oz.
Bantam female 680g/24oz.
Varieties: Black, Blue, Cuckoo, White.
Temperament: Docile.
Environment: Free range, but readily adapts to close confinement. Unsuitable for muddy conditions.
Egg yield: Up to 180 white to dark brown eggs per year. Some strains of bantams lay surprisingly large eggs.

easily. For exhibition purposes, the Dumpy is listed as a light breed. Light breeds are generally more productive birds than heavy breeds, and are therefore most likely to be kept for eggs than meat.

Examples of dumpy birds, or fowl with extremely short leg bones, have been found among archaeological excavations. This breed has also been known as "creepies", "bakies" and "crawlers" in response to its short leg length. An analysis of excavated Dumpy bones found in York, dating from the 10th and 12th centuries, was carried out by Dr Enid Alison. In her report she found that 31 per cent of those with reduced-scale leg bones were male, and 24 per cent were female bones. Along with these bones were others of varying leg length, assumed to be from the same species. Several other short-legged breeds exist around the world, including the white-lobed German Kruper and the even shorter black-legged Danish Waddler, so it can be assumed that as a breed and gene type, shortened leg bones are a long-established part of the poultry genotype. Today two versions of the Scots Dumpy exist, and so it can be assumed that

▼ A large Black Scots Dumpy hen.

this breed is extremely old. The long-legged Dumpy has legs that measure 6–7.5cm/ 2½–3in long, and the short-legged version has legs that measure just 4cm/1½in. This short-legged version has a lethal creeper gene, similar to that in Dexter cattle. If two short-legged birds are mated, 50 per cent of the eggs will hatch as short-legged chicks, 25 per cent will hatch with longer legs, and the remaining 25 per cent will fail to develop as a viable embryo, or will die upon hatching. In order to reduce the prospect of such a large quantity of eggs that fail, a long-legged Dumpy can be bred with a short-legged Dumpy. This will result in half of the

▼ A Buff Columbian Scots Dumpy bantam female.

brood having long legs and the other half having short legs. The long-legged Dumpys are not affected by the gene.

Large and bantam versions of this small breed can be found. Cuckoo, Black and White varieties are common in the large version, but plenty of bantam sports are known. That we now have bantams in a wide range of standard colour patterns may help to cement the breed's future.

Unlike the Scots Grey, this breed did not have a special interest club until 1993, a factor that could explain why many exhibition examples were bred to similar feather patterns as the Scots Grey. In the 1920s, the Scots Grey Breed Club secretary is known to have complained that the breed had lost many of the colour varieties seen in the late 19th century. Dumpy hens make excellent mothers and often go broody.

▼ A Black Scots Dumpy bantam female.

EUROPEAN FOUNDATION BREEDS

The earliest forms of European domesticated fowl have a shared ancestry with those of Western Asia, as well as with one or more species of jungle fowl. Red jungle fowl look similar to the native fowl of Northern Europe, with their characteristic light body weight and more agile nature. This group was distributed further afield along the Danube Valley and Atlantic trade routes that were exploited by Nordic and Viking explorers.

Nearly all of the ancient fowl and regional breeds of Europe are now classified as light in weight, and are significant because of their egg-laying capacity. The older members of this group probably have a shared ancestry with both the very lightweight Nordic Hamburg-type fowl and early crested types. Crested types appear to have had ornamental value for much of their known history. For example, the Swiss Appenzellar has a small, forward-sloping crest and horned comb, seen in early Roman poultry sculptures, combined with the typical Nordic light body shape and rudimentary spangling. At the other end of the size scale are some of the more statuesque Mediterranean Leghorn-type fowl, thought to be the result of an early introduction of Asiatic bloodlines.

Appenzellar Spitzhauben

The horn comb and forward-pointing crest are unique features of the Appenzellar Spitzhauben. Its body type, tightly packed body feathers and colouring of black markings on silver or gold ground leave no doubt of its relationship to breeds native to North-west Europe and the Eastern Mediterranean. Poultry populations that once existed in different localities as a patchwork of strains, such as the Yorkshire Hornet breed, which became extinct in the 1930s, were almost

> **ESSENTIAL CHARACTERISTICS**
> **Size**: Small with very lightweight frame. No bantams.
> **Varieties**: Black, Chamois, Gold-spangled, Silver-spangled.
> **Temperament**: Flighty, active.
> **Environment**: Happiest given the most free range conditions.
> **Egg yield**: Can exceed 220 medium or small white or tinted eggs.

identical to the Spitzhauben. "Spitzhauben" translates as pointed bonnet, a reference to its head feathers. A second variety from Appenzell in Switzerland, known as the Bearded Barthuhner, suggests there is local diversity within the breed's homeland. Those who reared the local fowl of the Appenzell district benefited from the region's remoteness in maintaining the purity of the breed. By temperament the breed is intolerant of confinement, and has a

▲ *The head of this male shows a well-developed horn comb. The forward-pointing crest is unique to the breed.*

lively nature well suited to living in trees and the mountainous terrain of its homeland.

This breed has the capacity to convert reasonably small amounts of food into numerous medium-sized eggs. It is now a rare breed; in Britain it is officially classified as rare, but international breeding groups are kept by conservationists in Switzerland and other European countries. Their alert appearance and attitude helps make them look far better in the open than in a show pen, and so this is a breed that appeals to the conservationist rather than the committed exhibitor.

▶ *A Silver-spangled Appenzellar rooster.*

Sultan

The very ornamental Sultan breed with its feathered legs and feet, which are more usually associated with Asiatic breeds, has sufficient characteristics to place it in the European group of crested poultry breeds. Look closely at the Sultan and almost every deviant from the genetic norm will be found – a combination found in no other breed. Feathered feet apart, the stiff hock feathers usually described as vulture hocks, the full crest, horned comb and cavernous nostrils are all features associated with regional breeds of Western Europe.

The Sultan came to Britain from Turkey in 1854 at the height of the first poultry-keeping boom at a time when interest in everything Asiatic was heightened following the importation of Chinese Cochins for Queen Victoria. From Britain the birds were taken to the USA. A single batch of birds was imported from Constantinople, and with such a tiny genetic base the breed was destined to remain rare, appearing fleetingly at

◄ Sultans are kept primarily as exhibition birds. They have a quiet disposition and can tolerate confinement. This is a large White rooster.

shows for the next century until early in the 1970s, when it was chosen as the breed logo of the newly formed British Rare Poultry Society. Almost all of the examples seen over the next decade were poor specimens lacking essential features. Eventually, one breeder working in Holland, Dr Boks, virtually recreated the breed by crossing and re-crossing breeds that each displayed one of the required features. At the same time he included the Breda, the duplex comb of which appears, at first sight, to be at odds with the requirement for the Sultan to produce a horned comb. Such is the complexity of the relationship between comb and crest that the Breda's duplex comb was an essential part of the genetic mix. Stock imported from this single source provided most of the really good examples seen over the next two decades. The breed is still available but requires the attention of dedicated breeders, who will find that its exhibition features make it one of the most ornamental of fowls.

▼ The Sultan has every additional feature including a flamboyant crest, long tail, horn, muffs, beard, feathered feet and a fifth toe. It can also fly. This is a large White hen.

▼ The Sultan's horn is usually covered by white feathers.

ESSENTIAL CHARACTERISTICS
Size: Large male 3.7kg/6lbs. Large female 1.8kg/4lbs. Bantam male 680–793g/24–28oz. Bantam female 510–680g/18–24oz.
Varieties: Black, Blue, White.
Temperament: Docile, friendly.
Environment: Copes with confinement well.
Egg yield: Can exceed 180 white eggs per year.

Poland/Polish

Breeds standardized as Poland or Polish, with a domed skull enhanced by full crest, were recorded as long ago as 1600. The remains of a fowl with a domed skull were found on a Roman altar site at the village of Uley in Gloucestershire, suggesting that the Romans knew the breed type and possibly held it in some esteem. The characteristic domed skull is in fact caused by a form of cerebral haemorrhage, and sets apart the fully crested breeds from related types that have varying amounts of feathers on their heads.

▼ *A frizzled large Blue Poland. Frizzled feather types are less common than standard feather versions.*

ESSENTIAL CHARACTERISTICS

Size: Male 2.7kg/6lbs.
Female 2kg/4½lbs.
Varieties: Black-crested White, Buff-laced, Golden, Silver, White-crested Black, White. Bearded or Non-bearded.
Temperament: Quiet.
Environment: Tolerates confinement. Requires protection in winter.
Egg yield: 80 per year.

Many breeds that may or may not have crests, but which have unusual comb forms, have cavernous nostrils. With 2000 years of development of this sort of fowl, it would be surprising if some of these traits had not been incorporated into other European regional breeds that would have developed alongside them. Neither is it surprising that a breed that had developed in more than one location had also acquired a number of names and differing descriptions. Recording the breed's homeland as Padua, Italy, Renaissance author Aldrovandi called them Paduan fowl, but crude woodcuts that have survived from that region show a female with crest muff and beard, and a male with full crest and wattles. The breed has a linked gene that suppresses wattles on bearded birds. None of the known names given to the breed have any connection with Poland or Polish communities. It is most likely that the name is derived from their "polled characteristics", a mutation that means that where the best crests are found, those birds have no combs.

Twelve colour variations are known for this breed, and all the colours are available as frizzles. The bird does not go broody and lays few eggs. These small birds make attractive and endearing pets, though they are more suited to people with experience of poultry keeping. The domed crest may obscure the bird's vision, and it may also hide pests that can affect the health of the bird.

▲ *Though known as Poland or Polish this breed is not thought to originate in that country. This is a White-crested black hen.*

Many of the birds that were the foundation of the Poland breed in the UK were imported from the Netherlands, where they were referred to as Polder fowl or Polderlanders. Other Dutch breeds that would have been far closer to Campines and Hamburgs were referred to in the same way. In the UK, bearded and non-bearded varieties are treated as one breed. However, much of the rest of the world treats them as different breeds or as varieties of the same breed. Some of our best strains descend from stock imported from Holland during recent years. The breed is a healthy and productive egg-layer. It is generally intolerant of wet conditions, and anyone wanting to keep this beautiful, ornamental breed at its best should provide housing with a covered run or open-fronted loose box.

The size of the popular bantam versions may be an issue to some. With crest size being an important exhibition feature, some winning bantams have very large crests that appear to be oversized for bantams.

▶ *The Poland is a visually distinctive breed, with the large crest providing the defining characteristic. This is a Black hen.*

La Fleche

Once raised as a dual-purpose bird and laying up to 180 eggs per year, La Fleche is now a rare breed that is kept for ornamental purposes. This bird hails from France and is thought to have Black Spanish and Crevecoeurs in its ancestry. Despite its black plumage, legs and feet, the flesh is white. The spectacular twin-horned comb that is the defining feature of La Fleche is always accompanied by cavernous nostrils and occasionally, though not a standard requirement, a few crest-like head feathers. Its other distinguishing features are the white earlobes and long red wattles. Just as beards usually suppress wattle development, very large, well-developed horn combs are rarely found on those birds that have fully developed, enlarged crests and skulls.

This is an active breed that likes to forage – a heavy bird that stands tall and proud. A bantam version of the breed is known.

ESSENTIAL CHARACTERISTICS
Size: Male 3.6–4.5kg/8–10lbs.
Female 2.7–3.2kg/6–7lbs.
Varieties: Black, Blue, Cuckoo, White.
Temperament: A restless bird.
Environment: Copes with confinement. Can fly so needs a high fence.
Egg yield: 180 white eggs.

◀ *The distinctive feature of La Fleche, a breed that is less commonly seen at exhibition, is the horned comb.*

Campine

In Britain exhibition Belgian Campine males are expected to have feathered tails. In Europe, the breed is known as Braekel and is usually found with a standard feathered male tail. This ornamental breed from the Campine region of Belgium was developed to lay white eggs. It is now a rare species kept for show purposes, partly because of the lustrous quality of its feathering. It has a neat and upright carriage and attractive feather pattern.

Campines are available as two varieties: Gold or Silver. Each variety has beetle-green pencilling or barring on the feathers, and densely packed feathering.

Campines prefer free-range conditions. They are flighty and inquisitive, active and intelligent.

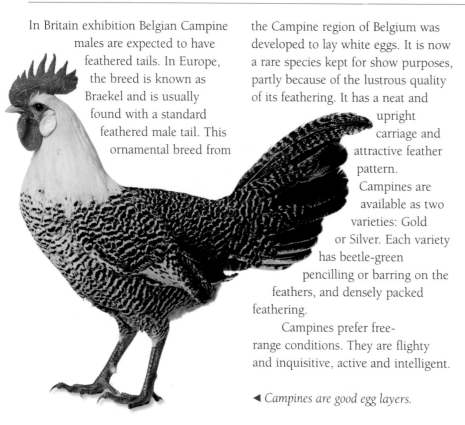

◄ *Campines are good egg layers.*

ESSENTIAL CHARACTERISTICS
Size: Large male 2.7kg/6lbs.
Large female 2.3kg/5lbs.
Bantam male 630g/24oz.
Bantam female 567g/20oz.
Varieties: Gold, Silver.
Temperament: Active, social.
Not appropriate pets.
Environment: Free range preferred.
Egg yield: Some early utility strains may have laid in excess of 220 medium-size eggs per year but exhibition strains may lay far less.

The breed rarely goes broody. In its original, less modified form it was used to make the original Cambar auto-sexing breed.

Lackenvelder

One of the better known breeds of the European foundation group, the German Lackenvelder enjoyed some popularity before World War II. Its name is Dutch and derives from the translation of white linen (*laken*) spread over a black field (*veld*). The breed was refined in Germany. Only one standard is recognized for this breed, although other colour variations are known. It has a black head and shoulders and black tail plumage, with the balance of the body feathers being white. The distinctive coloration is continued on to the large red comb, which always has five spikes. The legs are slate-coloured and the eyes are a dark

◄ *A Lackenvelder male with some black feathers in its saddle hackles.*

ESSENTIAL CHARACTERISTICS
Size: Male 1.8–2.3kg/4–5lbs.
Female 1.4–2kg/3–4½lbs.
Varieties: Blue.
Temperament: Wild, flighty.
Environment: Free range preferred.
Egg yield: 200 small to medium white or tinted eggs per year.

red-brown. Like nearly all of the European foundation group, the Lackenvelder is a prolific layer of reasonable-size eggs. It is a medium-size bird that is a good forager. It prefers to free range, but can tolerate confinement. As well as eggs, the breed is kept for exhibition. The breed is not closely related to the similar, but slightly heavier, Buff Vorverk breed.

Thuringian

Hailing from the Thuringian Forest region of Germany, this is an old breed known to have been around for at least two or more centuries. It is now a rare breed, even in its home country. Originally it was bred as a dual-purpose bird, with the hens laying an average of 160 eggs per year. Locally it was known as "chubby cheeks" because of the feather shaping at the sides of the face. This breed is cold-tolerant, lively and attractive. Thuringians are small birds, also available as bantams, and as they make good foragers, enjoy a free-range environment.

Gold- and Silver-spangled varieties are the most common, though plenty of others have been seen. This prettily marked breed is one of several similar local European breeds and varieties which, with closer contacts with breeders and shows, are likely to find their way to Britain. While each breed will bring something new to the show scene, each new arrival will have to recruit its own band of breeders willing to research the new breed's exhibition standard and genetic background. If they are to be fairly dealt with at show level, knowledgeable judges will have to be trained. The bantam version of Thuringian fowl seen at recent shows seem to be on the large side of a relatively small breed.

▼ *A Chamois bantam hen.*

▶ *Thuringians have a small beard and single comb.*

◀ *Thuringians are small birds with a distinctive upright carriage. This is a Silver-spangled bantam rooster.*

ESSENTIAL CHARACTERISTICS
Size: Large male 2–2.5kg/4½–5½lbs.
Large female 1.5–2kg/3–4½lbs.
Bantam male 737g/26oz.
Bantam female 623g/22oz.
Varieties: Black, Blue, Cuckoo, Chamois, Gold-spotted, Partridge, Silver-spotted, White, Yellow.
Temperament: Friendly.
Environment: Free range.
Egg yield: 160 white eggs per year.

Vorverk

This breed was created in the early 20th century in Germany by a breeder keen to establish a bird similar to the Lackenvelder but which had a dual-purpose role. Lackenvelder and Buff Orpington are two of the breeds that were used in this breed's selection, and in fact, the Vorverk appears as a black-buff version of the Lackenvelder, with black neck, collar and tail but with a buff body. The breed is rare today and is mostly kept by those interested in preserving a heritage breed. Considering its progenitors the breed should be heavier, and a newly-made bantam strain has added to confusion about the breed's size and identity. The bird is an active forager that converts feed to eggs economically. It has a rounded body, single serrated comb and orange-red eyes. The breed has a placid and alert nature.

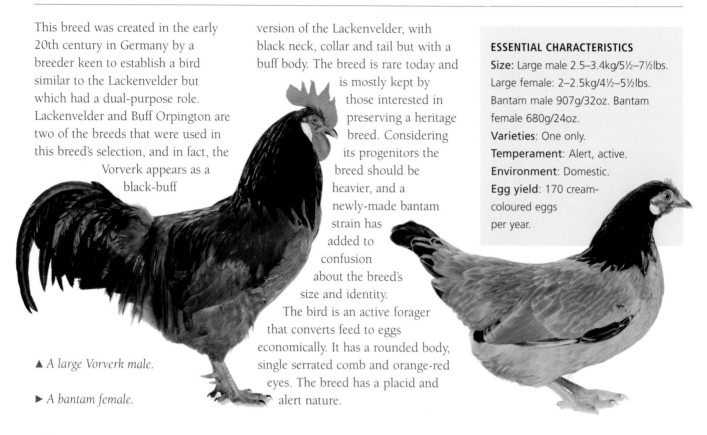

▲ A large Vorverk male.

▶ A bantam female.

ESSENTIAL CHARACTERISTICS
Size: Large male 2.5–3.4kg/5½–7½lbs.
Large female: 2–2.5kg/4½–5½lbs.
Bantam male 907g/32oz. Bantam female 680g/24oz.
Varieties: One only.
Temperament: Alert, active.
Environment: Domestic.
Egg yield: 170 cream-coloured eggs per year.

Friesian

This most attractive bird is an ancient breed from the Friesland area of Holland. It is classed as a large light bird, but is almost a bantam in size. Males typically weigh 2.5kg/5½lbs and females 2kg/4½lbs. For such a small size, this bird lays large eggs. All colours have slate-blue legs and, notably, white earlobes. It is this characteristic for which it has historically been valued. The breed is known to lay early and, for its size, lays masses of eggs. It is known to be a nervous and flighty bird, which does not cope well with confinement. It is available in several colourways including Chamois, Pencilled, Gold-pencilled and Silver-pencilled. These pencilled feather patterns give some indication of a genetic link to the similarly marked, but far larger, Campine and Braekel breeds.

ESSENTIAL CHARACTERISTICS
Size: Male 2.5kg/5½lbs.
Female 2kg/4½lbs.
Varieties: Chamois-pencilled, Gold-pencilled, Silver-pencilled.
Temperament: Friendly, inquisitive.
Environment: Adapted to harsh conditions in the Friesian Islands.
Egg yield:160–200 white eggs per year.

◀ This Gold Friesian female demonstrates the visual appeal of the breed.

MEDITERRANEAN FOUNDATION BREEDS

Mediterranean breeds are assumed to be those kept in Italy and Spain. However, the origin of this group remains something of a mystery. All of the Mediterranean breeds now known and kept were developed and bred to an agreed standard, and in most cases, they were named outside their country of origin. Dutch and English breeders or fanciers first chose to select breeds of the Iberian Peninsula for "head points", for example. As with so many regional populations, poultry breeders have been able to develop and capitalize on the genetic qualities that centuries of local development have provided.

While the ancient breeds of the rest of Europe have blue-grey legs and a similar body shape to red jungle fowl, Mediterranean and Iberian breeds have the upright stance and wing carriage seen in many of the domestic strains and breeds of Asia. The Leghorns and other Italian breeds also seem to have absorbed many features of other Old World groups. For instance, many Mediterranean breeds no longer have the broody traits that inhibited year-long egg production, a feature of other breeds that have a small amount of Asiatic blood in their genetic make-up.

Minorca

The Minorca breed was popular in the west of England. A single importation was taken to England from Minorca and became known in England as the Red-faced Spanish breed, a name that lasted for more than 150 years because of its similarity to the Spanish breed. With the decline of the Spanish breed, by the 1870s, the Minorca breed filled large classes at shows, competing for attention with huge Asiatic breeds and newly created Modern Game. In order to increase the size of the breed, breeders started to introduce unrelated genetic material to the Minorca gene pool. In addition, there was a perceived need to establish a distinctive wedge-shaped body and sloping back as a standard.

Over the years the breed became a popular contender for main show awards and for long periods it attracted some of the most competitive breeders, first in large fowl and then, when they were established, in a bantam version. Black, whites and blue have been popular colours, but contemporary bantams are now being seen in more complex colourways that look like examples of multi-coloured Minorca-type fowl as seen in early Dutch paintings. The large Minorca was never in the top rank of commercial layers, but it always had a following among urban domestic poultry keepers where it was found they withstood confinement well. The breed used to be a favourite of domestic keepers, with at least one known strain laying more than 230 eggs per year.

▲ *This bantam Minorca has attractive almond-shaped lobes.*

▶ *A large Black Minorca male with the breed's classic wedge-shape body, bold, upright comb and clean, almond-shaped lobe.*

ESSENTIAL CHARACTERISTICS

Size: Large male 4.3kg/9lbs. Large female 3.4kg/7½lbs. Bantam male 963g/34oz. Bantam female 850g/30oz.
Varieties: Black, Blue, Buff, White.
Temperament: Flighty.
Environment: The large comb makes the breed unsuitable for cold areas.
Egg yield: Large white eggs.

Dandarawi

Although indigenous to the eastern Mediterranean, the tiny Dandarawi also belongs to the European landrace group of breeds. The term landrace describes types of poultry (as well as other birds and animals) that are not necessarily formalized breeds, but represent a local population of poultry that has developed in response to the environment in which it lives. Its essential characteristics and visual appearance are determined by its ability to survive in its circumstances, whether the result of modifications or human intervention. Populations can be landraces and they can also be standardized breeds.

▼ This Grey male has a rudimentary buttercup comb and five toes.

The Dandarawi is a small bird. By nature it is flighty, and does not take kindly to close confinement. It is therefore not a bird to choose as a family pet.

Males are black with a white hackle and saddle and some white on the wings and body. Females are wheaten with white, grey or reddish-brown markings. This is an auto-sexing breed in which the young can be sexed upon hatching. Typically, the female can be identified by a black blotch on the head or stripes on the back; the male has no such blotches. The crest of this breed points backwards. These examples of a non-standardized population rather than a breed are included to illustrate the sort of local or village populations that exist throughout much of Northern Africa and the Near East. These populations are variously described as Berber and Bedouin fowl by those studying the origin of Mediterranean poultry breeds. They have rudimentary buttercup combs, which may provide some indication of the type of genetic material that went into making the Sicilian breeds which share the same feature. Dandarawis mature at about six months of age and may lay up to 150 eggs per year. Small groups of this sort of fowl occasionally turn up at shows, entered by enthusiasts. The birds are of interest to other enthusiasts, but will usually bemuse those exhibitors used to breeding fowl to exacting standards. In fact, this sort of fowl is best seen as an example of a population that evolved through environmental pressures. Conscious selection would soon diminish the population's overall genetic integrity.

◄ It is just possible to see a small lark's crest on this four-toed female. She looks to be duck-footed, a fault that appears occasionally in nearly every standardized breed.

ESSENTIAL CHARACTERISTICS
Size: Small.
Varieties: Not standardized.
Temperament: Flighty. Ability to survive on very low nutritional plain.
Environment: Free range. Naturally harsh and arid.
Eggs yield: Will improve given good nutrition.

White-faced Black Spanish

Much of the fowl once indigenous to the Iberian Peninsula seems to have been selected and standardized with large white lobes and a wedge-shaped body. It seems likely that fowl of this rudimentary form, later standardized in its homeland as Castilian, found their way into the Low Countries in the 16th century at the time of the occupation of the Spanish Netherlands. The White-faced Black Spanish is known to be an ancient breed, close in its breeding to the Minorca and Castilian breeds.

Huguenot weavers are said to have kept Spanish fowl in Spitalfields, London, in the late 1600s, and the breed was reported as popular in Bristol by the 1850s. While many of its breeders would have been obsessive in their selection for size and perfect texture of the white face, it seems likely that this one breed has always been in the hands of relatively small groups of dedicated fanciers. At several times in its long history it has come close to extinction.

The urge to perfect or even exaggerate some natural feature of a breed seems to be deeply embedded in some cultural groups. White-faced Black Spanish fowl have bigger white lobes than those of other fowl, and in some cases this white area extends to that part of the face that is normally red. It is likely that these are all

▼ A large Spanish showing the characteristic white face that is expected to extend above the eyebrows almost to the base of the comb.

features that have been exaggerated by early breeders. Because of its coloration the breed has also been known as the Clown-faced Spanish. Just what prompted an individual to select and develop this feature, until it extended over most and eventually all of the face, we will never know. Although the over-developed white earlobes are the most distinguishing feature of this breed, it also has black plumage and a single comb. It has four toes and lacks a crest.

As recently as 1970, the breed had diminished in numbers to just a handful in Germany. An international effort to save it was successful, and saw the breed recover to a point where breeders could spend time selecting and perpetuating its huge white face. There are still years when the breed all but disappears from the show scene, only for several excellent examples to return the following year.

Keeping its white face free from disfiguring blisters may mean that it needs protection from rain and wind. However, since generations of the breed have been kept in close confinement, it is more content than most other breeds in an urban environment, provided it is well cared for. Few breeds have had to wait so long for a bantam version, but its creation in 1980 means that those with limited space can now keep the smaller version of the breed. Both large and bantam versions lay quantities of snow-white eggs.

The breed does not go broody, and chicks are born with white facial feathering. The white face takes up to one year to develop fully, becoming more opaque as the bird ages. Selecting this unique, completely white face to exhibition-standard perfection means that breeders often only retain relatively small numbers of both males and females for future breeding. The downside of this search for perfection is that it could lead to a diminished gene pool, yet at the same time major show awards have been won by breeders who keep rather more hens for their utility, rather than exhibition, qualities.

ESSENTIAL CHARACTERISTICS

Size: Male 3.6kg/8lbs.
Female 3.2kg/7lbs.
Varieties: One only.
Temperament: Noisy, alert, friendly.
Environment: Copes well with confinement.
Egg yield: 150–220 large white eggs per year.

Blue Andalusian

The black poultry breeds native to Spain occasionally produce slate- or grey-coloured offspring. It is likely that the origins of the Blue Andalusian breed can be found in this lighter-coloured poultry. While it was once fashionable to claim foreign or exotic ancestry for every new poultry breed, it is likely that this breed was made and named in Britain. The Blue Dun Game poultry breed may have been included in some strains of its ancestry; however, most would have been "formula bred" by back-crossing grey sports of black Spanish breeds that would have been related on both sides. After a few generations, the colour of 25 per cent of the offspring would be a very pale grey splashed with the odd blue feather. When these were crossed with related black birds, all of the offspring had blue feathers with black edges. When these blue fowl were mated together they regularly produced 50 per cent of their offspring with "blue" plumage, 25 per cent with "splashed" feathers and the rest, black. The formula was

▶ The male Blue Andalusian has an upright comb and laced feathers on a ground colour that is difficult to perfect.

based on the work of Gregor Mendel. Blue Andalusians were successfully bred to this formula in the 1850s and 1860s. The early examples were vaguely blue-grey with rudimentary lacing, but over the years dedicated breeders have managed to produce birds with crisp blue-black lacing around a ground that is close to giving the illusion of being blue. It is this degree of breeding difficulty and the urge to create something beautiful that attracts many breeders. Yet, over the years, this breed has relied on three or four dedicated breeders to stop the breed from disappearing. A bantam

version could help create interest in the breed, but keeping enough Blue Andalusians to provide the necessary gene pool is a formidable task. By nature the Blue Andalusian is known as a noisy bird. It has a graceful gait and prefers a free-range environment to close confinement. In spite of their largely Spanish ancestry, they can be good winter layers.

◀ Many of the exhibition strains of the Mediterranean breeds are heavier than the original strains. The Andalusian, possibly due to an infusion of English or Spanish game in its ancestry, often carries more meat than Leghorns. Interestingly, black sports look like the native Spanish Castilian breed. This is a hen.

ESSENTIAL CHARACTERISTICS

Size: Large male 3.2–3.6kg/7–8lbs.
Large female: 2.3–2.7kg/5–7lbs.
Bantam male 680–793g/24–28oz.
Bantam female 566–680g/20–24oz.
Varieties: Blue.
Temperament: Active and agile. Likes foraging.
Environment: Free range.
Egg yield: 166–190 white eggs per year.

Sicilian Buttercup

The Sicilian Buttercup may represent a link between fowl native to the eastern Mediterranean, as its name suggests, and other Italian breeds that have played an important role in commercial poultry breeding, such as the Leghorns.

The first thing one notices about the breed is its unusual, and sometimes spectacular, comb, which is a feature common to the few other breeds that have a shared ancestry. On the body, the broken black barring or pencilling on a bay to rich golden ground is almost identical to that of many Egyptian fowl, such as the Fayoumi breed. The female is noticeably lighter in colour than the male, with a soft buff ground, while the male has a deep, rich orange ground. While Fayoumis usually have grey or slate legs, most of the Sicilian Buttercups have green or olive legs. This suggests that there has been a certain amount of interbreeding with other yellow-legged Italian breeds such as the Leghorns, which in turn, have had earlier contact with breeds imported from the Far East.

The Sicilian Buttercup first came to popularity during World War I when, for the first time, poultry was rationed as a food source. However, eggs were only rationed by price, and people wanting an abundant supply of eggs prior to the war were willing to pay premium prices for them. The Sicilian Buttercup breed was known for its vigour at egg production and as a result, it became a popular breed in wartime. For a while there was sufficient interest and demand for a Sicilian Buttercup breed club to be formed. During this time, a second Buttercup breed known as the mahogany-coloured Sicilian Flower emerged.

ESSENTIAL CHARACTERISTICS

Size: Male 737g/26oz.
Female 623g/22oz.
Varieties: One colour.
Temperament: Wild, flighty.
A good flier.
Environment: Free range.
Egg yield: 200 small white or tinted eggs per year.

With the return to peacetime, and the plentiful availability of large eggs laid by rapidly improving breeds such as the white egg-laying Leghorns, interest in the Sicilian Buttercup breed waned and there has been insufficient interest to maintain a worthwhile gene pool. Today the breed is so rare that one cannot rely on finding really good examples among the rare breed classes, even at the larger poultry shows. Aside from the breed's positive utility qualities, it does have an

▲ *The exhibition comb is expected to be as round and bowl-shaped as possible, with an evenly castellated rim.*

extremely flighty nature, a characteristic that many breeders will tolerate in order to keep a breed with an almost unique comb. The Sicilian Buttercup is a sufficiently good layer to breed the sort of numbers needed to select future breeding stock with very good combs.

While bantams with buttercup combs have been seen, these have never been classed as miniature Sicilian Buttercups.

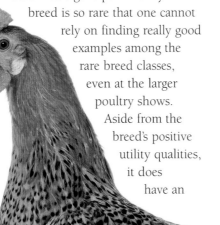

◄ *The hen's lightweight frame, rather elongated body shape and broken black barring or pencilling suggests a close relationship between this Sicilian breed and poultry breeds of the Eastern Mediterranean, such as the Turkish breeds as well as their Northern European Hamburg-type relatives.*

Leghorn

This is an old breed and one of the most well known. It is thought that the breed became known as the Leghorn in America because the first shipment that arrived there in 1853 came from the Italian port of Livorno, pronounced "leghorn" in English. One cuckoo-coloured and four white hens, formed the initial shipment, together with one rooster.

Whether as egg-laying fowl or exhibition birds, nearly all Leghorn poultry selection took place outside of Italy, notably in America, the UK and Denmark, where all colours of the breed have been developed to the most exacting standards. The majority of fowl varieties seen today are brown, white and intermediate colours with, as a rule, yellow legs, although many of the black variety have slate or black coloured limbs. The breed is exhibited with a wide range of differing standard colours.

The breed displays a natural reluctance to broodiness, a characteristic that the commercial egg industry has capitalized upon. Leghorns have historically been highly regarded for their egg-laying capacity. White hens can produce on average 250 pure white eggs per year, and as a result the breed's genes have been used extensively in commercial egg-laying hybrids.

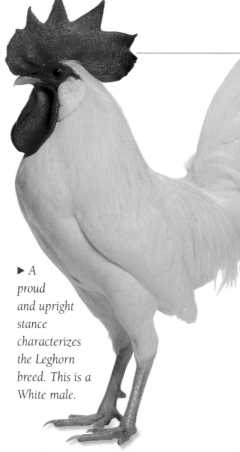

▶ *A proud and upright stance characterizes the Leghorn breed. This is a White male.*

▶ *This Brown bantam hen has the characteristic large floppy comb. Breeding birds to an exacting physical standard for exhibition means that the bird's egg-laying capacity is reduced.*

This selection of the breed for its egg-laying capacity saw the Whites reach a point in the 1930s where they were responsible for producing most of the world's commercially produced white eggs. White Leghorn-based hybrids convert poultry feed into eggs more efficiently than any other pure breed, which is particularly impressive when the breed's light body weight is taken into account. Breeding for the splendid perfectly modelled upright male combs, and female combs that flop gracefully to one side, may have detracted from the peak of utility performance. Many of the large fowl versions bred for showing may be bigger than they need be to fulfil a utility function, but this size has

enabled the creation of the bantam versions that are, in most colours, exact counterparts of their larger versions.

Selection to keep their size small in some bantam strains means that some families of Black Leghorn bantams, for instance, lay almost as well as commercial hybrid versions. All have an active disposition, but few are as flighty as many other light breeds.

As one of the great international breeds, Leghorns throughout the world vary more than any other poultry breed. Exhibition strains of the breed have built on the statuesque stance of the first White Leghorns imported to America. American breeders have favoured the marginally more horizontal body and gracefully sweeping tail carriage. German breeders, who only use the title Leghorn for the white variety, have bred a more horizontal outline. Other varieties are known in Germany as "Italians", and have an exaggerated horizontal tail and carriage.

ESSENTIAL CHARACTERISTICS
Size: Male 2.4–2.8kg/5½–6½lbs. Female 2–2.5kg/4½–5½lbs.
Varieties: Black, Black-tailed Red, Buff, Columbian, Dark Brown, Light Brown, Red, White.
Temperament: Flighty, noisy.
Environment: Prefers free range but utility strains have adapted to confinement.
Egg yield: Strains of utility Whites can lay up to 300 white eggs per year. Exhibition birds may lay fewer.

Ancona

The Ancona originates from the town of the same name in Italy, and was taken to England in the mid-19th century. It has similarities to the Leghorn and was initially known as a Mottled Leghorn. It is this mottling, the distinctive white ticking on black plumage, which is the distinguishing feature of this breed. As such, the breed standard for feather marking is exacting. Breeding to meet the precise feather patterns required may have saved some strains from excessive head point development. An alterative rose comb is more often seen in the Ancona breed than in Leghorns. The breed has a large, red single comb which may flop in females, and long red wattles. The legs are deep yellow and the build is slender.

By nature this bird is an active forager, easy to tame, and with a quick temperament. The earlier utility flocks of large Anconas may no longer exist, but some strains of the bantam version are capable of laying quantities of surprisingly large eggs.

▼ *The black feathers with white tips give a mottled appearance, and overall the plumage has an attractive greenish tinge. This is a bantam male.*

ESSENTIAL CHARACTERISTICS
Size: Male 2.7–3kg/6–7lbs.
Female 2.25–2.5kg/5–5½lbs.
Varieties: Mottled.
Temperament: Active, alert.
Environment: Free range but adapts to confinement.
Egg yield: More than 160 white eggs per year.

Fayoumi

The Fayoumi is an ancient breed that originated in Egypt. It is a small, lightweight bird: males weigh just 2kg/4½lbs and females 1.5kg/3½lbs. It is now kept for ornamental purposes, but it was traditionally kept for its egg-laying capacity, producing small, off-white eggs. The breed is characterized by a forward-thrusting neck and chest and an upright tail. Its flesh is slate blue, and the wattles, comb and earlobes are all red. This breed can move very quickly, is good at flying and dislikes captivity. If caught, this bird emits a noise similar to the cry of guinea fowl. Fayoumis are a hardy breed, being tolerant of extreme heat in keeping with their North African origins. As lightweight, good foragers they can have very low maintenance requirements, and when kept in well-ventilated conditions have much resistance to disease. These birds are quick to mature.

ESSENTIAL CHARACTERISTICS
Size: Male 2kg/4½lbs.
Female 1.5kg/3½lbs.
Varieties: Gold-spangled, Silver-spangled.
Temperament: Dislikes handling and is extremely flighty.
Environment: Free-range, even living in trees.
Eggs: Egg numbers can be high but are small in size and white or tinted.

◄ *Like many Fayoumis, this male has only a rudimentary barring on a golden ground colour.*

ASIAN SOFT-FEATHER FOUNDATION BREEDS

Many of today's domestic fowl are descended from Asian domesticated breeds, which historically were kept in densely populated areas, often in coastal margins. These are all massive birds, true to their original status, but it is likely that in appearance they have little in common with the first birds imported from Asia. These breeds have been selectively bred for their size, and have been used extensively to provide genetic material for other breeds.

Cochins and Brahmas have a significant amount of feathers that adds bulk to the visual appearance of these breeds. For all their size, however, they are gentle giants and make lovable pets for children as well as fabulous garden companions. Javas and Langshans have an equally attractive nature and like to range free. All will need large-scale housing and plenty of room in which to range. Due to their size they eat a large amount.

Cochin

The Cochin breed was responsible for creating a craze that became known as "poultry mania". Large fowl that were later reported as coming from Cochinchina, were probably the result of many different imports from various Chinese and Asian ports. The birds first reported in newspapers as being brought from Cochinchina, by Sir Edward Belcher, the scientist and explorer, were given to Queen Victoria in 1843. However, an analysis of his log on *HMS Sulphur* shows one reference to his loading fowl aboard in what is now Northern Borneo. Originally known as Shanghais, the five pullets and two roosters that he collected later became known as Cochin-Chinas. Later still, the name was abbreviated to Cochin. Cochin is a port in India and it is likely that the birds were named for this port on their

ESSENTIAL CHARACTERISTICS
Size: Male 5kg/11lbs. Female 3.9kg/8½lbs. For bantams *see Pekin*.
Varieties: Black, Blue, Buff, Gold-laced, Partridge, Silver-laced, Splash, White.
Temperament: One of the friendliest poultry breeds. Quiet.
Environment: Perfect for the home garden.
Egg yield: 120 dark brown eggs per year.

▶ *This large Black Cochin hen has feathered feet, a characteristic feature of the breed, and a propensity for extremely fluffy, almost silky, under-fluff.*

journey to the western world. The fowl Queen Victoria was given were reportedly good layers; this was borne out when a hen exhibited by the monarch in Dublin was reported to have laid 94 eggs in 103 days. The breed was also rumoured to lay two eggs per day, and because of its enormous size, was considered a good breed to rear for the table. Interest in the Cochin was heightened, and soon entrepreneurs were scouring the Far East for similar fowl. Northern Chinese ports were open to trade with the West, and fast tea clippers carried live birds from East to West. Unlike known European breeds, many of these birds had feathered legs. A second batch of birds was shipped from China in 1847. Although these were sold as Cochin, they bore little resemblance to the birds delivered a few years earlier. It is unlikely that the birds that were originally shipped from the East share any physical resemblance with the Cochin breed that we know today.

These early Shanghais were used to improve many local populations of European fowl, and the results became the basis of utility, brown egg-laying breeds such as Welsummer, Marans and Barnevelder. Desirable attributes of the Shanghai included foot feathers, and great numbers of fluffier feathers made the birds look enormous. These features were selected and bred into local poultry as well as altering the appearance of the Cochin breed.

The fact that such breeding tended to reduce the birds' natural utility was never a consideration for breeders of exhibition birds. The early boom in the breed had seen stock widely distributed, and if anyone wanted table fowl, a Cochin crossed with a Dorking-type fowl provided plenty of meat. Similarly, a pullet bred from a Cochin and a farmyard hen laid as well as any other bird. The craze for such poultry was short-lived when it was realized that although the birds appear large, it was merely the feathers that made them look bigger.

As an exhibition breed, Cochins had, by the 1890s, been selected to assume a shape, form and degree of feather that would be recognized as standard today. The breed now had the ability to produce attractive feather and fluff in a new range of feather patterns and colours. In China, the feathers were used for padding and insulation. Many of the fowl shipped from Shanghai may have been Black, but other imports

▶ *The Cochin breed was originally kept for its dark brown eggs and for its meat. This is a large Buff-coloured male.*

▲ *Cochins make adorable pets. This is a Blue-partridge rooster.*

included a natural Buff that had not been seen in the West previously; initially it was described as Cinnamon. This colourway was eventually refined to become a clear even buff that we now see in other breeds. The Partridge colour, with its intricately marked female form, was very different to the black-reds of either jungle fowl or native game breeds. This brought new complexities to exhibition varieties in other breeds. Whites that had previously been seen as weak when occurring as

sports in other breeds now became a feature to select, and a degree of whiteness is still a major show challenge in many breeds. Breeders introduced the gene of "Columbian restriction". Selection for overly soft feathers, body fluff and foot feather, which were seen as exhibition points soon detracted from the breed's original utility properties. For most of its existence, the Cochin has been anything but a commercial or even utility breed.

Today, the attributes that made the breed popular as a utility bird are those that make it an adorable, fluffy pet. Cochins have a gentle and docile personality, despite their large size. The bird has an aristocratic nature, and is identifiable by its size and the large cushion of feathers on its back. The male bird has a deep crow. When not bred for show, it is best seen as a delightfully placid ornamental companion in the garden or small paddock.

Brahma

A true giant among poultry breeds, the Brahma is thought to have the ancient giant jungle fowl, *Gallus gigantus*, in its ancestry. The breed originates from the Brahmaputra region of India, where one probable ancestor was known as Chittagong. It was first shipped to America in the middle of the 19th century, where it was given the name Brahma Pootra and eventually the name of Brahma. It is thought to have been selectively bred with a Malay-type breed in the USA, and the resulting offspring imported to Britain almost a decade later. Such breeding may have been responsible for producing a fowl with a pea or walnut comb as characteristic of the hard-feathered breeds of Asia. The comb soon became a standard point for show specimens.

In his book of 1855, entitled *Hen Fever,* George Burnham, an American breeder and entrepreneur, recalls how he selected a few large grey birds from a consignment of several hundred fowl of all grades and

▼ *A large Dark male, one of the original colour varieties that played an important part in creating the Sussex breed.*

▶ *A large Gold Brahma, taller and far more statuesque that the related Cochin.*

proportions imported from Shanghai, China. He crossed these with his existing fowl, which were likely to be heavy-boned breeds (Cochins) from different locations. "I selected from my best Shanghai chickens nine beautiful birds. They were placed in a very handsome walnut-framed case and having duly landed [from China]

▼ *Brahma bantams can be larger than other bantam breeds but are often similar to their large counterparts.*

were forthwith shipped across the big pond addressed as follows: 'To Her Majesty Victoria Queen of England'." The new birds, housed in London Zoo, fed the poultry mania sweeping the country.

Some of the original male American imports weighed up to 6.4kg/14lbs. The original grey colour of the imported birds was quickly distilled into Light and Dark varieties in the UK. The genetically created Silver-Columbian pattern provided a significant gene pool for the Light Sussex breed. The Dark variety later found its way into varieties of breeds that claim a wholly European ancestry. Over the years, Brahma breeders have been able to build on the original complex patterns to make

▲ *A Buff-Columbian female bantam, in which the black coloration is restricted to the hackle, tail and closed wing feathers.*

▲ *Brahmas have a distinct tail that is held aloft. This is a Gold Partridge hen.*

▲ *The Light Brahma variety has a restricted black feather pattern.*

and standardize new colours and feather patterns. Today there are several varieties, including the original Light, Dark, Gold, Black, White, Blue, Buff-Columbian and Blue-Columbian.

As Brahmas are so large, birds can take two years to develop to full size, and so were never a commercial breed. Some strains retained enough of their original utility properties – the bird was at first considered a dual-purpose breed – to be used to help make some of the first broiler crosses in the 1930s. Once a prolific egg layer, the additional colours that have been bred into the Brahma were at the expense of its egg-laying ability.

Nowadays the breed is considered a pet or is kept for exhibition, since its utility features are no longer so

important. The giant size, feathered feet and calm disposition make this an ideal garden breed. It is essential to train this breed from a young age however, since its large and weighty build may make it difficult to handle when it is mature.

For those with

limited space, the bantam versions, which were popular in the 1890s, can still be enjoyed. It is a most interesting, beautiful, challenging and hardy breed. Despite the size of this large bird, care needs to be taken that it is not bullied by other breeds, including much smaller birds that can sometimes take advantage of the breed's docile temperament.

ESSENTIAL CHARACTERISTICS

Size: Large male 5.4kg/12lbs. Bantam male 1kg/38oz. Large female 4.1kg/9lbs. Bantam female 907g/32oz.

Varieties: Black, Blue-Columbian, Buff-Columbian, Dark, Gold, Light, White.

Temperament: Calm and friendly. They make good pets.

Environment: Garden.

Egg yield: 120 brown eggs per year.

▶ *A large Dark Brahma hen with a coloration that in other breeds would be known as Silver-pencilled or Silver-partridge.*

Langshan

Most of the birds that early poultry keepers called Cochins (intending to capitalize on the early popularity of those delivered to Queen Victoria), were shipped through the northern ports of China. Many of the black examples came from what we now know as the port of Shanghai. Just how many of these black fowl were similar to the later importations of Langshans, or if any of these laid eggs with the characteristic plum-coloured bloom that become associated with the breed, is impossible to say. Since many of the birds that were originally imported from Asia were selected and bred from to produce new breeds for exhibition, each with specific visual characteristics, the utility value of many of these birds suffered. To find fowl with the original utility potential meant importing more of the ancestral fowl from the point of origin. However, finding the exact location would have met with some confusion. Shanghai, Lan-Chau, Yangtse or Langshan were all either native or European names for the same general region of China.

It would have been from this general region that Major Croad, in 1872, made one of the last (and arguably one of the least adulterated) importations; the breed is still believed to exist in that region of China. Major Croad concentrated on breeding the utility properties of his imported birds, and he eventually linked genes contained within his strain to produce what we now recognize as the Croad Langshan type. The breed was kept initially as a utility breed, and was developed for both its egg-laying capacity and its production of very dark brown eggs. Asiatic breeds lay browner eggs than those otherwise seen in Europe. Later breeders sought to emphasize the differences between most of the Asiatic breeds.

The bird has a broad outline and a large, upright body shape. It stands tall on its legs and carries a single upright comb. The black colour of

▶ *A Large Croad male with characteristic short back and lightly feathered legs.*

the plumage has an almost bottle-green sheen. It is now thought that the spectacularly U-shaped outline of the breed and the stiff upright tail carriage of the bird promotes the production of dark brown eggs – a fascinating genetic link. The upright tail feature is very different from the cushion tail associated with the Cochin standard.

Another interesting facet of this breed is the plum-coloured "bloom" that often overlays the surface of the brown egg, which always attracts attention at exhibitions.

Over the years there has been more than one competing Langshan breed, but the original Croad is still kept in sufficient numbers in both large and bantam forms to ensure the survival of the breed. The Langshan has an inquisitive but docile nature and can cope with confinement as well as free-range situations, making it an ideal pet. The breed is known to produce good mothers.

The original Croad Langshans were exhibited at the same time as the early Black Orpington, which was said to have some Cochin stock in its ancestry, and which looked similar to the Langshan at that time. In order to make the two breeds look different, some exhibitors bred taller birds. Those breeders of the original strain continued to promote what they saw as the correct type and formed the Croad Langshan club. Breeders of the tall birds named their birds Modern Langshans to distinguish their exhibition breed. Some examples had sloping backs and tail carriage and very scanty leg feathering, with certain authorities insisting that some had difficulty in standing. While the traditional Croads prospered, the Modern Langshans were scarce from 1920, and probably died out around 1960. However, prior to this date the breed was taken to Germany, and

▼ *Exhibition forms like this German Langshan have been exaggerated to a point where they look nothing like the original.*

from this stock the German Langshan was bred. From German Langshan stock it has been possible to recreate the original bird.

German Langshans, while tall, with clean legs, developed the same U-back and tail carriage as the Croad Langshans. The large German version is not quite the size of the Croad Langshan. A few large fowl have been seen at shows, but the bantams were soon established as one of the most popular and successful at exhibitions. The breed has been selected for utility and for exhibition, a process of selection that can lead to exaggeration in feather characteristics and perceptions of breed type. However, the tail of this breed is more rounded than that of the original birds.

▶ *A Black German Langshan bantam male, with typical upright tail.*

▼ *A Blue German Langshan bantam male with standardized clean legs.*

Croad Langshans are a heavy breed, but carry their weight gracefully. The head of the Langshan is small in comparison to the rest of its body. The crest is carried upright in male and female birds. The breed is active but docile and tolerant by nature and does not mind being handled, making it a good breed to keep if young children are around. The hens make excellent mothers. The breed is long lived, with some birds living up to 10 years. Egg-laying capacity is known to diminish rapidly after middle age, however.

The Langshan breed development mirrors much else that has happened in exhibition-based poultry selection. The original Langshan from Shanghai would have been very similar to those earlier useful fowl that helped to make what became known as Cochins. Those remaining with Major Croad's family retained a similar shape to the useful Croad still found today.

Java

This breed was imported to the USA from the East Indies in 1883 and was developed and refined there. Its Asian ancestry is unknown. The breed is little known on the world stage and is now quite rare in the USA. Nevertheless, the Java is one of the foundation breeds of modern poultry and is one of the oldest American breeds along with Plymouth Rocks and Jersey Giants, to both of which, it is known to have contributed genes. The Java belongs within the family of heavy, soft-feather breeds that had a wide distribution throughout much of Asia. Unlike those birds exported from China, the original fowl did not have feathered legs or feet.

In appearance, it is a large sturdy bird, with a long, low back and a plump chest. It is one of the largest poultry breeds. It has small ear lobes and a medium size comb, which starts quite low on the face suggesting that it has an ancestral link to breeds with a pea comb. Black and mottled varieties are available, though white was developed and later abandoned due to its similarity to another popular breed. White chicks do appear occasionally, and dedicated breeders, are keen to re-establish the variety. The black variety has beetle-green plumage, black legs and beak, while the mottled and white varieties have a yellow beak and legs and white flesh.

ESSENTIAL CHARACTERISTICS
Size: Male 4.3kg/9½lbs. Female 2.9–3.4kg/6½–7½lbs. No bantam.
Varieties: Black, Mottled, White.
Temperament: Docile.
Environment: Free range. Prefers a small flock.
Egg yield: Reasonable numbers of mid to dark brown eggs.

▲ *The breed was once known as Black Java, suggesting that black was considered the typical breed colour. It is still a popular choice of variety.*

This is a dual-purpose bird that is economical to keep if allowed a free-range lifestyle. The hens go broody and are known to make good mothers. Like most of the heavy soft feathered foundation breeds imported into Europe and the USA, the nature of the Java is that of a very docile bird. Cochins may also have originated in the same general area as the Java breed.

► *Most black varieties of fowl produce an occasional splashed or mottled sport.*

◄ *The Java hen is considerably smaller than the male of the breed.*

GAME BIRDS AND ASIAN HARD-FEATHER

The hard-feathered breeds of India, Malaysia and, to a lesser extent, Thailand, have had a significant influence on modern poultry development. These hard-feathered breeds have a high stature, but are devoid of fluff in their plumage and are poor and seasonal layers. They differ in practically every way from those breeds native to Northern Europe, yet intriguingly, they also differ from the jungle fowl that inhabit the same part of Asia. This harder, fluff-free feathering could have evolved as domestication took the descendants of jungle fowl to hotter lands, far south of their native regions. In the case of the Aseel, the feathering developed into a form of body armour. Indian or Cornish game were never used for cockfighting, but with the Aseel as one of their foundation breeds, they went on to develop a high muscle-to-offal ratio. Indian Game form part of the ancestry of the modern broiler fowl; the breed inherited much of its bulk from Malay-type fowl from Eastern India. Aseel is the ancestor of much of the world's economically important poultry stock. Breeders of fighting birds would have described all their fowl as "game". However, other often closely related strains were soon being described as separate breeds, named after their breeder or by their colour.

OLD ENGLISH GAME

Old English Game fowl are the descendants of the original pit-fighting birds bred by the nobility. They are highly prized, and extremely desirable, and exhibition varieties can command huge prices. When cockfighting was outlawed in England in the mid-19th century, the fighting birds were bred instead for exhibition purposes. At the time the country was gripped by a craze for the newly imported giant, soft-feathered Asiatic poultry, and the size of these imports had an influence upon the breeding of Old English Game. Soon exhibition judges were selecting the biggest and tallest birds for championship prizes.

Fowl that had been selected for the ability to survive the rigours of the cockpit evolved into strains. The strains developed according to type, size and colour, depending upon the characteristics that each breeder sought to emphasize. Each was influenced by his or her interpretation of the breed standard. The exhibition standard for the breed used a form of wording that reflected the breed's history as pit game, and this remained the only written standard used for this breed for almost a hundred years. In the 1930s the Old English Game Club split, and today, two distinct types of game are bred: Oxford and Carlisle.

THE SPLIT WITHIN THE OXFORD GAME CLUB

Writing about events that led to the formation of the Oxford Game Club, Herbert Atkinson, one of the original members, wrote:

"I fancy the general public believed the true Game Fowl to be a thing of the past …. Here let me say that it was solely among cock-fighters that he did still exist. Many of these had the same breed for generations. They were not led away by showing or fashion or moneymaking. Their requirements were purity of blood and courage, activity, strength and sound-ness of constitution." The adoption of an agreed standard in the 1880s for the Old English Game breed would have had to reconcile various concepts about differing strains. It would not have been the wording of that standard, but its interpretation, that led to splits within the game fraternity. The rift happened in the 1930s, and at that point separate Oxford and Carlisle Game Clubs were formed. Oxford birds are considered to be true to their cockfighting roots, whereas the Carlisle type are influenced by the giant Asian poultry being bred for exhibition, and are of a larger build.

◄ A Mealy-breasted Mealy-grey Oxford male.

◄ A Black-red Carlisle male.

Oxford Game

The game fowl categorized as Oxford type was the product of centuries of selection from local populations of game strains. Today's fowl are similar in bone structure and feathering to their ancestors, and are only slightly larger. Any increase in muscle development, weight and bone structure would have been kept in check by the bird's inherent need for speed and agility. The extent to which breeders incorporated the different hard-feathered Asiatic breeds, particularly Aseel, into their breeding programs varied considerably. Much depended upon each breeder's requirement to improve his stock in order to select the best of the breed, with the intention of matching the written standard. Oxford Old English Game are feathery. The small head is furnished with a single comb, small lobes and wattles. These game birds have large eyes and, appropriately for a fighting bird, a strong and powerful beak, a lean and muscular build, with short and strong

◀ A Grey male.

legs, powerful wings that slope down to the ground at an angle and a sloping back. These latter two characteristics help to distinguish the Oxford type from the Carlisle type. (An increasing number of shows put on classes that accommodate both Oxford and Carlisle types, and this helpfully allows the layman to see the differences between the two.) Unlike Carlisle Game, the Oxford fraternity stick rigidly to the upper weight limits of their standard for exhibition purposes.

Oxford Game are more numerous than Carlisle Game. The Oxford standard lists 32 colour combinations that often reflect a strain's earlier connection with a trade or district. Game men of all persuasions quote the old truism: "There is no such thing as a bad colour in a good game fowl".

The term "hard feather" is usually used to describe the tight feathering and glossy, watertight characteristics of the plumage. In relation to the Oxford Game birds, it seems to have been used to describe the quality of

the bird. Soft would have suggested an unfit or out-of-condition bird. It is customary to dub male game birds, which means removing part of the comb and wattles, originally so that they did not get damaged when the bird was fighting. Continuation of this tradition is likely to remain an issue.

◀ A Partridge hen.

▶ A Pile male.

ESSENTIAL CHARACTERISTICS

Size: Male 1.7–2.6kg/3lbs 12oz–5lbs 12oz. Female 1.8–2.2kg/4–5lbs.

Varieties: Black, Black-breasted Birchen-duckwing, Black-breasted Dark Grey, Black-breasted Dark Red, Black-breasted Red, Black-breasted Silver-duckwing, Black-breasted Yellow-duckwing, Brown-breasted Brown-red, Brown-breasted Yellow-birchen, Clear Mealy-breasted Mealy-grey, Cuckoo, Dun-breasted Blue Dun, Furness Brassy Back and Polecat, Hennie, Ginger-breasted Ginger-red, Muff and Tassel, Pile, Spangled, Streaky-breasted Light Red, Streaky-breasted Orange-red, Streaky-breasted Red-dun, Yellow-silver and Honey-dun, White.

Temperament: Agile and able to fly over most fences.

Environment: Free range.

Egg yield: More than 100, with some strains capable of laying far more medium-tinted eggs per year.

Carlisle Game

All Old English Game are light and flighty birds with a wild and alert quality. Most have powerful wings and can fly, and this should be taken into account when housing the breed. These are birds with a strong, athletic and muscular build. They have been bred for the pit and have an inherent instinct to fight. Male birds will fight to the death and should never be penned together. The hens are known to make good mothers.

The poultry fanciers who initially bred Carlisle game had collectively selected their birds to fulfil the exhibition requirements for larger fowl. As a result, Carlisle Game birds are larger birds than the Oxford type. Both versions incorporate Aseel blood in their genes. Many of the birds in Carlisle classes at exhibition exceed their breed's standard weight considerably. They also differ from Oxford Game in their posture, as Carlisle Game birds hold their back and wings horizontally. The birds have a deep breast, and because of this were considered meat birds, with a strong, robust flavour. Carlisle game are standardized in fewer colours than Oxfords, although there are 13 accepted varieties, more than for many other pure poultry breeds.

▼ A Black-red male.

▼ In order to assess their fowl, Carlisle Game fanciers hold the bird so that it faces towards their own chests.

▼ A Brown-red male.

▼ To assess overall balance and agility, judges and exhibitors of Oxford Game birds instinctively hold their lighter birds so that they face away from their own chests.

ESSENTIAL CHARACTERISTICS

Size: Male 2.9kg/6½lbs. Female 2.4kg/5½lbs.

Varieties: Birchen or Grey, Black-red (partridge), Black-red (wheaten), Blue-red, Brown-red, Crele, Cuckoo, Golden-duckwing, Pile, Silver-duckwing, Spangle, Blue-tailed wheaten, Self-white.

Temperament: Vigorous but not as agile as Oxford game.

Environment: Free range. Can fly.

Egg yield: Up to 130 smallish white or tinted eggs per year.

Aseel/Asil

The Aseel is an ancient breed originating in India. It is mentioned in the Codes of Manu, the ancient Indian legal texts, and is considered to be the oldest documented breed of poultry in the world. The name Aseel translates to mean foundation, original, regal or noble.

Merchant adventurers trading with India were attracted to the fearless fighting qualities of this breed, and it is they who were responsible for its export to other parts of the world in the early 1800s. Aseel-type fowl found their way into the cockpits of Britain. However, this arrival seems to have made little impact on English game breeds, which appear to have remained feathery and generally more like red jungle fowl than the Aseel. Nevertheless, the Aseel has had an influence on the development of some strains of Old English Game.

The breed almost certainly played a formative role in the development of the Indian/Cornish Game breed, which has added much to the shape and conformation of the broiler fowl that is used to supply much of the world with poultry meat.

In appearance the Aseel has strong and heavy muscles. It has an upright stance with a thick and muscular curved neck and a strong beak. It

▼ *Aseels are intelligent, aristocratic and pugnacious. This is a large Black-red male.*

holds its tail at an angle sloping to the ground, and the tail feathers fan outwards. It has long legs, thin thighs and powerful leg muscles.

The Aseel has a strong beak, small earlobes and a pea comb; wattles are absent. A unique breeding regime in its country of origin bestowed courage and stamina upon the breed with an inbuilt inclination to fight. Both male and female birds will fight to the death. Even young chicks will attack each other at just a few weeks old, and may also attack their mother. As such, they should only be put with other non-fighting breeds; and males should be separated from each other. Despite the inclination of the

▲ *The eyes are pearl-coloured and set at the side of the head, giving the breed a sinister appearance. It has a characteristic, powerful beak.*

young to fight, Aseels make good mothers, but are bad egg-layers. Along with other strains of breeds developed in isolation from mainline poultry, the Aseel brought hybrid vigour to the western poultry world. It has high muscle and meat content.

Rare and even obscure, many named strains of Aseel can be found at specialist shows, and the purest is likely to remain with specialists.

▶ *The Aseel has characteristics rarely found in other poultry breeds. For example, the duck foot shown here is allowed, but is considered a serious fault in any other breed.*

ESSENTIAL CHARACTERISTICS

Size: Male to 2.4kg/5½lbs. Female to 1.8kg/4lbs.

Varieties: Black-red, Black, White.

Temperament: A fighting bird, strong, muscular and hardy. Friendly towards humans.

Environment: Tolerates confinement or free-range conditions.

Egg yield: 20 tinted to brown eggs per year. They are large for the size of bird.

Shamo

The Shamo is indigenous to Thailand and was developed in Japan, where a number of forms exist. It is a protected breed in Japan and is that country's best-known game bird. Cockfighting is still legal in Japan, and the bird is bred there for fighting purposes. The name Shamo is a derivation of the Japanese word for Siam, the original name of Thailand. The Shamo breed name is used to describe several breeds, ranging from O Shamo, which is the tallest, through to Chu Shamo, Ko Shamo and Nanking Shamo. The latter two are bantams. Over the years, the Japanese have developed several other obviously related breeds, including the shorter and grotesque Yamato Gunkei. While the latter two are treated as bantams in Britain and Europe, in their homeland Japan they are seen not as

bantams but just as a smaller breed in a range of breeds that are each bred to conform to its own standard and weight range. This will help explain the wide range of sizes and weights often found among Ko Shamo entered in bantam classes in the West.

The breed reached Europe from the USA 40 years ago, where all of this group, as they appear in their present form, have been kept solely as exhibition fowl. The Shamo breed has been used to improve the table qualities of other breeds.

The Shamo is the tallest breed of poultry, with males regularly reaching 76cm/30in tall. The breed has an upright habit, with a long sloping back, broad breast, square shoulders and attenuated neckline. While it is similar to the standard-bred Malay, the Shamo is without the pronounced curves of that breed. It also has a thinner pea

▶ Like the Aseel, the Shamo has a pea comb, small lobes and barely has wattles. This is the Ko Shamo.

◀ A Black-red Shamo male. While superficially similar to the breed standardized as Malay in the Western world, the Shamo has a pea comb and flat back; features that are closer to those of the Kampong fowl of Northern Malaysia.

comb. This breed has particularly short and hard feathering, with the plumage failing to cover the breastbone and sometimes the shoulder area, and the face has harsh skin. Shamos look somewhat sinister with a medium-length hooked beak and pale orange eyes. The skin is red.

Breeders wishing to rear the Shamo for the sheer pleasure of keeping and conserving examples of some of the most unusual and rare breeds have to be constantly on their guard against those who try to steal them in the mistaken idea that they could still be used for cockfighting.

ESSENTIAL CHARACTERISTICS

Size: O Shamo Male 3.6–5.4kg/ 8–12lbs. Female 2.7–4.5kg/6–10lbs. Chu Shamo Male 3kg/6lbs 10oz. Female 2.2kg/4lbs 14oz (minimum). Nanking Shamo Male 1.1kg/2lbs 8oz. Female 737g/26oz. Ko Shamo Male 1.1kg/2lbs. Female 793g/28oz.

Varieties: Black, White, Black-breasted Red, Spangled, Dark, Brown-red, Wheaten.

Temperament: Docile, but males can be belligerent.

Environment: Tolerant of some confinement as adults but adolescent fowl need space to exercise.

Egg yield: Poor, 20–40 per year, but bantam varieties could lay more.

Malay

The Malay is a very striking bird, with long legs, a powerful stance, broad chest, long neck, gaunt appearance and cruel expression. These are birds to be wary of and are unsuitable for keeping as a family pet. These are instinctively aggressive fighting birds. Two roosters in a pen may fight to the death and inflict significant damage. A rooster may also become aggressive to hens. Because of their size Malays need room to roam, and they regularly dig holes. In its native region, the Malay is regarded as an ancient village bird that roams freely.

By about 1870, examples of these tall Asian Malay fowl had found their way to Britain and in particular to Cornwall, the first stopping-off point for ships returning from Asia. Malays made little impact until they were seen at the early poultry shows. Although standardized as

ESSENTIAL CHARACTERISTICS

Size: Large male 4.9kg/11lbs. Large female 4kg/9lbs. Bantam male 1.1–1.3kg/40–48oz. Bantam female 1–1.1kg/36–40oz.

Varieties: Black-breasted red Male, Clay, Cinnamon, and Red Wheaten Female. Creel, White, Black.

Temperament: Aggressive, but can be docile when regularly handled.

Environment: Free range. Requires room to exercise.

Egg yield: 30 medium light brown eggs per year.

Malay, the standard requirements of the neck, back and tail forming three curves, plus the walnut comb, suggests that most of these early imports were the taller strains native to states of British India rather than those states that are now part of Malaysia. As an exhibition fowl, the Malay was bred to an agreed standard by 1880, one which we would still recognize today. Its appearance is likely to owe much of its development to British, and, more specifically, to Cornish fanciers. It seems highly likely that both large and bantam Malays in their standardized form are a product of Cornish breeding.

The huge reach and weight of the large Malays may help to explain why some of the miniature versions are the largest of their class seen on the show circuit. As a breed type they may have donated many useful traits to the later heavy and specialized table breeds

▶ *A young Brown-red Malay male. Its tail has yet to develop the characteristic third curve.*

▼ A *Crele male: note the curved neck and back. The tail provides the third similar curve*

and strains. However, as exhibition-bred birds, both large and bantam versions are generally appalling layers. The older the hen, the fewer eggs she is likely to lay. Malays are also noted as bad mothers, in part because of their aggressive nature. They may inadvertently kill their young in the process of attacking another female.

The heavy weight and height of the full-size Malay will inevitably mean that its miniature version can be expected to be one of the largest of the bantams. As in the large version, reach is considered to be one of the most important breed points. Exhibitors tend to exhibit and breed from their tallest examples, which has led to over-sized examples being found both in Malay bantam show classes and breeding pens.

Modern Game

Within a few years of the various Acts of Parliament banning cockfighting, Britain became gripped by a craze for exhibition poultry. Breeders looked to exhibit their former cockfighting birds rather than use them for sport. Old English Game birds, which were the pit breed, were not judged appropriate for showing. Exhibition judges looked for birds that were taller than Old English Game, with a shorter back, more upright carriage and hard feathering. Initially, to increase the size of their game birds, breeders crossed them with the Malay poultry breed. With greater height, "reachiness" became a feature of the birds used to attract points at exhibitions. Fanciers managed to breed out the clumsiness of the Malay breed from these taller game birds, and produced a very elegant fowl. The scanty feathers and tail carriage of

▶ *All Modern Game birds have yellow or green legs. Males are dubbed on reaching adulthood. This is a Brown-red rooster.*

the new breed undoubtedly came from the Malay, however. It was with the formation of the Old English Game Club that these newly bred fowl become known as Exhibition Modern Game to distinguish the breeds, though later the word "Exhibition" was dropped from their name.

The popularity of Modern Game peaked by the early 1900s, after which Old English Game enjoyed a resurgence of popularity at the expense of Modern Game. The large Modern Game continued to lose popularity until its nadir in the 1970s when it could have been considered extinct. For the last 40 years, a small group of enthusiasts have largely replicated the efforts of the previous century, reinstating the bird to its full exhibition status. Very few examples are seen at today's shows, and because of this they are a fascinating reminder of the path that exhibition selection can take a breed. The birds are always likely to remain scarce, but will appeal to those who enjoy the competitive aspect of game exhibition.

The game bantams that were developed probably included smaller strains of the earlier cockfighting game, as well as some of the smallest crossbred bantams. Modern Game bantams remain one of the most

▼ *This Black-red Modern Game rooster is an excellent example of breed type. It is tall and slimline with a neat, compact body and short flat back. The bird has an upright, lofty carriage, and stands on long, tall legs. Its tail is whip-like.*

important, if challenging, bantam breeds. Victorian breeders would have wanted both large and bantam versions to be seen as exhibition birds, and while only standardized in seven colours at that time, they would have required each of these to conform to the most exacting rules for plumage pattern, eye and leg coloration. This range of colours has been extended by modern breeders. The bantam version remains in the hands of specialist breeders.

ESSENTIAL CHARACTERISTICS

Size: Large male 3.1–4kg/7–9lbs.
Large female 2.2–3.1kg/5–7lbs.
Bantam male 566–623g/20–22oz.
Bantam female 481–510g/17–18oz.
Varieties: Black, Blue, Birchen, Black-red, Blue-red, Brown-red, Gold-duckwing, Lemon-blue, Pile, Silver-blue, Silver-duckwing, Wheaten, White.
Temperament: Quiet, but exhibition birds will require careful handling.
Environment: The tiny bantams will stand confinement but may be less robust than other game bantams.
Egg yield: Up to 100 per year. Bantam eggs are tiny.

Old English Game Bantams

By far the most popular British exhibition bantam, Old English Game bantams would have been practically unknown until the late 19th century, and despite their name, would have evolved from the existing tall exhibition bantams that were later to become known as Modern Game. By the 1920s, photographs depict them as miniatures of the Oxford show game. In the UK a specialist national show is devoted to this breed. However, unlike most other breeds, a long period of separate development has seen these game bantams being treated as a completely separate breed.

As long as standard Old English Game birds remained on farms, country estates or smallholdings with enough room to display their natural athleticism, most flocks would have remained very like their pit-game ancestors. By nature, they are bold, proud and agile. The bantam version may initially have lacked some of the muscle and feather-hardness of the standard size. However, because of their diminutive size, they were far more likely to attract breeders with limited space for the birds to range. These bantams soon adapted to being kept in tiny pens that allowed their owners an easy opportunity to handle these small birds and assess firmness and shape. Before long, they had been bred to have the hard-feathered quality of their large counterparts. Other characteristics of the large Old English Game breed were also incorporated into the small breed. Some strains soon developed to a point where

▼ A Furness or Brassy-backed male.

▶ A Spangled male showing the sort of bend to its hock that is sometimes absent even in exhibition examples.

◀ When breeders started to select bantam versions of Old English Game, the birds would have looked more like this Ginger male. Such types are now occasionally exhibited as miniature Oxfords.

▼ *A Furness hen.*

ESSENTIAL CHARACTERISTICS

Size: Male 680g/24oz.
Female 623g/22oz.

Varieties: Barred, Birchen, Black, Black-breasted Red, Black-tailed Red, Black-tailed White, Blue, Blue Brassy-back, Blue Golden-duckwing, Blue Millefleur, Blue Quail, Blue-red, Blue-wheaten, Brassyback, Brown-red, Buff, Columbian, Crele, Cuckoo, Fawn, Fawn-breasted Red, Fawn silver-duckwing, Ginger-red, Gold-duckwing, Lemon-blue, Mealy-grey, Millefleur, Mottled, Porcelain, Quail, Red, Red-pile, Red Quill, Self-blue, Silver-blue, Silver-duckwing, Silver-quill, Spangled, Splash, Wheaten, White.

Temperament: Jaunty. The more developed strains are not good at flying.

Environment: Will adapt to free range. The exhibition strains that have been kept for generations in small runs seem happier than most fowl.

Egg yield: 80–100 very small tinted eggs per year.

of their feathers and overall body shape. As more breeders favoured and bred from birds that had a "flat, iron-shaped back and bullock heart-shaped body", the birds ceased to look and behave like miniature versions of Oxford Game. Later, as large Carlisle Game became popular, many saw Old English Game bantams as being their miniatures.

During World War II, large game birds almost disappeared from farms and smallholdings. Post-war food shortages meant that most poultry was kept solely for egg or meat production. Few could find room and precious food to keep a few tiny Old English Game Bantams. At exhibitions there have always been classes for Old English Game

they differed from the Oxford type, with those handling them beginning to describe their body shape as that of a "flat iron or bullock heart". Differences developed and the hard feathering led to a tighter and smaller tail. The breed standard asked for "wings held low to protect the thighs". However, a concentration on overall body shape soon saw a higher wing carriage become the norm for the bantam type. This in turn led to many breeders regarding "handling" as the most important aspect of the breed. Breeders who kept their birds confined to small spaces often owned birds that were more soft-feathered and fluffier than their large counterparts. The birds were continually assessed for the hardness

bantams. For most exhibitors, their interpretation of type, shape and feathering has been far more important than the colour of the bird. Some judges agreed, and often birds of no fixed or "off" colour were promoted to best in show.

◄ *A Silver-duckwing male showing the same sort of front and short back seen in some large Carlisle Game on today's show circuit. Note the wing carriage of this bird when compared to the Oxford type, particularly the Ginger male opposite.*

Indian/Cornish Game

Also known as the Cornish poultry breed, these fowl are the most solid and muscular looking of all poultry, with wide-set, strong, short legs, a deep-set breast and a solid appearance. The breed was developed for fighting and contains Old English Game, Malay and Aseel/Asil in its genes. However, it is a slow-moving bird, and its thick-set appearance means it was never agile enough to fight competitively, and although unsuitable for fighting, the bird was developed for the table instead. The massive size of the bird makes it particularly suitable for eating, and often it is crossed with the Sussex or Dorking breed for this purpose. Indian Game are poor egg-layers. Most cannot breed naturally because of their enormous body size and short legs, consequently they do not make good mothers.

Indian Game have yellow legs and flesh, which was once considered undesirable for the top end of the poultry meat market. They are slow-growing and only modest egg-layers, and are therefore undesirable as a commercial prospect.

ESSENTIAL CHARACTERISTICS
Size: Male 3.2–4.2kg/7–9lbs.
Female 2.7–3.6kg/6–8lbs.
Varieties: Cornish, Jubilee.
Temperament: Vigorous, active.
Environment: Back garden.
Egg yield: Up to 100 tinted eggs per year.

However, like their Aseel ancestor, when crossbred, Indian Game are capable of passing on useful genetic traits, such as abundance of breast meat. This in turn enabled poultry geneticists to incorporate Indian Game genes into some of the most successful meat birds found on our supermarket shelves.

In spite of their ancestry, the Indian is a docile and friendly

▲ *A large Jubilee rooster.*

fowl and makes the perfect pet. The bantam versions are exact miniatures and are suitable for a small garden.

▶ *A Dark Indian Game bantam hen.*

THE CHANTECLER BREED

Indian Game was one of five breeds used to create the Chantecler breed, a dual-purpose fowl able to withstand the hard winter frosts of Canada. The initial cross was of a Dark Indian Game male with a White Leghorn hen, and then a Rhode Island Red male with a White Wyandotte hen. Each cross produced white or off-white pullets with tiny pea combs that were thought desirable in extremely cold conditions. The offspring of these two crosses were mated. Some of the very best resulting pullets were later mated to a White Plymouth Rock. In total it took nine years to produce the perfect Chantecler breed. While for a time widely kept by Canadian farmers, the breed is now rare.

Rumpless Game

Few breeds of poultry have a rumpless variety, and most are considered to be quite rare. Rumplessness, where the breed effectively has no tail feathers and instead has a rounded rear, is caused by a genetic defect in which the end of the vertebrae and what is usually known as the parson's nose, from which tail feathers grow, is missing. The oil glands that would serve the tail feathers are also missing.

Rumpless game are a tailless version of the Old English Game bird. They are available as large or bantam versions, though the large versions are much rarer. They are also known as Manx Rumpies, and are thought to have descended from

ESSENTIAL CHARACTERISTICS

Size: Male 2.2–2.7kg/5–6lbs.
Female 1.8–2.2kg/4–5lbs.
Bantam male 623–737g/22–26oz.
Bantam female 510–623g/18–22oz.
Varieties: All game colours. Few birds have identical coloration.
Temperament: Game characteristics.
Environment: Free-range.
Egg yield: Ornamental value.

◄ *This is a Blue-red male bird.*

Persian rumpless game, although the exact origins appear to be lost.

Rumpless game birds have an upright posture, a forward-thrusting carriage and a rounded body that slopes down and back. A wide variety of colours are known, and it is unusual to have two identically coloured birds. The breed has a single comb, red earlobes and no standard leg colour. While the bantam version is virtually a rumpless version of the Old English Game breed, they are not customarily dubbed, and should, when exhibited, be entered in the rare breed classes. They may, however, be found to be less quarrelsome than many of their standard feathered counterparts.

► *A Blue-wheaten bantam hen.*

▼ *A Rumpless Game. Also known as Manx Rumpies and Persian Rumpies, they are thought to originate from what is now Iraq.*

A DIRECTORY OF TRUE BANTAMS

The defining characteristic of a true bantam is that, unlike other poultry breeds, it does not have a large counterpart. Smaller versions of large breeds are often incorrectly known as bantams, but should in fact be termed miniatures. The true bantam classification covers a handful of breeds, each with distinguishing characteristics, which are admired by many breeders. These small birds are often available in a wider variety of stunning colours, and their visual appearance can be immensely appealing, adding ornamental value to the garden.

Such small birds make good pets for young children. In addition, true bantams are the perfect pets for those with limited space; they require smaller housing, taking up less room. They also inflict less wear and tear on the garden environment. These birds have lively and perky characters, with a gentle and friendly nature. They are feisty and can be extremely entertaining to watch. True bantams lay eggs that are smaller than those of standard hens, providing a practical purpose for keeping them as well. They will need to be well protected from predators such as cats and foxes.

▲ *True bantams have a bold but gentle disposition and respond well to humans.*

◄ *Available in a wide range of colours, the plumage of true bantams is often appealing to breeders with an interest in perfecting unusual varieties.*

WHAT IS A TRUE BANTAM?

Weighing no more than 750g/1½lb, these small birds are the dwarves of the poultry world. For all their small size, these are fowl with large personalities, lively dispositions and friendly natures, making them suitable pets for those with less room to spare.

In 1970, the term "true bantam" was adopted to describe all poultry breeds that do not have a large version. All of the true bantams, standardized as such throughout much of the world, are thought to have descended from an ancient population of tiny fowl that may have existed for centuries in the Javanese islands of Indonesia, before being spread through both East and West along the trade routes. The term "bantam" derives from Batavia, the Dutch name for Jakarta, a port on the island of Java, which was used by the Dutch East Indies Company to trade with Europe. It is likely that sailors brought the small fowl that they found in this location back to Europe; these original bantams would then have naturalized in Northern Europe. It is plausible that imported true bantams were crossbred with existing undersize

strains of English game or Hamburg-type breeds. Elegant strains of miniature game fowl, far removed from the early pit game, would seem likely to have developed almost entirely from these bantams.

Nowadays, the word bantam has become the accepted term for any tiny or diminutive fowl. Small

◄ Belgian bantams are bright and perky by nature.

versions of large fowl are often wrongly known as bantams, but these are in fact miniatures, despite the fact that many miniature versions of large breeds can be anything but miniature in size. True bantams were used in some initial crosses that formed the foundation of many miniature versions of large fowl breeds.

Bantams are ideal for poultry keepers with limited space. Their food requirements are similar to those of other poultry but in smaller quantities. Their eggs are half or even a third of the size of those of standard breeds.

Group characteristics

All members of the true bantam group have a different shape to those of miniature versions of large fowl. They characteristically have very short backs and a low wing carriage. In some instances the wing carriage is almost perpendicular to the back of the bird and the wings nearly touch the ground.

Group classification

The Victorian craze for exhibition poultry led to the concept of breeding fowl to conform to a written standard. As a result, breeds were grouped according to type. Apart from game breeds, the early administrators chose the terms "sitters" and "non-sitting breeds", referring to the breeds' inclination, or not, to sit on their eggs

◄ True Belgian bantams have many characteristics of standard breeds including muffs and beards.

▲ *Dutch bantams are available in many varieties and appeal to those who choose poultry with unusual colours.*

▲ *With their rounded body shapes and attractive personalities, Pekins make appealing pets.*

▲ *Feather-legged Booted bantams need to be kept in an environment where the foot feathers will not be damaged.*

and rear young, as the classifications of choice. Shows classified miniature versions of sitters and non-sitters as variety bantams. Today, breeds are classified as heavy and light, according to weight, rather than as sitters or non-sitters, with plenty of categories within each class to further distinguish birds by type and by origin.

For most of the 20th century, the breeds that had partly or wholly derived from the Javanese true bantams were listed along with Pekins/Cochin bantams, Poland bantams and so on, as "ornamental bantams". By the 1970s, the miniature versions of the soft-feather breeds were classified as dwarves, and

there was a growing awareness of the need for a system that classified all the bantams derived wholly or largely from the original Javanese imports as true bantams.

The breeds

Today, the breeds that make up the true bantam classification have been selected and perfected in different areas of the globe. Like some large breeds, there are true bantam breeds with feathered feet, beards and muffs, long saddle, hackle and sickle feathers, distinctive feather patterns, modifications and coloration. There are a variety of combs, and different stances. There is even a breed with short legs, and a few that are rumpless. In fact, all the true bantam breeds are easy to distinguish from each other because their appearances are so individual. Many make good broodies and will look after the eggs of other poultry breeds.

◄ *Belgian bantams make good pets for people who want eggs but have little space. They are available in a huge range of colour varieties.*

Sabelpoot/Booted Bantam

Those Booted Bantams shown at exhibitions today are likely to be descended from Continental strains, principally from the Netherlands, where they have long been standardized as Sablepoot. Yet fowl similar to Booted Bantams were referred to in British books around 1850, exhibiting a fuller tail than those currently being shown as Sabelpoots. The Booted Bantam hails from the Netherlands where it is known as the Sablelpoot or Sapelpoot. This is an old breed. Booted Bantams are historically and genetically linked to the feather-footed Belgian bantams.

▼ A White male.

They were was crossed with the Barbu d'Anvers breed to make the Barbu d'Uccle breed. In their homeland the breed is relatively common. True to its name, the main distinguishing feature of this breed is the extravagant feathering on its feet. The breed has a majestic appearance, with an upright stance, deep curving chest, wide and upright tail feathering and a single red comb, full wattles and red earlobes. It is

◄ The feet feathers can easily become damaged if not looked after. A deep litter hen house may help to protect the feathering.

available in a wide number of varieties, all of which are attractive. As a result of the feathering on the feet, this breed is less likely to cause damage to flowerbeds than other breeds when left to range free in a garden environment. Booted Bantams do have a foraging nature, however. These birds have a calm and friendly temperament and make great family pets.

Booted Bantam genes were used to create Cochin bantams in 1884. A descendant of their progeny was crossed with American Cochin bantams in 1890. It is a measure of the way true bantams have helped to create miniature versions of the large breeds.

▼ A Buff-mottled hen.

ESSENTIAL CHARACTERISTICS
Size: Male 850g/30oz.
Female 750g/27oz.
Varieties: Black, Blue, Cuckoo, Millefleur, Mottled, Porcelain, White.
Temperament: Docile.
Environment: Needs dry housing to protect the feathered feet from wet weather.
Egg yield: 80–100 eggs per year.

BELGIAN BANTAMS

The Belgian bantams, made up of the Barbu d'Uccle, Barbu d'Anvers, Barbu d'Everberg, Barbu de Grubbe and Barbu de Watermael are the only true bantams to be standardized with two or more ornamental appendages. These small fowl with feathered legs are thought to have found their way to northerly regions of Europe from Asia during 300 years of trade with the Dutch East Indies Company. The original imports are thought to have been beardless and muff-less, and it seems likely that today's breeds are derived from the careful selection and crossing of their descendants with other tiny bantams brought back to the same region. The feather-legged Barbu d'Uccle and clean-legged Barbu d'Anvers quickly found favour, while the rumpless Barbu de Grubbe and Barbu d'Everberg were largely ignored. Along with the crested Barbu de Watermael, these three breeds remained minority varieties for many years, even within their homeland. Four of the five breeds are standardized with the same colours. Exhibitors need to understand all the details of their most complex colour patterns, as well as the shape of every variety. Belgian bantams make the best of pets and are perfect "chatty" garden companions.

Barbu d'Uccle

The Barbu d'Uccle, also known as a Booted Bantam, is characterized by its feathered feet and beard. The hen has a muff and beard, with the features forming distinct tufts. Both male and female carry a neat, and relatively small, single red comb. This breed has abundant feathering, with the hackle feathers reaching down to the saddle area of the back. The males have a tail sward that is carried in an open configuration. The breed has a low posture with wings that are also carried low to cover the vulture hocks. All these features combine to create a breed with a proud stance.

The breed has a gentle and docile nature. It is placid and undemanding, except during the breeding season, when males have been known to attack humans, other birds and animals. The hens go broody and make good mothers.

▼ *There are strong historical connections between colour and variety. Many people wrongly assume that the Millefleur colour is specific to this feather-legged breed. This is a Millefleur rooster.*

> **ESSENTIAL CHARACTERISTICS**
> **Size**: Male 800g/28oz.
> Female 550g/19oz.
> **Varieties**: Black, Blue, Cuckoo, Lavender, Millefleur, Porcelain, Quail, White.
> **Temperament**: Tolerant.
> **Environment**: Care is needed to ensure that the leg feathers do not get broken.
> **Egg yield**: 80–100 white or tinted eggs per year.

▼ *Male birds are tolerant toward each other, and can be housed together except in the breeding season. This is a black rooster.*

Barbu d'Anvers

The stance of the Barbu d'Anvers is distinctive. It is that of a bird standing to attention and showing off,

▲ A Quail hen.

▶ Some of the colour varieties of Belgian bantams can be difficult to perfect.

with the chest puffed out and upright. The male carries his tail at a perpendiuclar angle and the wing and wing feathers point downward almost covering the clean legs. Belgian d'Anvers are capable of flying. The breed has thick hackle feathers, which in the male look like a mane and in the female like a ruffle. The body is short. The males have a tail sward rather than sickle-shaped feathers. Like all the Belgian bantams, this breed has a crest and beard that suppresses the wattles. It has a broad rose comb that ends in a leader. This is an attractive breed that makes a good pet, and fowl will become tame with handling.

ESSENTIAL CHARACTERISTICS
Size: Male 680–790g/24–27oz.
Female 570–680g/20–24oz.
Varieties: All of the standard Bearded Belgian colours.
Temperament: Cheerful, chatty.
Environment: Can be kept in a small pen.
Egg yield: 80–100 white or tinted eggs per year.

Barbu d'Everberg

The Barbu d'Everberg is regarded as a rumpless subvariety of the Barbu d'Uccle breed. Like all rumpless varieties, it would have originated from spontaneous sports of fowl with standard tails, in this case a Barbu d'Uccle. Rumpless breeds are few and far between in the poultry world. This particular breed was first recorded in

ESSENTIAL CHARACTERISTICS
Size: Male up to 800g/28oz.
Female up to 600g/21oz.
Varieties: All the standard Bearded Belgian colours.
Temperament: Perky.
Environment: Can be kept in small pens. Requires a dry floor area.
Egg yield: 80–100 white or tinted eggs per year.

1904. The rumpless gene is a dominant one, so whenever the Everberg is crossed a rumpless form will always result. Where the rumpless characteristic is found to be the result of a dominant sport or mutation, it offers the possibility of creating new colours. Rumpless breeds have the last two vertebrae missing. It is to these vertebrae that the tail feathering is usually attached. The rest of the body is covered in abundant feathering. The back is covered in long saddle feathers; the feet also have feathers. This breed has a crest and beard, small single comb and no wattles. The rumpless feature is appealing.

◀ The characteristic rounded boule is as much a part of the Barbu d'Everberg as its beard and muff.

Barbu de Grubbe

This is another rumpless true bantam, of the Barbu d'Anvers genetic line. This breed has a soft and gentle temperament, though not in the breeding season, when males are known to become aggressive.

The Barbu de Grubbe is a small breed that has a pert, upright stance and wings that slope to the ground. It has a short, thick neck, a beard and muffs, single red rose comb, and a wide, rounded rear body shape. As in Belgian bantam varieties with beards and rose combs, the de Grubbe should not have any wattles. A similar but probably far larger fowl illustrated by Aldrovandus (an Italian naturalist regarded as the father of natural history) in 1600 was labelled as a Persian fowl, and later, rumpless fowl were recorded near Liège in Belgium, identified as hedge fowl. These were valued because, having no tails, they were more likely to escape from predators such as foxes.

ESSENTIAL CHARACTERISTICS
Size: Male 650g/23oz. Female 550g/19oz.
Varieties: All Belgian bantam colours.
Temperament: Perky Belgian character.
Environment: Can be kept in small runs and houses.
Egg yield: 80–100 white or tinted eggs per year.

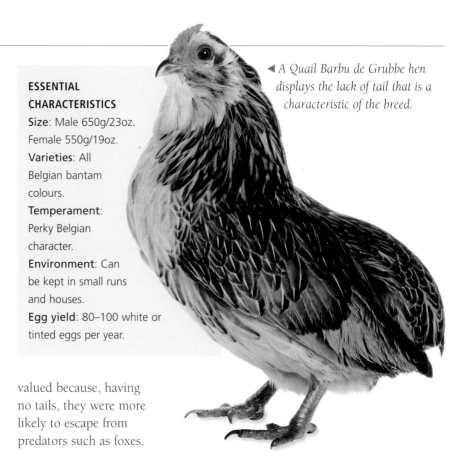

◀ *A Quail Barbu de Grubbe hen displays the lack of tail that is a characteristic of the breed.*

Barbu de Watermael

ESSENTIAL CHARACTERISTICS
Size: Male 600–700g/21–24½oz. Female 450–550g/16–19oz.
Varieties: All Belgian colours.
Temperament: Perky, cheerful.
Environment: Small runs and houses.
Egg yield: 80–100 white or tinted eggs per year.

The Barbu de Watermael is the smallest Belgian bantam. It has a small square rose comb, which is unique in having three leaders. It has a tri-lobed beard and clean legs, and is the only member of the bearded Belgian bantam family with a crest. The crest may in some way inhibit the development of the characteristic boule. The unique tri-lobed beard adds its own distinctive feature.

▶ *This breed has clean, unfeathered legs.*

◀ *A Lavender Quail male with a unique tri-leader comb.*

Dutch Bantam

The tiny Dutch Bantam is one of the smallest of all the true bantams, and is the most popular poultry breed in its native Holland. It is probably descended from a Dutch native breed, but may include Indonesian ancestry. The Dutch East Indies trading company had closer and longer trading links with Indonesia, and it is likely that sailors included poultry on their vessels to provide food as well as for trading. Asian poultry brought back to Europe by these sailors could have become absorbed into local landrace bloodlines. Because local landrace poultry was commonplace, the Dutch Bantam was not recognized offically as a breed until 1906.

This is a breed that lays tiny eggs, and it may have been selectively bred for this characteristic. It is believed that in past centuries, large eggs had to be passed to the kitchen of the local landed gentry, and farmers were only allowed to keep those that were small in size.

▲ *A Silver-blue Partridge hen.*

Dutch Bantams found their way to Britain in 1970, but appeared much earlier in the USA. The breed died out in the USA due to lack of interest, but has since been successfully reintroduced. Breeders soon established a club and strong show presence. Dutch Bantams often win top awards when shown competitively.

This tiny fowl is a perfect miniature, free from any of the appendages and exaggerations that are essential to the anatomy of many other true bantams and ornamental fowl. Unlike the Rosecomb breed, the earlobe of the Dutch

ESSENTIAL CHARACTERISTICS

Size: Male 550g/19oz.
Female: 450g/16oz.
Varieties: Birchen, Black, Blue, Blue-partridge, Blue-yellow partridge, Buff Columbian, Crele, Columbian, Cuckoo, Gold-partridge, Lavender, Millefleur, Mottled, Partridge, Pile, Quail, Salmon, Silver-partridge, Silver-blue Partridge, Yellow-partridge, Wheaten, White.
Temperament: Flighty, friendly.
Environment: Back garden.
Egg yield: 160 cream or light brown small eggs per year.

Bantam is small and unexaggerated. It has slate-blue legs and relatively large wings for its size. This is a breed that can fly. The modest single red comb is not expected to sit tight to the head as in most true bantam breeds, but is allowed to "fly away" slightly. Initially bred in the Black-red and Silver-partridge colours, the varieties now number at least 15. Their colours are thought to be the exact counterparts of rudimentary game bird patterns. All are carefully standardized colour combinations that make the breed one of the most colourful additions to the show bench or garden.

By nature the Dutch Bantam is alert and flighty. The breed has a friendly disposition, making it a good bird to

▼ *A Black male.*

► *A Gold-partridge hen.*

▲ *A Lemon-porcelain male.*

◄ *A Gold male.*

▼ *A Gold-partridge male.*

keep as a pet. In addition, it lays a good number of eggs considering its small size, which makes it a practical breed to keep. The breed is broody, and is known to make a good parent.

The Dutch Bantam adapts to being kept in a relatively confined space, but like all bantams kept in close confinement, regular interaction with humans is essential for the wellbeing of the bird. The breed is hardy and remains one of the least complicated and most satisfactory tiny garden fowl.

Nankin

Nankins are thought to be the result of early crosses between Javanese imported poultry and some of the small strains later standardized as Hamburgs. However, there is also speculation that the breed hails from Nanjing in China. Nankin or nankeen was also an early description of the colour of a fabric imported to the West from the Far East.

This is an old breed thought to date back to the 1700s, and is considered by some authorities to be one of the foundation breeds used to establish Sebright bantams.

Nankins are only found in a natural two-tone form of buff colour, and are available in two varieties, single comb and rose comb. They made little impact

ESSENTIAL CHARACTERISTICS
Size: Male up to 680g/24oz.
Females up to 625g/22oz.
Varieties: Single comb, Rose comb.
Temperament: Cocky, bouncy, less placid than other true bantams.
Environment: Will be happy to range free.
Egg yield: 120–140 smallish tinted eggs per year.

on the exhibition scene and had more or less disappeared until they were rediscovered in Britain in 1970. The breed remains under the protection of the Rare Poultry Society in Britain. The Nankin retains the type, bounce and character of all true bantams and is probably as good an example as we are likely to find of yesteryear's bantams of the countryside.

▲ *A single comb male.*

▲ *A Buff rose comb hen with a natural two-tone pattern.*

Japanese/Shabo

This is an ancient breed, recorded more than 1000 years ago in Japan. However, for centuries Japan was not open to trade with the western world, so the breed did not arrive in Europe or America until the 19th century.

This is a distinct bantam breed. The breed standard requires a precise tail carriage that in the males is somewhere between upright and veering beyond perpendicular to the body. It also has extremely short legs and weak thighs. An interest in the grotesque may have led Japanese breeders to select for and accentuate the shortening of leg bones. In Europe, dwarfism had been noted in Scots Dumpy populations. Like this

ESSENTIAL CHARACTERISTICS

Size: Male 510–600g/18–20oz.
Female 400–510g/14–18oz.
Varieties: Birchen-grey, Black, Black-tailed Buff, Black-tailed White, Blue, Brown-red, Cuckoo, Mottled, White.
Temperament: Placid.
Environment: Dry, protected.
Egg yield: 60–120 small cream or white eggs per year.

European breed, the Japanese bantam also suffers from a lethal creeper gene. Both parents have the long and short leg gene. If both pass the short leg gene to the offspring, those embryos will fail to thrive. This happens in 25 per cent of the offspring. Another 25 per cent will be born with long legs. This feature alone makes this fowl a difficult breeding proposition.

The breed has a deep and full breast, a short round body, long saddle feathers, and wings that touch the ground. It also has some unique and challenging colour combinations. Because of its short legs the breed has a low carriage, and requires protection from cold and wet.

The last few years has brought greater movement of breeding lines out of Japan, along with a better understanding of the culture behind the breed. This same movement of ideas and stock has seen more frizzle-feathered examples, as well as the emergence of a silky-feathered variety. The Japanese bantam is one of the most important exhibition breeds. However, the breed is always likely to remain in the hands of experienced breeders and dedicated exhibitors. Like so many of the true bantams, where breed type and style have developed in the hands of fanciers and exhibitors, the Japanese bantams are content to spend much of their life in reasonable confinement. The breed is reliant on its owners and is happiest when given plenty of attention.

▶ *A Grey male. Note how the tail is held upright even when the bird is sitting.*

▼ *A White frizzled hen.*

Rosecomb

Rosecombs are an old breed, which may have been developed in England in the 15th century. They are kept primarily for exhibition or ornamental value in the garden, since they are known to be poor egg layers and not worth keeping for their meat. Exhibitors probably spend more time preparing their birds for show than breeders of any other fowl.

Early illustrations depict black and white varieties with single or rose combs and either red or white lobes. However, the term "Rosecomb" was once used to describe several breeds that had a rose comb, rather than one specific breed. English breeders were largely responsible for refining the breed, introducing Hamburg genes to improve the quality of the feathering. When shown beside a Hamburg, the two breeds do have similarities. Perfect rose combs and smooth white

▼ *The white lobes are smooth with a velvety texture. This is a black male.*

lobes were developed to become the most important defining features of the breed. By the turn of the 20th century, Rosecombs had reached a stage of development that would be recognized by today's breeders.

Black, White and Blue are the most common varieties since breeders concentrated

on perfection of head points rather than colours. In profile, the breed has a short back, arched neck and proud, upright stance. The tail has wide feathers and is carried upwards at an angle, slightly higher in the male than the female. The wings are held low and at an angle but do not obstruct the leg visibility.

British Rosecombs are almost identical to those shown in Holland as Javas.

▼ *The comb may be disproportionately large in the Rosecomb breed. It should have a square front with the central area covered in protrusions. The long tapering leader leans back.*

◄ *Rosecomb hens rarely go broody and may be difficult to breed. Chicks may have a high mortality rate either before or just after hatching. In addition, males may have low fertility rates. This is a Black hen.*

Pekin/Cochin Bantams

In Britain the breed of bantam called Pekin and treated as true bantams, is known as the miniature Cochin throughout most of the rest of the world.

A single pair of Pekin bantams was sent to Britain with other booty after the sacking of Peking's (Beijing's) Summer Palace by Anglo-French forces during the Second Opium Wars of 1860. At that time, any poultry from distant regions was thought to be the indigenous breed of that district, hence the naming of the breed for its point of origin. By 1863 the offspring of this single importation were out-crossed with a White Booted Bantam. With just this one line to breed from, some breeders resorted to out-crossing the breed with Nankin bantams. All the breeds used to create the early Pekins would have been true bantams. W. F. Entwistle, who is generally credited with making many early miniature versions of large fowl, used these birds to cross with others that he had imported from Shanghai in the 1880s. By 1890 he co-operated with American breeders, loaning one Buff rooster which was reported to have sired 30 chicks. Reading his notes, there can be little doubt that the intention was to create miniature Cochins. All the illustrations that he made show birds that are exact

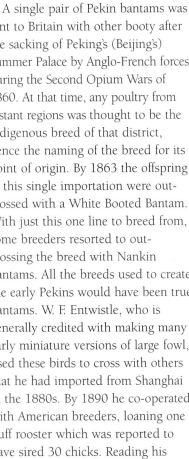

▼ *A Blue male with long saddle and tail feathers extending over the cushion.*

miniatures of the large Cochins of the period. He wrote "Cochin bantams should be exactly the same as the larger Cochins, whilst as regard size and weight one fifth the weight of large Cochin fowls."

At this time many exhibition strains were developing a noticeable forward "tilt", with an outline not unlike a wedge of cheese. It was this type that was later favoured by British breeders, who regarded their birds as true bantams rather than miniature fowl.

For many years poultry exhibitions were dominated by large fowl. Most Pekin breeders had to exhibit their birds in the "variety" bantam classes. From the 1950s, shows were dominated by bantam entries and

▼ *The Silver-partridge hen could be seen as a rather exaggerated Cochin type.*

▼ *This Mottled hen is a good example of a British Pekin type and tilt.*

▼ *A Blue-mottled frizzled example has a fluffy outline.*

▲ *Top row, left to right: Lavender hen, Silver-partridge hen, Lemon-cuckoo hen. Bottom row, left to right: Millefleur hen, Black male, Cuckoo hen.*

bantam exhibitors, with specialist shows attracting large numbers of Pekin bantams entries.

In appearance the Pekin is a bundle of plumage, with an abundance of soft underfeathers. The back has a significant rounded cushion of feathers. It has a characteristic forward tilt to its body with short legs and feathered feet and toes. The breed makes a good broody and a good mother. They may be as tolerant of confinement as any true bantam but, given the run of a garden on a fine day, a little group will adopt many of the sedate mannerisms of large Cochins.

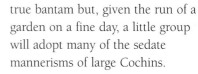

ESSENTIAL CHARACTERISTICS
Size: Male 680g/24oz.
Female 570g/20oz.
Varieties: Barred, Birchen, Black, Blue, Blue-mottled, Buff, Columbian, Cuckoo, Lavender, Mottled, Partridge, Red, Silver-partridge, Wheaten, White.
Temperament: Calm, gentle.
Environment: Copes with confinement. Requires grass on which to forage.
Egg yield: 60–130 small cream, tinted or brown eggs.

▶ *A Partridge hen.*

Sebright

The Sebright breed was named after its creator, who intended to produce an entirely ornamental bantam breed with laced feathering. It was the search for perfection in lacing, previously seen only in a rudimentary form in strains of the Poland breed, that led him to make an initial cross between the Poland and an unnamed "common" bantam. It is now thought that Hamburg and Rosecomb were also used in the genetic material of the breed. The offspring were bred and selected from until almost perfect lacing had been obtained and the crest of the Poland had been bred out. In spite of having Poland blood in their ancestry, the Sebright remains a typical true bantam.

In the Sebright breed the exhibition male should be "hen-feathered". This means that rather than having the curved and pointed sickle in the tail, and the narrow saddle hackle feathers that cover the back, each of these feathers is expected to be rounded like a hen's feathers, thus enabling every feather to be evenly laced. Not all males are hen-feathered, and those that hatch as such sometimes revert to standard feathering after a moult. Hen-feathered and standard-feathered males are both used in breeding programs by the more knowledgeable breeders.

After 200 years of inbreeding from a very limited gene pool, some strains of Sebrights have less than perfect immune systems. Additionally, some hen-feathered males are less fertile, making breeding Sebrights to reproduce to an exacting standard difficult, and ensuring that exhibition breeds are likely to remain in the hands of skilled and dedicated enthusiasts.

Sebrights have distinct rich black lacing on a clear and even silver or gold ground. In total it took almost two decades to perfect the quality of lacing and to fix the breed type, though once it had been achieved, the breed quickly became a popular ornamental show bantam.

The breed has an upright and alert carriage, with a rounded breast carried forward and downward-pointing wings. The male has a rose comb. The skin is blue and the legs are clear of feathering.

▼ *A Gold-laced male with an upright posture and a bright and alert eye.*

▶ *A Silver-laced Sebright hen. In their early days, Sebrights were often referred to as Sebright Jungle fowl.*

ESSENTIAL CHARACTERISTICS

Size: Male 625g/22oz.
Female 570g/20oz.
Varieties: Gold-laced, Silver-laced.
Temperament: Alert.
Environment: An active and ornamental breed than can be quite hardy but is difficult to breed.
Egg yield: 50–80 small white eggs per year.

Serama

The Malaysian Serama evolved from a program of crosses between Japanese Bantams, Silkies and tiny Malaysian bantams known as Ayam Kapans. The genes of the Serama put it firmly in the true bantam camp. The breed was created in 1971 by the Malaysian Wee Yean Een, and named after the 16th century Thai king, Sri Ama. They are described as game-like because of their Malaysian bantam ancestry. The breed is so tiny that in its homeland it is often treated as a house pet, outnumbering cats and dogs. It is a good breed for urban areas, requiring just a small amount of living space.

This breed of poultry is, in fact, the smallest in the world, and selection for size is a significant factor in breeding programs. In Malaysia it is exhibited in three different weight bands.

The breed is a relatively late export to the western world and is currently growing in popularity.

It has a pert and upright stance, a long, upright tail and equally long wings. In type the breed shows a "V"-shaped body posture, albeit in an exaggerated form, more than any of the other true bantams originating from the Far East.

As a relatively new breed, albeit distilled from ancient Malaysian true bantam populations, the Serama may take time to settle or be accepted into a Western show culture.

▲ *Spangled male.*

While they have been exhibited in a range of size bands, in Britain at least, the maximum weights seem likely to be adopted as the show standard for this tiny breed.

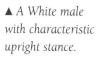

▲ *A White male with characteristic upright stance.*

▼ *A silkie Buff hen.*

▼ *A Millefleur hen.*

ESSENTIAL CHARACTERISTICS
Size: Male 500g/17½oz.
Female 300g/10½oz.
Varieties: No fixed colour varieties.
Temperament: Docile, friendly.
Environment: Said to require a very protected environment and to be difficult to breed.
Egg yield: White to dark brown.

A DIRECTORY OF MANMADE BREEDS

Manmade poultry breeds make up a distinct portion of all pure poultry breeds. These are the breeds that were created for commercial purposes by crossbreeding existing breeds, with the aim of producing offspring that benefit from the desirable traits of each parent, such as large body size and quantity of meat, their productive egg-laying capacity, or because they are economical to keep. Such breeds preceded the development of the modern hybrid, and for the most part were intended to provide maximum food for least cost. These fowl have been perfected over time by selecting and breeding from the best, and many have been used in the creation of new breeds. Today many of these breeds continue to have a commercial role, although most are not able to compete with the egg-laying capacity of hybrids. Like foundation breeds, those developed for exhibition purposes have less utility value, though the character and visual appearance of many attracts enthusiastic breeders and amateurs.

▲ *Burford Browns are good dual-purpose birds laying dark brown egg, but are not yet bred to an agreed standard.*

◄ *Lavender Orpingtons are a new variety of a well-known and popular manmade breed.*

WHAT IS A MANMADE BREED?

A manmade breed is a breed of poultry which has been developed by taking genetic material from at least two established pure breeds with the intention of creating a new breed that will inherit the most desirable qualities and characteristics of the parents.

The concept that a new poultry breed could be created out of two or more existing breeds was initially an American one. American breeders did not have any native chickens until immigrant settlers took fowl with them to the New World. The birds travelled as deck cargo to provide eggs and meat on the long sea journey. It is possibly because of this limitation that American breeders had far fewer inhibitions about making and naming new breeds of poultry from existing breeds than did breeders in other countries. In England, for instance, as late as the early 19th century the concept of a manmade breed was thought to be close to heresy. The idea that a breed could be created, stabilized and refined to an agreed standard that would then conform in certain external features such as size, comb, leg colour, and

type (shape), completely altered the way poultry keepers thought of poultry breeding. The driving motivation was purely commercial.

American breeders were prepared to use any breed in the breeding pen that could produce enough eggs in a

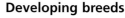
▲ *Marans are a French fowl developed for the very dark brown eggs that they lay.*

harsh climate to satisfy New York's ever-increasing demand for eggs. Unlike other parts of the Western world, since there was no local prejudice against yellow flesh, breeders could include an optimum proportion of Asiatic bloodlines in their table fowl breeding pens to produce the type of bird with plenty of breast meat that would satisfy market demand.

Developing breeds
The development of manmade poultry breeds followed two different, but parallel, courses. The first development was that of the "formula breeds", those where breeders included established breeds in their breeding pens with the aim of cross-breeding them to create new breeds

◄ *The extremely long tail of some Japanese breeds is a feature that has been selected in breeding programs.*

RHODE ISLAND RED x LIGHT SUSSEX: A MANMADE SUCCESS STORY

The British Light Sussex is an ancient foundation breed that evolved from management and selection of regional Surrey and Kent fowl. It has a high commercial value because it is a productive egg-layer. The Rhode Island Red is an American manmade breed created using genetic material from fowl imported from Europe and Asia. It, too, has a strong commercial value as a dual-purpose bird.

Rhode Island Red males were crossed with Light Sussex females to produce brown pullets and white males. The female offspring inherit their feather colour and egg-laying capacity from the Rhode male, and will produce up to 75 per cent of all eggs sold in Britain. The white or silver-coloured males inherit the Light Sussex coloration and enough of her body conformation to make them a worthwhile table fowl.

This feather-colour sex-linkage allows early visual determination of chick sex,

and this cross is the basis of much of the world's brown egg-laying hybrid flock. This egg production gene is carried down the male line. Added to that, the Light Sussex is a very productive hen. The two breeds crossed together therefore produce a high egg yield. The more commercial strains of the Rhode Island

▲ *The Light Sussex (left) and Rhode Island Red is a classic pairing with offspring that are prolific egg-layers.*

Red family are some of the most productive hybrid strains and they are one of the success stories of modern agricultural development.

encompassing the best features and character traits of each breed. Good examples of type were required for the original breed stock. The second course saw new breeds such as the Rhode Island Red gradually evolve out of a mixed population of fowl from all over the world, rather than from specific breeds. Using genetic material from a greater pool, it became possible to perfect the traits of the offspring. The new breeds were developed to adapt to local conditions as well as to meet market demands. The breeding program for each type is rigorous, with the requirement that the resultant offspring are stable and will breed true to type, if required. When it became generally accepted that the standard breeding formulae could be altered to create new colours, poultry breeding and

exhibiting became a more creative pastime, attracting fanciers with an interest in perfecting colours. At that time poultry farmers understood the concepts of varieties within a breed, the various strains and the importance of utility selection, but at that period emphasis was on breed type and breed standard, rather than on hybridizing.

Lasting legacy

The implications of rearranging breed formulae to create new colours, as well as bantam counterparts of most breeds, have been considerable. Often, many manmade bantams are now more popular than the original large breeds. The ethos behind the creation of many of these miniatures was to recreate, as closely as possible the large breed characteristics. When

bantam versions of large breeds were created, the wings were held far higher and at a more horizontal angle.

Crosses of Rhode-type males with hens descended from and not dissimilar to the original Light Sussex are the basis of many of today's black-tailed brown hybrid hens. A similar "recessive white" female line, descending in part from single-combed sports of White Wyandottes and white sports from Rhode Island Reds, is crossed with a typical Rhode Island Red male to produce the common pink- or white-tailed brown hybrid hens. Many of the almost black hybrids that are popular with small producers are the product of crosses involving Rhode Island Reds and Barred Plymouth Rocks. The significant manmade breeds still influence modern poultry breeding.

AMERICAN MANMADE BREEDS

American manmade breeds are the results of experiments which took place probably while the new nation was forming. With no indigenous chicken breeds in North America, American breeders had few qualms about creating fowl, that combined the best characteristics of existing breeds. In the early days, such breeders were driven by purely commercial interests. Farmers and breeders selected from a wide variety of breeds to create new dual-purpose types that would be prolific egg-layers and also satisfy the growing demand for meat caused by rapid urban expansion. Unlike European consumers, no prejudice against yellow poultry meat was felt. This meant that breeders were free to use Asian fowl in their programs. Crosses between Asian, European, Mediterranean and British fowl yielded breeds such as the Rhode Island Red, today probably the world's most successful poultry breed. The first American poultry show was held in 1849. The American Poultry Association was founded in 1873, arising from a need to set standards for poultry breeds and to appoint judges. Only one year later, the first *American Standard of Perfection* was published, and it remains one of the best-respected poultry breed handbooks in use today.

Dominique

The origins of the Dominique probably represent one of the earliest examples of the fusion of the ultra-light Northern European breeds with one of the massive Asiatic breeds. Unlike the later, similarly marked and formula-bred Barred Plymouth Rocks, no written account of how Dominiques were created exists. This suggests that similar fowl occurred whenever black Asiatic fowl were introduced to an area where Pencilled Hamburg-type fowl had a predominant influence on the local fowl population. The Dominique has the Hamburg's rose comb and yellow legs. The lack of foot feather suggests that the breed has clean-legged Java-type fowl in its ancestry. The breed has significant amounts of feathering. Such breeds had existed in the USA since 1835 and would have figured more prominently than any of the Cochin or Shanghai alternatives in any breeding program. However,

ESSENTIAL CHARACTERISTICS

Size: Male 3.2kg/7lbs.
Female 2.3kg/5lbs. If bantams existed they would be expected to weigh 20–25 per cent of the large versions.
Varieties: One only.
Temperament: Reasonably quiet.
Environment: Tolerates confinement. Likes to forage. Cold hardy.
Egg yield: Up to 230 medium-size brown eggs per year.

the addition of these genes could have resulted in the breed's red face.

Single-combed Dominique-type fowl are thought to have played a part in the later creation of Barred Plymouth Rocks. This suggests that fowl type may have been well known among poultry breeders. These early crosses would have inherent hardiness from their north European ancestry, and size and productive egg-laying properties from the Asiatic family.

Dominiques are an interesting, active, garden-worthy breed, and are good dual-purpose birds. Hens are known to go broody and make good mothers; the sex of the chicks can be determined upon hatching. This breed was never reared commercially.

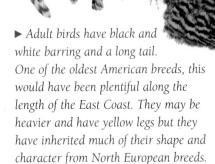

▶ *Adult birds have black and white barring and a long tail. One of the oldest American breeds, this would have been plentiful along the length of the East Coast. They may be heavier and have yellow legs but they have inherited much of their shape and character from North European breeds.*

Jersey Giant

As its name suggests, the Jersey Giant is a large fowl that originated in the US state of New Jersey. When first bred in the 1870s, it would have evolved to help meet the increasing demand for large, well-fleshed table fowl, as called for by the New York and Philadelphia markets. Unlike the British breeders, whose market was prejudiced against fowl with yellow legs and yellow flesh, and thus were inhibited from using large proportions of Asiatic genes in their breeding programs. American poultry breeders could maximize their use of Asian breeds with yellow flesh, such as Brahmas and Javas in their breeding programs, as American consumers had no prejudice about skin or flesh colour.

The breed was admitted to the American standard of perfection in 1922 as Jersey Black Giants, after the name of the original breeders, John and Thomas Black. Black was the original colour of the fowl, although later Whites were produced and then Blues, with all varieties possessing legs with an underlying yellow or willow pigmentation. Over the years, however, the term Giant has been called into question by those comparing the size of the breed with large fluffy breeds such as the Orpington, which have been bred to an even larger size.

▼ The Jersey Giant is a massive bird, but has been surpassed by other breeds in terms of size since it was developed.

The breed's creators used Black Java, Cornish Game, Dark Brahma and Black Langshan in its genes. When they did so, they would have been seeking to create a breed with not just size and weight, but weight in the right proportions and on the areas of the carcass that make a good roasting fowl, with the intention of marketing the bird as table fowl. This was a bird that was intended to compete with the turkey as a roasting fowl of quality. The original Jersey Giants would also have been made or have evolved to fill a gap which had formed when breeds such as the Rhode Island Red were developed as egg-laying breeds rather than table fowl. The Jersey Giant has remained a good enough egg-layer to produce enough chicks to meet this demand for table fowl. The breed has never been sold commercially as an egg-laying breed, however, since the ratio of food it eats to the number of eggs it produces makes it non-viable. Conservation of the breed is left to the enthusiastic amateur.

Jersey Giants are friendly and docile, and the males are rarely aggressive. They adapt well to both confinement and free ranging. Housing is required for roosters of up to 5.9kg/13lbs as well as room for hens up to 5kg/11lbs in weight. As a result of their size, this breed requires a reasonable amount of exercise from an early age for the birds to develop the legs, bone structure and musculature needed to carry the sort of weight expected of a breed labelled "giant". Perches will need to be placed reasonably close to floor level, and where adult birds are found reluctant to perch, any sleeping or resting area will need to be covered with clean wood shavings or similar material. When held, they are "lumpy". The breed has a well-developed breast and carries considerable amounts of meat which are distributed across its wide, flat back. There would be little point in creating a bantam version, because it might well be bigger than the large versions of many other breeds.

ESSENTIAL CHARACTERISTICS
Size: Male 5.9kg/13lbs. Female 5kg/11lbs.
Varieties: Black, Blue, White.
Temperament: Extremely quiet, slow-moving.
Environment: Large housing required.
Egg yield: 135–150 eggs per year.

Plymouth Rock

A dual-purpose fowl, the Plymouth Rock is a highly successful breed of poultry. The Barred variety saw American poultry breeders embark on a new chapter in poultry breeding. A program of crossbreeding fowl created hybrid offspring with beneficial vigour. Breeders hoped to encapsulate this trait, along with the benefits of the parents' pure and identifiable breeds in their offspring.

Plymouth Rock No 1 was created from a three-way cross between a Black Java, an unidentified Asiatic hen and a barred Dominique. The offspring from this cross was bred with a White Brahma.

Plymouth Rock No 2 was the result of a cross between a Dominique male and a Black Java female. The offspring of this union were feather-legged, and played little part in any later breeding program.

▼ A Partridge Plymouth Rock bantam hen.

A Minorca was mated with a Cochin cross, the offspring of which was back-crossed to Plymouth Rock No 1 to produce Plymouth Rock No 3. In turn, this was mated with a Dark Brahma to produce Plymouth Rock No 4. The final step was a back-cross between Rock numbers I and 4 to produce the first Barred Plymouth Rock.

While the type (shape) and colour of the Plymouth Rock would have been established with these preliminary crosses, the complex work of selecting strains that combined all the desirable qualities of their ancestors within the package

▶ The Barred Plymouth Rock is one of the most popular colourways for this breed, which was developed as a dual-purpose bird.

of a single strain was only just beginning. Initially, these first Rocks would have enjoyed enormous amounts of hybrid vigour along with the potential to produce the odd rogue bird that carried less useful traits, which then had to be eliminated from the breeding program. Contemporary American sources refer to the emergence in 1878 of an Essex strain, which, like most strains, either merged with other strains, became too inbred or had to be out-crossed to lose the breed's original genetic intensity.

Over the years, every really successful breed has relied for its creation on countless, often inbred, strains that could later be crossed to create new strains. In the case of the large Plymouth Rocks, there have been strains developed as table fowl and others selected for an ability to lay well, as well as to excel as parents. Most of the black hybrids favoured by many smaller-scale poultry keepers contain at least 50 per cent utility Barred Rock in their ancestry. More controversially, the search for the

finest possible barring saw some
exhibition strains with very narrow
feathers, bred to such an extent that
the overall vigour of the more
exaggerated examples was lost. While
the Buff Plymouth Rock, created
from Buff Leghorns, Buff Cochins and
Light Brahmas, had a completely
different ancestry, the development
of strains, each modelled on the
Plymouth Rock type, saw them
quickly accepted as a variety of the
same breed.

The Barred version of the
Plymouth Rock probably represents
one of the first successful attempts
at using a formula to create a new
breed containing the most desirable
characteristics of its parent breeds.
White sports that appeared among
some strains and families of Plymouth
Rock were back-crossed to form
emerging strains of Buff Rocks.
Later, some of the heavier white
sports, sometimes known as Albions,
were used in the complex mix that
went into the creation of the later
broiler strains.

Both the Partridge and the
Silver-pencilled varieties would have
had an infusion of similarly coloured
Wyandotte blood. Many unusual
varieties are likely to remain scarce

particularly in large fowl; they are
often more abundant as miniatures.

The same format that allowed
breeders to create new colour
varieties enabled miniature versions
to be developed, with the Barred and
Buffs becoming some of the most
popular exhibition varieties. The
Partridge variety, which is one of the
most attractive as well as one of the
hardest to perfect, is now found in a
form that can rival any Wyandotte in
terms of egg production. With
feather-free legs, these bantam
versions are reasonable layers and a
most attractive and garden-worthy
miniature fowl.

In appearance this dual-
purpose bird is large,
with a long and
broad back, a

▲ *A Black Rock is a commerical hybrid
developed from the Plymouth Rock
breed. It has been a successful breed,
readily producing a good egg yield.*

moderately deep breast, and yellow
legs, beak and skin. The hens possess
a deep abdomen, which signifies a
productive egg-layer. The face is red,
with red earlobes and a single comb.

This is a hardy and long-lived
breed. In nature it is docile and the
hens make good mothers. The hen

▶ *Plymouth Rocks are
one of the world's best-
known and popular
poultry breeds.
This is a Partridge
rooster.*

has been most
useful in producing
sex-linked hybrid
crosses, meaning that the
sex of the offspring can be
identified by the colour of the chick's
down on the first day of its life.
The most famous hybrid that the
Plymouth Rock hen has produced is
the Black Rock. Fine exhibition
examples exist, but selecting birds for
the quality of their barring tends to be
at the expense of the egg-laying gene.

Wyandotte

While utility considerations seem to be the driving force behind the creation of most breeds of poultry, rather more exotic aims drove the focus of attention that eventually led to the Silver-laced Wyandotte, and later to the whole family of Wyandotte varieties. It seems that the original intention was to improve Cochin/Pekin bantams by crossing a male Sebright bantam with a Cochin hen. When the result turned out to be too big for a bantam, the offspring were sold as Sebright Cochins. A second cross between a Silver-spangled Hamburg and Buff Cochin was made. The offspring of these two crosses, when mated together, resulted in American Sebrights. However, without any agreement on comb type, admittance to the American Standard was refused in 1876. At about the same time, a cross between a Silver-spangled Hamburg and a Dark Brahma hen produced a more desirable pea comb and was given

▲ *The original colourway is the Silver-laced variety, shown here on a large hen.*

the provisional breed name Eurekas. The original ancestry of the Wyandottes included Pekins, Cochins and Silver Sebright bantams. The resulting breed has been endowed with a mixture of all the necessary genes used to develop some of the most spectacular

exhibition fowl, as well as some of the most productive utility strains. When these were bred with the offspring of an earlier Silver-spangled Hamburg-Dark Brahma cross, the result was a uniform rose comb that became an essential part of the breed standard. They were admitted to the American Standard as Wyandottes in 1883.

Given that Buff Cochin went into the original mix, one could have expected the odd Gold-laced example to turn up as a sport. However, the breeder Joseph McKeen of Wisconsin claimed to have first produced a Winnebago breed from a Partridge

▼ *A large Lavender hen.*

► *A Partridge bantam hen. It is the quality of lacing and the even distribution of lacing over the body that is the feature most difficult to perfect.*

▲ *A Buff-laced bantam hen.*

▼ *A Blue-laced bantam male.*

Cochin, a rose comb Brown Leghorn and a Gold-laced Sebright. The Winnebago was crossed with a Silver Wyandotte to make the Gold-laced Wyandotte.

The Cochin would have given the breed its cushion tail, its curvaceous outline, and the rose comb with neatly downturned leader. The Silver-pencilled variety could owe much to the original Dark Brahma genes, and the Partridge to the Partridge Cochin.

Even without further genetic input, all the elements were now in place for the breed, with selection, to fulfil almost any role. The Silver- and Gold-laced varieties that arrived in Britain in the 1890s were soon established as good egg layers. The Whites and Blacks, as sports, had been noted for laying during the winter months (always a desirable characteristic), and strains of Whites had broken egg-laying records.

Bantam versions, probably resulting from the original true bantam Sebright input, remain exact replicas of the original stock. Unfortunately, the faults inherent in the breeds used in the original formulae can still manifest themselves in the offspring; parents with perfect combs can produce chicks with single ones.

Many miniature breeds are on the large size for bantams. Most Whites have the capacity for excess feather and fluff that, while welcomed by most exhibitors, can lead to the more exaggerated examples being extremely unproductive.

Some of the more intricately marked examples are often found to lay well. The breed is a quiet domestic fowl that is content with less space than some other large exhibition fowl.

▼ *A large White male.*

▼ *A large White hen.*

▼ *A Partridge hen.*

New Hampshire Red

The early New Hampshire Reds had the same genetic basis as the Rhode Island Reds, which in turn owe much to the work of the Rhode Island Experimental Institute. New Hampshire Reds are made solely of Rhode Island Reds, but have been selectively bred to create a bird with different strengths. Work done at the University of New Hampshire first encouraged the selection of the New Hampshire Red as a separate breed. It was the vision of poultryman A. W. (Red) Richardson, who recognized that mountain-bred poultry stock had sterling properties, and encouraged scattered breeders to collaborate with a common aim. In 1935, the breed was

▼ *A miniature hen.*

standardized in a natural orange-brown colour with limited Columbian-black markings.

The breed made little impact when first imported into Britain in 1937, but that changed in the 1950s when

it found its way into the hands of a long-established Sussex breeder, who discovered that the breed made better cross-breeding fowl than Rhode Island Reds. The first results were too unremarkable to attract anyone other than those looking for the most commercially viable breeds, but shortage of bloodlines saw the importation of much rounder and more feathery strains, first from Germany, and then from Holland. The result was a much rounder, more comfortable-looking fowl that had very attractive coloration. It attracted enough interest for breeders to form their own breed club. In its present form, the New Hampshire Red averages nearly 200 eggs a year. Unlike the Rhode Island Red, breeders were intent on producing a bird that matured quickly and had good meat quality. As a result this breed is now a less productive egg-layer than its ancestors.

In appearance the New Hampshire Red is similar to the Rhode Island Red, but with lighter coloration. It has a single comb, red wattles and lobes, and is an easy-going fowl that is close to being a perfect domestic breed because of its dual-purpose characteristics.

The bantam versions may be even better egg-layers than the large variety, and are beginning to gain recognition on the show circuit.

◄ *The exhibition New Hampshire Red still retains many of its recent ancestors' utility properties. It is a lighter, brighter red than the Rhode Island Red, and is less fluffy and more mobile than the Buff Orpington. The New Hampshire Red remains one of best all-round fowl seen on the exhibition circuit.*

ESSENTIAL CHARACTERISTICS

Size: Male 3.9kg/8½lbs.
Female 2.9kg/6½lbs.
Varieties: One only.
Temperament: Placid nature, good for a garden environment.
Environment: Tolerates confinement.
Egg yield: 200 brown eggs per year.

Buckeye

The American Buckeye is a dual-purpose breed with lustrous red plumage. The breed was first bred in Ohio and was developed in the last decade of the 19th century by Mrs Nettie Metcalf of Warren, Ohio, who crossed a Buff Cochin with a Barred Plymouth Rock hen. The female offspring were crossed with black-red game males, and the resulting generation formed the basis of selection for the new breed.

The Buckeye breed has a unique body shape, although the breeder was aiming to replicate the Indian/Cornish Game breed. It is reported, however, that the Cornish breed was not included in the genetic composition of the new breed.

The body is broad and squat, with a back that slants towards the ground. As a dual-purpose bird, the breed was developed to have strong, meaty thighs, and well-developed wings and breast. In colour it is deep red, which may cause confusion with the Rhode Island Red breed. However, a degree of the Buckeye retains the dark-coloured barring of its original parent in the soft downy underfeathers

on the back. Rhode Island Red feathers, in contrast, are uniformly red. The feathers are tightly packed – a trait that characterizes all birds in the American class. The Buckeye has yellow legs and skin, red lobes and comb and a pale brown beak. Its pea comb signals that this is a hardy breed and can tolerate cold winters.

There was talk of calling the Buckeye a Pea-combed Rhode Island Red, but it quickly became apparent that the name would be detrimental to the breed's popularity. Instead, the name Buckeye was chosen in honour of the state in which it was bred. This breed was developed prior to

▼ *A large hen with characteristic rounded chest and substantial, solid appearance. With a diminished gene pool, some, like this example, are found with less than perfect pea combs.*

the Rhode Island Red, and it is possible that the Buckeye was used to improve the genetic base of the Rhode Island Red. The new breed was admitted to the American Standard in 1904. However, it is now regarded as critically endangered in the USA. The breed is an active bird, which is friendly towards humans, and so makes a good family pet. It will tolerate a variety of environments but prefers a free-range setting where it is able to forage for food. It does not particularly thrive in close confinement.

▲ *A large male. The tail feathers of the male are particularly long.*

ESSENTIAL CHARACTERISTICS

Size: Male 4.1kg/9lbs.
Female 2.9kg/6½lbs.
Varieties: One only.
Temperament: Friendly, active.
Environment: Dislikes confinement, tolerates cold.
Egg yield: 150–200 medium-size brown eggs per year.

Rhode Island Red

Early breeders of the Rhode Island Red – the poultry farmers of New England and Rhode Island – were motivated to produce poultry that would meet the increased commercial demand for eggs and poultry meat made by the expanding local urban population. Unlike breeders of other poultry breeds, their interest was focused on producing a bird that met the requirements of their customers rather than to comply with a written standard for their breed. It would have been the Rhode Island Red's early development as a dual-purpose fowl, that led to it becoming the world's most successful breed.

For most of the 20th century, the Rhode Island Red was the most important brown egg-laying breed of poultry. One of the first farmers and market traders to start creating a purpose-bred strain was William Tripp, who, in 1854, obtained a large black-red Malay rooster that had arrived from a South-east Asian port. He bred this with his scrub hens and noticed that the resultant chicks were far superior to other local fowl. The

▲ *A rose comb version of the Rhode Island Red.*

▲ *The single comb of the Rhode Island Red male stands upright.*

birds produced better meat and the hens laid more and bigger eggs. His friend, John Macomber, who lived in Westport, Massachusetts, became interested and the two

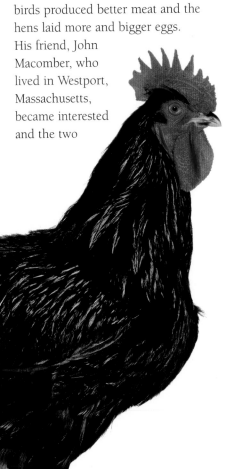

▶ *The Rhode Island Red has a docile, friendly and quiet temperament, and as such, makes a good family pet. However, males are known to attack strangers.*

worked together for a time crossing and exchanging their best birds to avoid too much inbreeding. After Macomber died, the work was taken up by others who sought to breed fowl that would produce bigger and browner eggs while at the same time providing a larger proportion of meat. Malay, Cochin, Langshan, Hamburg and Leghorn genes are all thought to be included in its genetic composition. The aim was to produce the hardiest stock that would prosper under any conditions, including the rigorous New England winter.

Much of the work to stabilize the breed was done by the Rhode Island Experimental Station, which selected and collected birds from a wide area. When Rhode Island Reds were first seen in Britain, they were reported as being pea-combed, even though many of the early imports into the United Kingdom were described as rose-combed. In the USA the single comb was admitted to the standard in 1904. The rose comb was standardized as Red American in 1905, but by 1906 the American Poultry Association recognized both combs in the breed, as did the British Rhode Island Red Club when it was formed in 1909.

ESSENTIAL CHARACTERISTICS

Size: Male 3.9kg/8½lbs.
Female 3.4kg/7½lbs.
Varieties: Red.
Temperament: Good family pet, though can be aggressive to strangers.
Environment: Likes to free range, and is cold hardy. The comb can become susceptible to damage in extreme cold.
Egg yield: At least 200 brown eggs per year, though, like many breeds, productivity drops in very cold temperatures.

▼ *Rhode Island Red bantam hens like this one are highly productive egg-layers, including those birds bred for exhibition purposes.*

While some British breeders would have selected strains to meet their own interpretation of the standard, the original wording remained the basis of birds selected to be utility and commercial laying fowl. When entered in laying trials, the foremost utility strains would often lay more than 280 eggs, making this breed one of the best for farmers, smallholders, and domestic keepers.

While most of the large Rhode Island Reds seen at shows today may be too big and not lay enough eggs to be described as utility, the exhibition-bred bantams are excellent layers of reasonably sized brown eggs. For those who still want to keep useful representatives of the best-known historic fowl, some of the old commercial stock is still kept, including one known strain that has remained as a closed flock since winning a National Laying Trial gold medal in 1954.

The Rhode Island Red has rust-coloured plumage that can be as dark as mahogany or significantly paler; the male can have black on the wings. The breed has a pale brown beak and pale yellow legs. With its rectangular shape, broad, flat back and medium-length tail, this fowl is often described as being brick-shaped. It is a medium-weight poultry breed and makes a good family pet. It is especially suitable for owners interested in egg production, although strains bred for exhibition are notably less productive than those that have retained their utility value. By nature the breed is docile and friendly, particularly to those responsible for feeding it, though it can be aggressive to strangers. It is an alert bird that likes to forage and free range. These birds often remain together as a group.

The breed fell out of favour with those keeping hens for egg production in the 1970s, when hybrid birds were proved to lay greater quantities of eggs for less feed than standard breeds. However, the breed is still the best known in the world, and is often used as the parent of many of today's hybrids. The male, in particular, is considered useful since the egg-laying gene is passed down the male line.

▶ *Rhode Island Reds make good, if large, pets that add a valuable contribution to the garden when allowed to free range.*

Araucana

The Araucana breed is considered to be South America's only native fowl. Its most distinguishing feature is its blue eggs. Throughout the world there are many different types of fowl, all with differing visual characteristics, that are capable of producing blue eggs, and all are known as Araucanas. This is because the blue egg-laying trait or gene is more dominant than most external breed characteristics and, for this reason, the trait is used to determine the breed type. Two are native to Chile: the ear-tufted Quetros breed and the rumpless Colloncas breed. In 1914 it was suggested that the blue egg-laying gene could come from a wild fowl, the Chachalaca breed, which had reportedly hybridized with domestic fowl in Chile.

A number of forms of the Araucana are found in the USA, though a rumpless version with unique ear tufts on the ends of unique fleshy or gristly ear appendages is generally thought of as being the true descendant of the Chilean Araucana. This descendant, like many original forms of other ancient fowl populations, is not large enough to be generally accepted as a large type or as small as most other bantams. More unfortunately, the gene that seems to be linked to ear tufts also results in varying proportions of chicks dying

before they hatch. Rumplessness also gives rise to fertility problems, so if these versions are the purest form of Araucana, they seem destined to remain in the hands of a small group of enthusiasts.

Versions of the breed with a tail are generally free of inherited weaknesses and will be the best choice for those attracted to rearing breeds that lay blue eggs. Those standardized as British Araucanas have a small head tuft. A similar tuftless breed is standardized in the USA as Ameracauna. The most distinguishing feature of the breed, the blue egg, is the reason for its popularity; blue eggs sell well in farmers' markets, and their saleability has encouraged the poultry industry to attempt to produce enough similar blue eggs to supply the commercial market. However, like most small-scale poultry keepers before them, the industry has found that the Araucana and its descendants are remarkably resistant to laying large quantities of very large eggs. Strains of the standard breed are available that lay fairly large numbers of mid-size eggs; in order to increase the egg yield, the breed has been crossed with other breeds. First-generation offspring resulting from outcrosses with white egg-laying breeds lay pale blue eggs. The same crossing with brown egg-laying breeds produce olive or greenish coloured eggs. For those interested in exhibiting eggs, a large deep blue egg will take many prizes. The bantam version, which can be quite small, may also lay lots of pretty blue eggs. The breed's cross-bred form has been

▲ *The blue egg-laying Araucana remains the basis of nearly all of the fowl that lay the majority of blue eggs.*

used to create commercial breeds. The inclusion of the Araucana breed in the Crested or Cream Legbar had a lasting commercial impact.

ESSENTIAL CHARACTERISTICS

Size: Male 2.7–3.2kg/6–7lbs.
Female: 2.25–2.7kg/5–6lbs.
Varieties: Black, Black-red, Blue, Crele, Lavender, Gold-duckwing, Pile, Silver-duckwing, Spangled, White.
Temperament: Alert, active, hardy.
Environment: Garden.
Egg yield: 270 green or blue eggs.

▶ *Large and bantam versions are standardized in a wide range of colours.*

EUROPEAN MANMADE BREEDS

European poultry breeders have always viewed the utility and commercial aspects of poultry breeding in a rather different light from their British and American counterparts. The French saw the quality of their regional table fowl as being of primary importance. They had long thought that quality of meat far outweighed considerations of poultry size. When creating the Faverolles and Houdan breeds, the British Dorking was also included in the genetic composition; a sign that French breeders recognized the quality of its meat. As a result both breeds had a fifth toe like the Dorking. Both the French and Dutch, who each had a surprisingly large share of the British egg market, later developed breeds to meet the British preference for the darkest brown egg in the hope of selling into that market. The fact that the market was willing to pay a premium for dark brown eggs influenced the development of both the Dutch Welsummer and Barnevelder, and the French Marans breeds.

Houdan

The Houdan is an old French breed named after the town of that name which is situated 40 miles from Paris. The town of Houdan was where the important poultry markets which supplied the Paris meat markets were located. The breed's origins can be traced back to the start of the 18th century. The Houdan was originally raised as a dual-purpose bird. It is heavy enough to produce a meaty carcass and its meat was and still is considered to be that of a quality table fowl with

▲ *The breed has an interesting "leaf" comb and pretty mottled feathers.*

succulent white flesh. It also lays approximately 160 small- to medium-sized white eggs per year, converting feed to eggs at a very economical rate. In its ancestry, it is thought to have Poland and Crèvecoeur, which gave the breed its crest, and Dorking, which gave the breed its five toes. Most poultry have four toes. It is now regarded as an ornamental fowl, and can be particularly spectacular to look at with its attractive crest, beard and muffs. It has small ear lobes and wattles, which remain mostly hidden by the head plumage. Many breeders concentrated on the ornamental points of the Houdan, at the expense of its utility value. The Houdan is a docile breed that can cope well with confinement, although care needs to be taken to protect the crest. It is an excellent breed to keep in the garden and will happily forage for food. Total free-range conditions are not always desirable, particularly for the rooster, since his crest can obscure his vision making it difficult for him to see predators and move out of the way.

◄ *The Houdan (pronounced oodan) is an attractive bird that makes a good family pet. If handled from a young age, it responds well to being petted.*

ESSENTIAL CHARACTERISTICS

Size: Large male 3.1–3.6kg/7–8lbs.
Large female 2.7–3.1kg/6–7lbs.
Bantam male 680–793g/24–28oz.
Bantam female 623–737g/22–26oz.
Varieties: Mottled, White.
Temperament: Quiet if handled young.
Environment: Free range, but crest needs protection from rain.
Egg yield: 160 small to medium white eggs per year.

Barnevelders

The Barnevelder breed evolved from landrace poultry that were kept in the Barneveld district of the Gelderland province in Holland. In 1930, a World Poultry Congress report stated that the breed origins were those of local farm fowl crossed with Cochin hens. The offspring of these hens were crossed with Brahmas and later with Langshans to produce the bird that we know today. In 1906, the breed was crossed with Buff Orpington and in consequence its colouring changed to that of Partridge. However, the breed standard had been established long before this report. A photograph of a pen containing four hens and a male, which were winners at the Utrecht, Netherlands, show of 1922, shows a foppish breed with the same pronounced U-shaped back that forms part of the breed's standard.

The popularity of the breed was due to the desirable brown eggs, which were in great demand. The breed's standard was at one time prefaced with the note: "The egg is part of the standard, no more no less". The coffee-brown egg is mainly due to the Langshan genes, although the egg of the present Barnevelder is larger. The breed also remains productive throughout the winter.

▼ Crisp double lacing on a rich red-brown ground makes the Barnevelder hen one of the most attractive utility fowls.

Breeders kept Barnevelders firstly for utility value and secondly for feather colour. Early reports stated that the breed laid very dark brown eggs. Today, however, Welsummers and Marans both lay darker brown eggs than the original Barnevelders ever did. Show breeders now concentrate on visual features rather than on egg colour. Originally it was egg size that seemed to be a feature of their participation in laying trials. One pullet from the Bethnal Green Utility Poultry Society laid 201 "specials", 39 "firsts" and 1 "second" when entered in the Middlesex trial of 1934. In build the Barnevelder is medium-size, producing a good carcass of meat.

Both Partridge and Double-laced varieties were bred in Britain. The Laced variety soon established itself as one of the most attractive colour patterns that is still compatible with a utility breeding program. Partridge examples are still seen on occasions:

some birds of this strain give the appearance of having been bred from a laced ancestor. It is unlikely that a breed that, in its large form, at least, has a relatively small gene pool, can fully support two complex colour varieties while maintaining the breed's other important characteristics. Blacks that used to be bred in some numbers still turn up as sports from the double-laced variety, probably a throwback to the earlier Langshan ancestry, but this would probably be very difficult to maintain in both sexes with the required yellow legs. This is a neat and compact bird with a very upright stance and a single comb.

Few pure breeds are now kept commercially. The Barnevelder, in both large and bantam forms, remains one of the most attractive breeds that could still, with careful selection, pay its way in a domestic situation.

ESSENTIAL CHARACTERISTICS

Size: Large male 2.7–3.6kg/6–8lbs.
Large female 2.3–3.1kg/5–7lbs.
Bantam male 680–793g/24–28oz.
Bantam female 566–680g/20–24oz
Varieties: Black, Double-laced, Partridge, Silver, White.
Temperament: Quiet, docile.
Environment: Small runs and free range.
Egg yield: 160–200 large brown eggs per year.

Welsummer

Like most of Europe's poultry breeds, nearly all of Holland's indigenous fowl would have laid white or tinted eggs. Dutch poultry breeders were among the first to recognize the commercial importance of dark brown eggs, which were perceived to be a healthier choice than white eggs. The Dutch Welsummer breed is famed for its dark brown eggs. The main source of brown pigmentation in the shell is derived from the heavy Asiatic fowl that were imported into mainland Europe during the 19th century. There also appears to be a link between the U-shaped back outline of the Asian Langshan breed and the dark egg colour of the Welsummer.

The original fowl that were the foundation of the Welsummer breed were from an area north of the river Ysel. They were reported as being of very mixed colours and types, with some even having five toes. By 1917, breeders had established some breed uniformity, with only red cockerels with the markings of the partridge-coloured breeds being used in breeding pens. It is likely that crossing this landrace breed with Barnevelders also created colour stability, although Brahma, Cochin, Wyandotte, Leghorn and Rhode Island Red could also have added to the gene pool.

The Welsummer is a large, upright bird with a deep breast, broad back and large tail. It carries a single red comb, large wattles and has yellow legs. This is the breed that appears on the famous cereal packet. Welsummers are active, friendly and placid birds that suit a garden environment. Bantam versions are available, but they produce a lighter tinted egg.

By 1930 the British Welsummer Club was formed, and from the outset there seems to have been much rivalry between Dutch and British breeders and considerable controversy over breed standards. Since the breed was imported to the UK before it was fully established, this left plenty of scope for the breed to develop in parallel in Holland and in the UK. Not only did those who first imported birds from Holland hope to corner some of the market for dark brown eggs, they also hoped to make money by supplying breeding stock to other poultry keepers at a time when there were no restrictions on importing birds. In Britain, breed development has focused on the competitive

◄ A Partridge bantam pullet.

element of exhibiting the dark brown eggs. Without the same stimulus of egg shows, the breed as now kept in Holland lays only mid-brown eggs.

Most small-scale poultry keepers would be happy to find a strain of large Welsummers that lay 180 dark, matt brown or "flower-pot red" eggs, each weighing 70g/2½oz. However, the darkest eggs are laid by pullets which produce fewer eggs. It makes no sense commercially to have a hen that produces dark brown eggs unless it lays a reasonable number. The breed is standardized as light but is weightier than some heavy breeds.

► Described in Holland as being Rust Partridge, the female Welsummer is enhanced by a rich chestnut-brown breast and golden-brown neck hackles.

ESSENTIAL CHARACTERISTICS

Size: Large male 2.7–3.1kg/6–7lbs. Large female 2.2–2.7kg/5–6lbs. Bantam male 1kg/36oz. Bantam female 793g/28oz.

Varieties: Partridge, Silver-duckwing.

Temperament: Active, but quiet.

Environment: Free range or grassed runs.

Egg yield: 160–200 dark brown spotted large eggs per year.

North Holland Blue

The Assendelft breed of poultry had been kept for centuries in an area north of Amsterdam, and were considered typical of the small fowl of northern Europe. This breed was tolerant of wet land, but laid small eggs. When breeders looked to improve the egg size of the breed, the Belgian Maline breed provided the perfect genetic qualities to introduce to the breeding pen. The Malines had a similar tolerance to wet ground, but were distinguishable from the Assendelft by their leg feathering. This breed was also used in the genetic composition of the Marans, and would have been responsible for adding greater weight to both breeds.

Standardized as North Holland Blue more than 100 years ago, some of the first birds that arrived in Britain still had feathers on their legs. Poultry judges of the time decided that the breed would be indistinguishable from Marans unless it was devoid of leg feathers. Leading utility judge W. Powell Owen persuaded the British Poultry Club to standardize this Dutch breed as having feathers on its legs. However, when British poultry farmers imported large numbers of chicks from Holland, they found that nearly all of these were clean-legged, and with the British table market in mind, they continued to select for clean legs. As long as the breed remained on poultry farms, those wanting to exhibit their birds were likely to find a farmer willing to part with the occasional bird that had feathers on its legs for them to use as breeding material.

In many ways, these imported North Holland Blues were perfect domestic fowl, true to their Dutch origins and tolerant of the wet conditions found in many intensive runs. They enjoyed considerable commercial success as good layers of light brown eggs. As a breed that matures quickly and to a heavy size, males also make good table birds. Their white skin is particularly appealing to European markets. Only one variety of the breed is available, that of the black and white barred cuckoo pattern. The male has slightly lighter colouring than the female bird. The breed is sex-linked, meaning that the sex of its offspring can be determined at one day old by a lighter head spot, even when the North Holland Blue is bred with an unbarred breed. Feather-legged versions of North Holland Blues are now unknown in their homeland and are rare in Britain.

When hybrid hens replaced nearly all commercial breeds and the clean-legged version disappeared from British farms, the exhibition breed almost died out. Dutch North Holland Blues look very like British Marans, so any attempt to admit them to UK poultry standards is still likely to run into the same opposition that the original breeders faced more than 50 years ago.

ESSENTIAL CHARACTERISTICS
Size: Male 3.1–4kg/7–9lbs.
Female 2.7–4kg/6–9lbs.
Varieties: Cuckoo.
Temperament: Very quiet.
Environment: Will tolerate damp conditions.
Egg yield: Early utility strains lay more than 200 eggs per year.

◄ *North Holland Blues have attractive plumage.*

Faverolles

In many ways, the early development of the French Faverolles mirrored that of some strains of the Sussex breed. The breed was developed within a local area to meet the growing demand for quality white-fleshed table fowl in the 19th century. Small-scale farmers would have crossed local indigenous fowl with a variety of other breeds, with each successive cross intended to improve the quality of the breed.

The Faverolles are said to be descended from an indigenous five-toed French breed, crossed with various proportions of Polish, Crèvecoeur and Houdan fowl. The result is a lightweight, very white-fleshed, quality table fowl. The requirement for the breed to have a larger carcass saw the introduction of heavy strains to the breeding pen, such as Dark Dorkings and Light Brahmas. Like their Sussex counter-parts, Faverolles' breeders eliminated any yellow-skinned birds resulting from the Brahma outcross. After several generations, a sizeable table fowl emerged that retained the five toes of its ancestors, along with some vestige of feathered feet from the Brahma. It was the Faverolles' beard

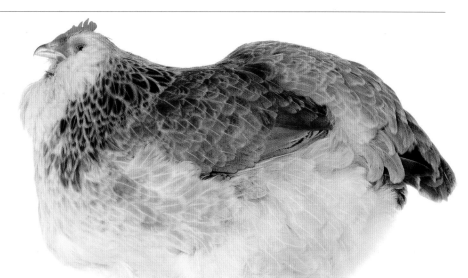

▶ *A classic Salmon Faverolles hen.*

inherited from either its Houdan or Polish outcrossing that became the breed's badge of distinction, to the point when later some saw this to be the breed's most important exhibition feature.

The breed became popular in Britain as a utility breed during the post-World War I expansion in table fowl production. For a while its "cloddy" handling (meaning lumpy – the word is still in the breed's standard) became a feature of both exhibition and utility fowl.

Today the appealing Salmon variety attracts exhibitors as well

as those looking for a large and unusual garden fowl. Several other colours exist, in large and miniature versions that fully reflect the breed's ancestry. The bantams are some of the heaviest varieties available.

Selection for beards and fluff may have detracted from the utility merit of some strains, but there have always been breeders willing to select on the basis of early maturity and table type.

Faverolles are strong and hardy birds, with a calm disposition and gentle nature. They can be bullied if kept with more aggressive birds. They are ideally suited to a back garden environment, though they cope well with being confined.

▼ *A large Cuckoo Salmon male*

▼ *A pretty Buff bantam.*

ESSENTIAL CHARACTERISTICS
Size: Large male 3.1–4.9kg/7–11lbs.
Large female 3.1–4kg/7–9lbs.
Bantam male 453g/16oz.
Bantam female 396g/14oz.
Varieties: Black, Blue-laced, Buff, Cuckoo, Ermine, Salmon, White.
Temperament: Placid, quiet.
Environment: Copes with confinement.
Egg yield: 150 eggs per year.

Marans

Cuckoo-pattern feathers and very dark brown eggs are synonymous with the breed of fowl standardized as Marans. The irregular and indistinct barring pattern standardized as Cuckoo is typical of breeds where there has been interaction between an Asiatic colour gene and that of the Pencilled varieties of northern Europe. The coloration is typical of many breeds and local populations that evolved in Holland and Belgium, but not in France.

The development of the Marans as a wholly French breed started in the Aubiers region of Deux-Sèvres. By selecting only from those birds that laid the darkest eggs, breeders had, by 1931, made a new breed of hen, the Marans. It is likely that the strains that made up the local breed were crossed with English Game, before later having Asian fowl added to the gene pool.

However, brown eggs imported from France and labelled as Marans, had appeared on the London market from the 1920s, creating doubt about the origin and sequence in importation of parent stock. The breed that was to

◄ A large Cuckoo hen.

ESSENTIAL CHARACTERISTICS
Size (British clean-legged standard): Large male 2.7–3.6kg/ 6–8lbs. Large female 2.7–3.1kg/ 6–7lbs. Bantam male 793–907g/ 28–32oz. Bantam female 680–793g/24–28oz.
Varieties: Black, Cuckoo, Dark-cuckoo, Golden-cuckoo, Silver-cuckoo, Wheaten, White.
Temperament: Docile and calm.
Environment: Hardy bird, tolerates wet conditions.
Egg yield: 150–200 large, chocolate-brown eggs per year.

become the most successful brown-egg layer owed much of its British development to Lord Greenaway, a poultry patriot who believed the British poultry breeders should have the resources to compete with the rest of the world. Frustrated by the reluctance of the French to part with breeding stock or even fertile eggs,

even after Lord Greenaway met them at the Paris exhibition of 1929, his manager, Parkin, seems to have successfully imported clean-legged Belgian "Coucou de Flandre", some of which laid dark brown eggs. From these he developed his own Cuckoo

▶ A large Wheaten hen. This is a French standard feather-legged Marans.

Marans. A Marans club was formed in 1950, and the written standard followed soon after. It ensured that poultry keepers had a breed that laid large, dark brown eggs and was also a first-class table fowl. While never really challenging the established laying breeds, strong support from egg exhibitors and specialist egg producers ensured that this version of the Marans became a well-known breed. The exhibitors selected their birds for breeding almost exclusively on the basis of their ability to lay eggs with extremely dark shells. Because of this, some strains may have lost some of their laying productivity.

Marans bantams lay an egg that is just as good as that of their large counterpart, but over the years they have struggled to maintain the required weight. Commercial interests created a Marans-based speckled hybrid that rarely lays an egg as brown as the true breed or in such numbers as a hybrid hen. Meanwhile, the French continued the development of their own original Marans, and standardized the lightly feathered leg and rather different body shape.

Russian Orloff

The Russian Orloff is an ancient breed; named in honour of a Russian nobleman named Orlov who was responsible for promoting the breed. It originated in Persia (modern-day Iran) and was widely distributed across Europe and Asia by the 17th century; German breeders are responsible for its development. It was included in the American Poultry Standard in the late 19th century, but did not arrive in Europe until the turn of the 20th century. It was introduced to Britain in the 1920s. Today it is considered a rare breed.

It is thought that the Malay breed is partly responsible for the genetics of this bird, although others have suggested that the Thuringian breed has added to the gene pool. In appearance, the Orloff has an owl-like face, with a round head, muffs and a beard. It has a small strawberry comb.

This is a large and heavy breed developed as a table fowl; the bantam version was not developed until the 1920s. It is tall, with plenty of feathering, particularly around the head and neck, and generally has a game-like appearance.

The breed has yellow legs, tiny wattles, bay or brown eyes and a small and strong curved beak. The Russian Orloff is a hardy fowl, able to withstand cold temperatures. The breed has a number of recognized colourways.

◄ The Russian Orloff is able to tolerate harsh, cold climates in keeping with its development in the steppes. This is a bantam hen.

ESSENTIAL CHARACTERISTICS
Size: Male 3.6kg/8lbs.
Female 3kg/6½lbs.
Varieties: Black, Cuckoo, Mahogany, Spangled, White.
Temperament: Calm.
Environment: Copes with confinement.
Egg yield: 160 light brown eggs per year.

► Russian Orloffs have a distinctive appearance. These are large birds with a strong physical presence and an "owl-like" appearance.

► The breed has a strawberry comb, which looks like half a strawberry that is situated at the top of the beak and at the centre front of the face.

BRITISH MANMADE BREEDS

Dedicated British poultry breeders were renowned for selecting existing and imported breeds and then refining character traits and marketability, to the point where physically they bore little resemblance to the original breeds. Despite this, for a long time there was considerable resistance to the concept of making and naming a new breed of poultry. Sussex poultry breeders, for example, were happy to make use of the local strains of Kent and Surrey fowl as a foundation for the birds that they bred and perfected to become the Sussex breed. William Cook, a skilled poultryman, was the first to standardize and

market his newly made Orpington breed in the late 19th century. Exhibitors have since selected and altered his original breed. The Buff Orpington was developed to become a breed in its own right, and is perhaps one of the world's best-known breeds. The Marsh Daisy was created at the beginning of the 20th century, followed a few decades later by the Ixworth. It was not until the 1970s that British breeders created more new breeds. Many of these have been successful locally, but none of those developed have been as commercially successful or as popular as breeds created in other parts of the world.

Orpington

William Cook's introduction of Black Orpingtons in 1886 heralded the first of a family of differently coloured Orpingtons and a new departure in how the British perceived poultry breeds and poultry breeding. Cook,

an astute businessman and skilled poultry keeper, having previously advocated and marketed crosses between different breeds, must have seen the acceptance of the new

◄ *This is a heavy breed, with a short back and curvy U-shape, in which the thick feathering almost entirely obscures visibility of the legs. This is a Black pullet.*

ESSENTIAL CHARACTERISTICS

Size: Large male 4.5–6.5kg/10–14lbs.
Large female 3.4–4.5kg/7½–10lbs.
Bantam male 907g–1kg/32–36oz.
Bantam female 793–907g/28–32oz.
Varieties: Black, Blue, Cuckoo, Jubilee, Spangled, White (Buff).
Temperament: Docile, friendly.
Environment: Large space required. Needs protection in wet weather.
Egg yield: 90–150, often quite small, light brown eggs per year.

American breeds as an opportunity to make and market his own breed. Unlike the earlier American breeders, he kept the exact breeding formula of his new breeds to himself, and he saw each new introduction as a new breed rather than a new colour variety. Black Minorca males were crossed with Black Plymouth Rock pullets, and the offspring were mated with a clean-legged Langshan to form the basis of the original Orpington fowl. It is likely that the breed also has some Hamburg ancestry. Cook claimed that Langshans, and his later single-combed Black Orpingtons, descended from urban fowl.

When analyzing how those breeds that were created from a mixture of other breeds have developed, it is usually found that, once the genetic composition is in place, it is how subsequent generations are selected that shapes the future of the breed. Many of the Black Orpingtons were developed to became shorter in the leg, and with enough extra feather and fluff to look like clean-legged Cochins. Once a trend in exhibition poultry has been established it is difficult to stop, and given a tendency for most exhibition strains of heavy, soft-feather breeds to become over-feathery, the Black Orpingtons soon assumed the style and body type that we recognize today. The Buff Orpingtons, which still have their own separate breed club, retained a far more active stance.

It seems likely that the White Orpingtons were derived from sports of the Buff Orpington. Early publications illustrate White Orpingtons as being flat-backed and with rose combs. Interest in this colour strain has varied over time. The Jubilee Orpington was introduced in time for Queen Victoria's Golden Jubilee (1887), but failed to make much progress. Blue Orpingtons are difficult to breed, but every year there are a few Blue large and bantam fowl that are good enough to compete with Blacks.

▼ *The Lavender is one of the latest colour varieties, and is so new it has yet to be admitted to the Poultry Club standards.*

Cuckoos were never as feathery or fluffy as the Blacks and never really established, but recently, good Spangled varieties have reappeared, to be joined by new Chocolate and Gold-laced varieties.

The Orpington story still has room to develop. They are all very large and heavy birds, with equally large appetites, and require specialized or adapted housing. Few will be even moderate egg-layers, though the breed does go broody and hens make good mothers. Since the breed has been largely bred for exhibition, it is no longer considered to be a table fowl, but there are still those who like to have a large, placid fowl in the garden, and for those with less room, the bantam version, which in some instances is as big as some large fowl breeds, has all the style and character of its larger counterpart.

▼ *A large Lavender hen.*

▼ *A White hen.*

▼ *A Black hen.*

Buff Orpingtons

Committed fanciers may see the extremely heavily feathered and rather rounded shape of the Black Orpington as the ultimate exhibition strain, but for most of the poultry-keeping world, Orpington is synonymous with Buff Orpington. One reason why many with only a passing interest in poultry keeping know the name Buff Orpington is that, unlike the Black variety, it combines an extremely placid disposition with an ability to lay enough eggs to make it worth keeping. It can be found in suburban and country gardens as well as on smallholdings.

William Cook, the breeder, was not keen to publicize just how he bred his Buff Orpingtons, but contemporary reports suggest a Gold-spangled Hamburg was crossed with a Buff Cochin, and the female offspring of that match was mated with a Dark Dorking male. The subsequent off-spring was mated with a Buff Cochin to produce the Buff Orpington. Other reports suggest that he included the non-standardized, but popular, Lincolnshire Buff in his breeding pens. For most of the 20th century,

▼ A huge young Buff Orpington male, with a wealth of feather that rivals that seen on the best exhibition Blacks.

breeders and exhibitors accepted that in order to fulfil the utility aspirations of many poultry keepers, the breed would have to retain a different body type to its Black counterpart.

By the 1980s, few poultry keepers expected pure-bred fowl to lay well, and at the same time, hobby keepers were beginning to look for a bird that would compete with the Black Orpington. British judges officiating at Dutch shows recorded the emergence of strains of Buffs of a type not dissimilar to Black Orpingtons. Importation began from Holland in 1983, and later, from Germany. The result is that the Buff Orpington now being shown is as large and feathery as the Black Orpington. While some may deplore the disappearance of the earlier bird, far more Buff Orpingtons are now being kept. The emerging bantam Buffs are an exact counterpart of the large version. Many bantams weigh more than hybrid hens although they are small. They often lay more, proportionally larger, eggs than their large counterparts, making them the perfect garden companion. Many have fallen in love with the shape, quiet demeanour and colour of this variety of Orpington.

▼ A large Buff Orpington hen.

ESSENTIAL CHARACTERISTICS

Size: Large male 3.6–4.5kg/8–10lbs.
Large female 3.1–3.6kg/7–8lbs.
Bantam male 907g–1kg/32–36oz.
Bantam female 793–907g/28–32oz.
Varieties: Buff. The colour may fade in bright sunlight.
Temperament: Docile, friendly.
Environment: Dry run.
Eggs: 120–160 sometimes rather small, tinted to brown, eggs.

Australorp

The Australorp provides one of the best examples of how different strains of a breed can develop to the point where they become separate breeds. When William Cook bred his first Orpingtons, he seems to have selected the original single-combed Black Orpington on the basis of its laying ability. Other breeders would have used varying amounts of Cochin blood in the breed, and it is from these lines that most later Black Orpingtons descend.

All of these strains would have had an early wide distribution throughout Australia, where it is likely that breeders had a different attitude to exhibiting and selection. Selecting fowl from the better-laying families led to many Australian strains of Orpington developing along utility lines. Australian Orpingtons were developed for their utility qualities, and include modest

amounts of Minorca, Rhode Island Red, Leghorn and Langshan in their genetic composition. Some strains of large Australorps are satisfactory egg-layers. An Australian Orpington broke the laying record with 302 eggs in 1920. Few Black Orpingtons would have been even modest egg-layers. First and second generations of importations from Australia in the late 1920s saw all perform well in British laying trials.

The description Australian Orpington was soon shortened to Australorp, and this was eventually the name accepted for the breed by Australian poultry societies.

Later, the breed lost popularity to the best Rhodes and Wyandottes. However, the breed's reputation as being a first-class smallholders' fowl was added to

▲ *A Black bantam male.*

during World War II, when domestic poultry keepers found them to be excellent layers even when fed on wartime rations. Competition ensures that all exhibition breeds provide individual challenges, but the bantam version now found in Black, Blue and White varieties has gained a reputation as being among the best miniature fowl for those with limited space. In common with the strains of most breeds now being kept by enthusiasts, few lay as many eggs as their ancestors, but with some selection this quiet fowl could still be a useful addition to many gardens.

▶ *A large Australorp hen with the firm stiff tail, rising from a neat cushion, that distinguishes this variety from the fluffier Orpingtons.*

ESSENTIAL CHARACTERISTICS

Size: Large male 3.8–4.5kg/ 8½–10lbs. Large female 2.9–4kg/ 6½–9lbs. Bantam male 1kg/36oz. Bantam female 793g/28oz.
Varieties: Black, Blue, White.
Temperament: Calm, docile.
Environment: From free range to intensely housed.
Egg yield: 120–180 tinted to mid brown eggs per year.

Lincolnshire Buff

Poultry from Lincolnshire, England, was used extensively to supply meat to the London food markets. It is likely that Dorking-Cochin crosses formed the basis of many breeding pens in that county, but the breed remained unrecognized outside its home country.

▶ *The five toes and body shape of this adult male reflect the Dorking part of the breed's ancestry.*

In the 1980s, Riseholme College, an agricultural college in Lincolnshire, began a program of refining the breed. This work was continued by local fanciers until such time as the breed could be bred to an agreed standard. By the time a breed club had been formed in 1995 the breed would have found new friends among those for whom the Buff Orpington had become far too feathery to meet their requirements for an all-round utility fowl.

The Lincolnshire Buff may remain largely confined to its home county, but seems to be here to stay, albeit in large form only. In appearance, the breed has a long back and carries its tail at a low angle. It has five toes, and tighter feathering than the Buff Orpington, whose previous role as a an all-round useful and attractive, buff-coloured fowl it is beginning to replace. The two-toned buff pattern is one of the least demanding to breed and maintain.

ESSENTIAL CHARACTERISTICS
Size: Large male 4–4.9kg/9–11lbs.
Large female 3.1–4kg/7–9lbs.
Bantam male 1.1kg/40oz.
Bantam female 963g/34oz.
Varieties: One only.
Temperament: Quiet.
Environment: Free range.
Egg yield: 120–150 medium tinted eggs per year.

Norfolk Grey

The Norfolk Grey was the creation of Fred Myhill of Norwich, whose poultry-breeding enterprises were interrupted by a spell in the World War I trenches. Norfolk Greys were widely advertised in the poultry press but the exact origins of the breed are unclear. Leghorn and Game, with an infusion of either or both Black Orpington or Australorp, seem to have been the genetic base of stock being offered in the 1930s. The breed never became popular, and little seems to have been seen or heard of the breed until the formation of the Rare Breed Society in 1970, when four birds not unlike large Grey Old English Game appeared at shows. These four birds were responsible for the breeding pens that are known today. While still rare, this regional poultry breed has made something of a recovery.

The breed is an excellent meat bird, no doubt the game element of its genetic make-up accounts for its good flavour. The Leghorn ancestry ensures that the breed is a reasonably productive egg-layer.

Norfolk Greys are black with silver hackles, black or grey legs, a single

◀ *A Norfolk Grey male looking very like a large, table-type, Old English Game bird.*

red comb, lobes and wattles. The bird is classed as a heavy breed, although its weight suggests otherwise. This is a hardy breed that likes to forage. Like other British breeds, the Norfolk Grey was marketed for a new audience between the two world wars that wanted a smaller plump carcass.

ESSENTIAL CHARACTERISTICS
Size: Male 3.2kg/7lbs.
Female 2.7kg/6lbs.
Varieties: One only.
Temperament: Quiet.
Environment: Free range.
Eggs: 140–180 tinted to brown eggs per year.

Marsh Daisy

The Marsh Daisy evolved, like several other minor British breeds, out of the search for an ideal dual-purpose fowl, which saw poultry keepers introduce both Indian and English Game breeds to their breeding pens. John Wright of Marshside, Lancashire, originally used both Old English Game and Malays, along with Hamburg and Leghorns, and then bred their offspring together as a closed flock, to ensure there were no further introductions of new blood into the flock. Breeding from older hens probably resulted in the breed's later recorded longevity. In 1913, having previously turned down offers for his stock, he sold some hens to Charles Wright from Doncaster, who first introduced a pit game cock and later added Sicilian Buttercup to the mixture. From this beginning, the Marsh Daisy breed developed into one which has gained a surprising degree of commercial success. A

▲ *The Marsh Daisy is considered to be a rare breed.*

reputation for laying large eggs into old age could be the result of the original breeder only breeding from old hens. This, combined with a plump game conformation, saw the breed remain on some farms until just before World War II. Now rare, this green-legged breed is still seen at the occasional show.

ESSENTIAL CHARACTERISTICS
Size: Male 2.4–2.7kg/5½–6lbs. Female 2–2.4kg/4½–5½lb.
Varieties: Buff, Red-wheaten.
Temperament: Active.
Environment: Garden.
Egg yield: Once good, and recorded in 1939 as laying large eggs into old age.

Ixworth

The Ixworth was created by well-known waterfowl and duck breeder Reginald Appleyard in Ixworth, Suffolk, in the UK, in order to fulfil the pre-war commercial demand for white-fleshed poultry, using the carcass of the Indian or Cornish breed.

Starting with Jubilee Indian Game and White Sussex, Appleyard is said to have added both Pile Old English Game and White Orpington blood to his breeding pen. Not wishing to be influenced by appearances, he is said to have made all his final breeding selections in the dark, by feeling the muscle, bone and flesh structure of each bird. Not standardized until 1939, few Ixworth birds survived World War II. Those that are exhibited today are often large and excellent examples of the Ixworth. The breed is also an excellent egg-layer.

◀ *An Ixworth male displays much of the useful conformation of a game fowl without the excessive bone of some Indian Game birds.*

ESSENTIAL CHARACTERISTICS
Size: Male 3.8–4kg/8½–9lbs. Female 2.7–3.1kg/6–7lbs.
Varieties: White.
Temperament: Quiet but game-like, hardy.
Environment: Free range.
Egg yield: 150–180 eggs per year.

Only one colourway, White, is available in the Ixworth breed. The birds have pink legs and a pink beak. The eyes are orange and it has a red pea comb.

The breed is an active forager and prefers a free-range environment. The Ixworth is a hardy breed that is reported to provide the best-quality meat of any modern pure breed.

LONG-TAILED JAPANESE BREEDS

Native Japanese poultry known as "jitory", have a body type similar to the native fowl of northern Europe and, in some breeds, to the early feathery forms of English game fowl. As poultry meat and eggs were not widely consumed in Japan before the mid-19th century nearly all early poultry selection in that country was made purely on the basis of the perceived aesthetic qualities of the bird. The native poultry had single combs and white lobes. They were crossbred with breeds imported from China and Thailand to produce a group of fowl with long tails.

Japanese poultry keepers selected their birds for their long tail feathers. Ten long-tailed Japanese breeds with varying combinations of comb forms and either red or white lobes are known. Once a non-moulting gene within the Japanese group of fowl had been identified, poultry could be bred with tails that could reach quite extraordinary lengths. The incorporation of the non-moulting gene into the genes of the native Onaga-dori long-tailed breed meant that that breed could only survive in the most artificial of environments.

Yokohama/Phoenix

Long-tailed Japanese fowl arrived in Europe in 1860, and from the Onaga-dori breed and the Minohiki breed, German poultry breeders created the Yokohama breed. Early illustrations of the new breed show a diversity of comb and type that could suggest it has a genetic relationship with several Japanese long-tailed breeds.

In Britain new poultry breeds were generally named after their port of dispatch: in this case, the breed was sent from Yokohama in Japan. In Germany the single-combed versions became known as Phoenix fowl, after a mythological

▶ A large Silver-duckwing male has the non-moulting mutation that allows some birds to attain very long tails. The breed requires attention, since the tail may hamper natural movement.

bird said to rise up from a fire's ashes. Later German breeders called their long-tailed, walnut-combed, game-type fowl Red-saddled Yokohama. That breed had features in common with, but had no exact counterpart, among the long-tailed breeds now being kept in Japan. The brilliant

red-backed males and uniquely pink chequered-breasted females make Red-saddled Yokohamas one of the most attractive of the long-tailed group.

◀ A single-combed Yokohama exhibiting the breed's characteristic wealth of saddle and hackle feathers.

YOKOHAMA ESSENTIAL CHARACTERISTICS

Size: Large male 1.8–2.3kg/4–5lbs.
Large female 1.1–1.8kg/2½–4lbs.
Bantam male 566–680g/20–24oz.
Bantam female 453–566g/16–20oz.
Varieties: Game colours.
Temperament: Tame if handled.
Environment: Very long-tailed males will need total protection.
Egg yield: 80–100 small white eggs.

ONAGA-DORI

Onaga means long tail and *dori* translates as fowl. The development of these long tails seems to have been encouraged by the use of long tail feathers in the processional train for the attendants of the Shogun's court in Japan. In total, there are up to 25 pairs of long tail feathers in a complete Onaga-dori tail. These are enhanced by up to 200 non-moulting saddle hackle feathers. Records from 1830–43 show the breed had a tail that reached 3m/3¼yds long. Between 1863 and 1922 an extra metre was added to the length of the tail. By 1930, several birds were reported with tails greater than 6m/6½yds long, and by the late 1950s it had increased to 8m/8¾yds.

The male Onaga-dori's long tail develops over many years; and then only when the bird is kept in such a way as to let the tail continually hang down. Since the breed moults if the bird is allowed to spend much time in more usual poultry conditions, it is unlikely that the western world will ever see this sort of development in their Onaga-dori breeds.

▶ *Some examples of the legendary Onaga-Dori of Japan have tails that are several metres long. Such lengths are attained by older male birds, many of whom will spend most of their life standing on a high perch, with the tail allowed to hang down freely.*

By the early 1900s, the single-combed breed standardized in Britain as Yokohama was popular enough to have its own breed club. Most of these birds had white lobes and would have been very similar to the Japanese Shokoku breed. Some illustrations show red-faced, pea-combed breeds that suggest the importation of other Japanese varieties, but as the similarly shaped Sumatra Game had also found its way to Europe, some of the early long-tailed examples could be the result of early outcrosses.

An importation into Germany in 1976 probably represents one of the few times the Onaga-dori has been seen in Europe. While these produced offspring with very long tails, the expertise to delay moulting by more than a couple of years seems to have eluded exhibitors. Animal welfare considerations are likely to see those males kept in more natural conditions in Europe with a reasonable amount of trailing feathers. In fact, while they are likely to be seen primarily as

RED-SADDLED YOKOHAMA
ESSENTIAL CHARACTERISTICS

Size: Large male 1.8–2.3kg/4–5lbs.
Large female 1.1–1.8kg/2½–4lbs.
Bantam male 566–680g/20–24oz.
Bantam female 453–566g/16–20oz
Varieties: Game colours.
Temperament: Active.
Environment: At its best on free-range grass. Some strains are intolerant of confinement.
Egg yield: 80–100 small white eggs.

exhibition fowl, all forms of the large Japanese long-tailed fowl standardized in Europe (including the bantams made from them) have more

range and freedom than most breeds. The bantam forms of both the Red-saddled and single-combed breed seen at recent shows seem to have been bred from smaller examples of large versions, and while perhaps on the large side, have displayed an exceptional wealth of feather.

◀ *A Red-saddled Yokohama bantam male. Many examples shown as bantams exceed the standard weights. This breed is unknown in Japan.*

Ohiki

Japanese long-tailed poultry breeds are found across a considerable size range. The concept of a miniature or bantam version bred to conform to a percentage of the size of a large version does not really exist in Japan, where each breed is seen as having its own ideal weight. The long-tailed Ohiki, however, is a true bantam, one that has much in common with the Japanese Bantam/Shabo breed. It is thought to be developed from the Onaga-dori breed crossed with the Japanese bantam. Like the latter breed, the Ohiki has very short legs and a long, trailing saddle hackle, with long, soft downy feathers beneath, meaning that the exhibition Ohiki has to spend much of its life confined to a clean, shaving-covered pen in order to protect the tail. The tail feathers can measure any length from 60–150cm/2–5ft and are held initially upright from the body, then dragging behind the bird at a low angle. The breed has an abundance of plumage, including hackle feathers, giving it the appearance of a full and round breed. The wings are long and carried low to the ground. The bird walks with a horizontal carriage.

◄ *The breed has a single comb, white earlobes and willow legs. This is a Black-red male.*

ESSENTIAL CHARACTERISTICS
Size: Male 0.9kg/2lbs.
Female 0.7kg/1½lbs.
Varieties: Black-breasted Red, Ginger, Gold-duckwing, Silver-duckwing, White.
Temperament: Calm.
Environment: Tolerant of confinement, males will need a dry run with a clean floor.
Egg yield: Kept for ornament.

Kuro Gashiwa

Another long-tailed breed from Northern Japan, with feathering that drags behind the bird. The bird is completely black, with slate-coloured legs and feet. The most distinguishing feature of this bird is its crowing, which is long and deep. Long-crowing roosters have over the years had almost cult status among enthusiasts in many countries, where length and tone of crow is deemed to be at least as important as breed type. Standardized forms are found in Germany, Belgium and Brazil, where they have an Asiatic game form. All have a sloping back like the Japanese Kuro Gashiwa. Japanese legend has it that such poultry was first introduced from China to act as alarm clocks – a long, loud crow would have been seen as a desirable attribute.

▼ *The Kuro Gashiwa is an unusual addition to the garden.*

ESSENTIAL CHARACTERISTICS
Size: Male 2.7kg/6lbs.
Female 2.3kg/5lbs.
Varieties: Black.
Temperament: Friendly.
Environment: Free range, but neighbours may complain about noisy crowing.
Egg yield: 50–100 white or tinted.

Sumatra

Named for the Indonesian Island from where it originates, this poultry breed has had a chequered development since arriving in America in the mid-19th century. It was imported to Europe from Canada in the late 19th century. This is a game bird used for cockfighting in its native country, though it is better suited to crossing with game birds for the genetic heritage it provides its offspring. The breed's arrival in Europe coincided with the end of cockfighting, and thus it never gained the popularity of other game birds. The triple spurs found on some males may be seen as an indication of purity but are not an essential part of the breed standard.

However, at the time of its importation there was interest in long-tailed Japanese breeds. Some breeders saw the tail of the Sumatra as the breed's most important feature. Its tail is held low, and in the male has a very impressive long sweep made up of many pointed feathers. These long, pheasant-like tail feathers may have assisted the Sumatra's semi-domesticated ancestors in flying out of harm's way. This breed can still fly.

Sumatras have an upright, pheasant-like carriage, small pea comb, almost non-existent wattles and small earlobes. It is their beetle-green feathering that sets this breed apart from any other. A dark or plum-coloured face is a breed characteristic.

Few breeds will enjoy total freedom to range or sleep in trees as they may have done in their native environment. Given a fox-free run Sumatra are capable of looking after themselves. The Black Sumatra has no equal as a broody, and is often crossed with the Silkie breed to make the perfect foster mother for exotic chicks. With a bantam version now available, those with less room will be able to keep one of the poultry world's most interesting, and slightly unusual, fowl.

▼ *A large black hen with firm game-like outline and almost whipped tail.*

▼ *This type of pea comb is similar to that reported in the breed when it was introduced to the West. Early examples shown in Europe were described as having eyes the colour of a horse chestnut.*

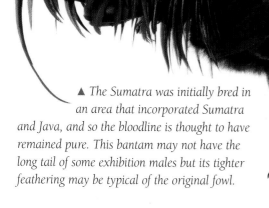

▲ *The Sumatra was initially bred in an area that incorporated Sumatra and Java, and so the bloodline is thought to have remained pure. This bantam may not have the long tail of some exhibition males but its tighter feathering may be typical of the original fowl.*

ESSENTIAL CHARACTERISTICS

Size: Large male 2.2–2.7kg/5–6lbs.
Large female 1.8–2.2kg/4–5lbs.
Bantam male 737g/26oz.
Bantam female 623g/22oz.
Varieties: Black, Blue, White.
Temperament: Bold, but at times, wary.
Environment: Exhibition males may want some protection. Adult breeding stock will enjoy free range.
Egg yield: 100–130 smallish white or tinted eggs per year.

MODIFIED FEATHER BREEDS

Feathers with changes in their structure are likely to occur from time to time within any group of fowl. Some of the more extreme examples are associated with early civilizations. The long pheasant-like tail feathers of the Sumatra breed may have helped its semi-domesticated ancestors to fly out of harm's way, but the extremely long tail feathers of the Onaga-dori breed, which are enhanced by a non-moulting gene, mean that the breed would only survive in the most artificial environment. Similarly frizzle-feathered fowl are a prime example of a modification that would have little chance of survival other than in the most protected environment. Silky-feathered fowl would not have retained their unique characteristics without selection, and the unique genetic package that includes black skin and dark flesh that has been selected and standardized as the Silkie breed would have soon become diluted by crossing it with fowl of different-coloured skin. At the other end of the scale, Naked Neck sports seem to have occurred regularly and make up a large proportion of the fowl that survive in quite harsh environments. This group contains some of the most genetically interesting and spectacular varieties.

Silkie

The origin of the Silkie is wholly Asiatic; Marco Polo, the Italian traveller and merchant who introduced Asian cultures to Europe, first sighted fowl with similar feathers to the Silkie breed towards the end of the 13th century, while travelling through Asia. He reported them as "Hens which have hair like cats, are black and lay the best of eggs". As did later 16th-century reports, mainly from Sumatra and Java, he noted that the fowl had black skin and legs. These features are still retained in the breed standard, along with its

▼ *A Black unbearded hen.*

ESSENTIAL CHARACTERISTICS
Size: Large male 1.8kg/4lbs.
Large female 1.4kg/3lbs.
Bantam male 623g/22oz.
Bantam female 510g/18oz.
Varieties: Bearded and non-bearded.
Black, Blue, Buff, Partridge, White.
Temperament: Docile and friendly;
the perfect pet, but often persistent
broodies.
Environment: Needs a covered run.
Wet, muddy and hot conditions are
unsuitable. Copes with confinement.
Egg yield: 100–120 cream eggs
per year.

feather silkiness. Since the breed is small it does not have the carcass of a meat bird. Its black skin, flesh and bones are not to Western tastes, but in China the meat is considered to have all manner of health-enhancing and medicinal properties.

Silkies, like their name suggests, are associated with silky feathers that feel like down. It is a feature that was once unique to this breed. In the best specimens, such downy feathers almost replace standard feathers. This attribute, however, ensures that Silkies cannot fly. Its other distinctive characteristics include a modified walnut-type comb, and five feathered toes. The silky feather type has now migrated to other breeds that do not have these additional characteristics. An unusual feature of this breed is the turquoise earlobes, which are quite striking.

Unlike Frizzles, when mated, two good silky feathered specimens will always produce all their offspring with this same feather characteristic. While the breed does not lay a massive quantity of eggs, broodiness is a strong characteristic. In fact, the smaller versions are a broody of choice for those looking to naturally incubate eggs from other poultry, or for small waterfowl breeds that do not go broody. Silkies naturally make good mothers. Some breeders use pure-breed Silkies to produce crossbreeds that almost always inherit the legendary maternal instincts.

Silkies have been a feature of our farmyards and gamekeepers' rearing pens for a long time, but they are not widely represented across broad geographic regions. Often these slightly undersized birds are impressive at first sight because they appear to be so unusual.

Without a bantam counterpart, and being a small breed, Silkies were often considered to be large bantams. The creation of a bantam version (with weights as low as 510g/18oz for females), which is rare in Europe but popular in the USA, helps to dispel this misconception. Dedicated work by skilled breeders may make bigger strains of the large breed in the future (with weights up to or exceeding 1.8kg/4lbs for males). Japanese breeders have spent years perfecting their bantams so that they have become very silky.

White birds generally dominate the exhibition classes. However, the original black varieties can be just as

◀ *A White male Silkie. It is not just the silky or almost wool-like feathers that have long defined the Silkie as a breed. The complete package includes black skin, five toes and a mulberry or walnut comb.*

stunning. The arrival via Europe of a Bearded variety that has been perfected in America will add future interest and variety to the show scene. This new variety is a "cloddy" type, which lacks the bright-eyed and alert stance of the traditional type. Not everyone will want to exhibit Silkies, however, and this ornamental breed makes a perfect pet. Docile and calm by nature, the breed should be put with non-aggressive birds since it is susceptible to bullying.

▼ *A muffed and bearded black Silkie bantam hen.*

Frizzle

The Frizzle is standardized as a feather type which may be bred into any poultry breed. In Britain, the Frizzle is also classified as a distinct breed. Frizzled feathers curve backward, whereas standard feathers curve forward. They provide the bird with a shaggy, rather than smooth, appearance. The perfect, wide, reflexed feather remains a challenge for breeders to perfect. This feather modification provides a bird with little chance of survival in any other

▲ *A frizzled Pekin male.*

▲ *A large White Frizzle.*

ESSENTIAL CHARACTERISTICS

Size: Large male 3.1–3.6kg/7–8lbs.
Large female 2.2–2.7kg/5–6lbs.
Bantam male 680–793g/24–28oz.
Bantam female 566–680g/20–24oz.
Varieties: Many.
Temperament: Quiet, friendly.
Environment: Good housing and a dry run.
Egg yield: 80–150 white tinted or brown eggs per year.

than the most protected environment. Frizzled fowl were described as early as 1600. Early naturalists agreed that frizzled feathers were an Asiatic characteristic, possibly originating in Japan. It is thought that frizzled breeds came to Europe via the Dutch trading port of Bantam. Nearly all imported birds with this feather characteristic conformed to a type later categorized as true bantam.

The frizzle feather can often be found in commercial strains of large heavy breeds like Rhode Island Reds and White Rocks, as well as broiler breeding strains. These large Frizzles, in all other respects, match the standard for their particular breed. All large frizzled fowl are classified as heavy for exhibition purposes. The original bantams are now shown as miniatures of the heavy versions, rather than true bantams.

As poultry keeping becomes an increasingly international hobby,

the world is likely to see more breeds adopt a frizzled variety. It is now usual to see frizzled Polish, and perhaps more controversially, frizzled Cochins and Pekins, and long established breeders see this as being an unwelcome departure from their standard of perfection. Many poultry fanciers will get pleasure from a quaint and unusual variation of the standard breed.

FRIZZLED FEATHERS

The frizzle feather type provides an excellent example of Mendel's theory, with regard to dominant and recessive genes. Two mated Frizzles will produce offspring in which 50 per cent have frizzled feathers that match the parents. Of the rest, 25 per cent will have a standard feather type, and the balance will have feathers that are over-frizzled, meaning that they will be so extremely curled and fluffy that the chicks would be unlikely to survive in a challenging environment. This over-frizzled category, however, if crossed with their standard feathered siblings, can be used in a breeding program that allows the frizzled feather gene to "migrate" to standard-feathered breeds.

► *A Buff Frizzle male bantam.*

Transylvanian Naked Necks/Turken

The most dramatic changes in the feather structure of poultry are most likely to be perpetuated with human assistance. However, the opposite is true in the case of the Naked Neck breeds. Related groups of these birds seem to occur spontaneously. The most significant visible characteristic of the Naked Neck, as its name suggests, is that the neck area is devoid of feathering. These breeds also have less feathering across the breast bone. Most of the diverse populations of Naked Neck fowl seem to have emerged in response to difficult conditions. Such conditions do not add to a bird's chance of survival, and in many cases the naked neck characteristic will prove counterproductive to an ideal life in challenging, or even habitual, environments. Naked Neck birds are more likely to survive in domestication.

In spite of the prefix Transylvanian given to the breed name, populations of fowl with nearly or completely naked necks have a wide distribution, though there may once have been some connection between the breed and Central Europe. It may have originated in Hungary, though it was largely developed in Germany. Its alternate name of Turken is thought to have arisen from a belief that this breed, with its naked neck, was a hybrid between a chicken breed and a turkey.

In the early 20th century, an agricultural adviser to Grenada reported that the breed was preferred in the West Indies to imported birds because of its superior hardiness and other qualities. It seems this hardiness also attracted subsistence farmers in the French-African colonies, who kept Naked Necks under the name Barbary Fowl. Later, French scientists noticed that as table fowl this breed was practically devoid of visible surface or skin fat.

The fat issue was of great interest to health-conscious consumers, and led French poultry geneticists to breed commercial strains of the breed. The Naked Neck breed has since been found to be linked with a useful gene that disperses fat through the dry meat areas in table birds. It also gives a wonderful texture to the meat.

◄ *The breed is said to have survived the Wartime siege of Malta, because their vulture-like necks enabled them to dig into rubbish for food.*

▲ *The neck of the Transylvanian Naked Neck breed should be a deep red colour, in order to achieve high marks at exhibition. The skin turns red when exposed to sunlight.*

Hybrid table strains that retained the characteristic naked neck could be used to create new strains that, with selection, may conform to the exhibition standard for Naked Necks. This demonstrates the value of conserving the diversity contained in the most unusual forms of poultry. This breed is known to be resistant to many poultry diseases. Naked Necks have fewer feathers than other breeds, including those over the rest of the body.

The bantam versions make both unusual exhibits and curious additions to any poultry yard. This is a good dual-purpose bird converting feed to eggs at an efficient rate.

ESSENTIAL CHARACTERISTICS
Size: Male 3.1–3.6kg/7–8lbs. Female 2.4–2.9kg/5½–6½lbs.
Varieties: Black, Buff, Red, White.
Temperament: Friendly.
Environment: Free range or confinement. Needs protection in cold weather.
Egg yield: A good layer of light brown medium-size eggs.

A DIRECTORY OF OTHER DOMESTIC FOWL

Ducks, geese and turkeys are bred to be shown at exhibitions by specialist and hobby enthusiasts. They are also kept as domestic pets. For small-scale and amateur breeders, the appeal of keeping these birds may stem from a fascination with the character traits, personality and physical appearance of the species. It may represent the chance to own an old-fashioned breed familiar to one's grandparents, as well as the opportunity to keep the breed alive for future generations. Ducks, geese and turkeys are all quite vocal species, which is worth bearing in mind if you intend keeping them in an area close to neighbours.

Each breeder will look for specific features that he or she considers important in their fowl, then select the best of their stock. Selected birds will be used to breed the next generation in an attempt to produce offspring that perfectly fit the accepted breed standard for exhibition fowl.

▲ *Ducks make unusual pets, but are most usually associated with a rural, rather than urban, environment.*

◄ *Call ducks make charming pets and can be accommodated in a relatively small space, such as a large garden.*

DUCKS, GEESE AND TURKEYS

All of today's breeds of domestic fowl would have been identifiable in varying shapes and sizes by the middle of the 19th century. It was at this time that written exhibition standards for domestic waterfowl were drawn up, and breeders perfected their birds.

There are less breeds of turkeys, ducks and geese than there are of chickens, but this has not quashed breeder interest. Standards of perfection are high among this diverse group of birds.

Ducks

All the domestic breeds of duck, with the exception of the Muscovy (*Cairina moschata*), descend from the wild mallard (*Anas platyrhynchos*). The mallard is a migratory bird and breeds with all known duck species, including domesticated ducks.

It is not known for certain when ducks were first domesticated. It seems likely that as soon as humans started growing crops and living in agricultural settlements, wild mallard ducks arrived to share the harvest. Their presence was tolerated because the occasional bird provided meat, feathers for padding and insulation, and eggs for eating. Ducks would eventually have laid second and

third clutches of eggs in order to compensate for the loss of eggs. Over time, more productive ducks would have evolved and became the basis of lightweight laying breeds.

Evidence suggests the ancient Egyptians may have bred ducks for food and also to sacrifice in religious ceremonies. In South-east Asia they were being reared before 500BC, and roast duck was certainly a dish prized by the Romans. Centuries later, the Normans introduced selected heavy

▼ *Rouen ducks have the same colouring as the wild mallard.*

◄ *Call ducks are small birds, and are ideal to keep in an urban environment.*

strains of mallard-coloured and white domestic ducks for the table. Monastic records from this time indicate that waterfowl were more important to the diet than poultry. While many of the ducks that were bred had a modified mallard pattern, birds with white feathers and bill were understood to represent a bird with quality meat.

Before 1890, flocks of ducks were hardly ever kept as egg-layers, even though domestic ducks were more prolific egg-layers than their wild ancestors. The tall, ultra-lightweight "Runner"-type ducks first introduced by the Dutch from the East Indies allowed the creation of breeds that laid greater numbers of eggs than did hens. Within 30 years, vast numbers of lightweight ducks, all related to, or partly descended from, Indian Runners were kept. Food shortages during and after World War I brought attention to lightweight ducks that could lay far more eggs than any hen of the period. The Khaki Campbell and Indian Runner became the breeds of choice for small-scale poultry keepers. Yellow-billed Pekin ducks imported from the East offered the possibility of strains that both laid well and grew quickly, qualities desirable to breeders.

Geese

Traditionally associated with the storybook farmyard, geese are large and strong birds, renowned for their noisy and aggressive behaviour. They are kept for their meat and eggs.

In Europe, North Africa and western Asia, domestic geese are descended from the wild Greylag goose (*Anser anser*). Those of eastern Asia are thought to be descended from the wild Asiatic Swan goose (*Anser cygnoides*). Known as Chinese geese, they can be distinguished from European geese by the large knob at the base of the bill. However, both kinds have been widely introduced in modern times, and many flocks in both regions now contain either type.

The recent boom in small-scale poultry keeping has sparked similar heightened interest in keeping geese. Specialist breeding companies are able to supply goose eggs to hatch, or goslings just a few days old, to poultry keepers who want to keep geese for meat and eggs. European breeds are particularly fashionable. For pure breeds the best source of stock is a small-scale breeder.

Turkeys

The wild turkey, *Meleagris gallopavo*, originated from Mexico. There it was domesticated by the Aztecs and other

▼ *Pilgrim geese have a useful auto-sexing characteristic.*

Mesoamerican peoples for meat and eggs, and also for its feathers, which were used for decorative purposes. The species was brought to the attention of Europeans through the Spanish colonization of the Americas in the early 16th century. From its homeland, the turkey was introduced to Spain, and from there, to the rest of Europe. All domestic turkeys are descended from the wild species brought to Europe. Following its introduction into Europe, a number of distinct breeds were developed.

Domesticated turkeys were taken back to the USA by European

▲ *Beltsville White turkeys are an American breed and now quite rare.*

migrants almost two centuries later. These immigrant settlers bred and selected heavier domesticated strains of turkey that became associated with the feast of Thanksgiving, and later with Christmas dinner. The breed is now popular with commercial livestock farmers the world over because it is cheap to rear for the amount of meat it yields.

▼ *Sebastopol geese have softly curled feathers on their bodies.*

DUCKS

From the tiniest Call to the large and feisty Rouen, ducks are an attractive species to behold, and will undoubtedly add substance and character to any backyard. With such an array of sizes, temperaments and physical appearances, there is sure to be a duck variety that will suit your purposes, whether you want to keep ducks for meat, eggs, or ornamental value. All ducks need space to wander and a body of water in which to swim, although small ducks need no more than a paddling pool-size area in which to dip their feathers. For those with a small garden and no expanse of water, the small ducks may appeal.

In exhibition terms, ducks are classified according to their weight – heavy, medium and light. However, accepted bird weights differ from country to country. As with poultry, new breeds have been created to fulfil a commercial requirement for meat or eggs, and the utility varieties frequently have slightly different characteristics from the exhibition types.

By definition, ducks have a broad and low body shape, usually a long neck, strong scaly legs and bill, and wings that are set back on the body, supported by strong muscles. Males and females have a different appearance.

Aylesbury

Like all ducks except for the Muscovy, the Aylesbury is descended from the wild mallard. A relatively recent introduction to the duck family, the Aylesbury was developed at the turn of the 19th century for its utility qualities, and later for the exhibition scene. The true Aylesbury has snow-white plumage with a pinky-white or flesh-coloured bill and legs, the latter placed mid-way along its undercarriage, giving it a boat-shaped body and horizontal carriage. The keel should almost touch the ground when it stands upright.

By the beginning of the 20th century, Aylesbury ducks had become one of the world's best-known breeds. Nowadays, there are two distinct types of Aylesbury: exhibition birds, which remain true to the written standard for the breed, and those developed for the table. Often the latter are Aylesbury-Pekin crosses, and are distinguished by their bright yellow beaks. To create these crosses, some breeders in the Aylesbury district were recorded as having introduced a percentage of

Pekin blood into their strains. The Aylesbury-Pekin cross became the duck of choice for those seeking to supply the mass market, and after generations of selective breeding, this is the basic duck now used to produce most of the world's duck meat. However, as with other breeds developed for the quality of their meat, white-fleshed skin is more appealing to the consumer, and white feather stubs produce the least amount of blemishing to the skin.

Utility breeds of the true Aylesbury are desirable for those who want duck eggs and meat, although most

> **ESSENTIAL CHARACTERISTICS**
> **Size:** Drake 4.5–5.4kg/10–12lbs.
> Duck 4–4.9kg/9–11lbs.
> **Varieties:** One (white).
> **Temperament:** Slow, ponderous.
> **Environment:** Needs space, and water for mating.
> **Egg yield:** 150 blue, green or white eggs per year. Exhibition strains lay fewer.

birds are kept as garden pets. Utility lines may produce 150 eggs per year, but most produce considerably fewer. Most convert food to meat at a good rate and are ready for the table when they reach 1.8–2.2kg/4–5lbs, usually at eight weeks.

Since the Aylesbury is one of the largest duck breeds, it needs considerable space. Its size prohibits it from mating on land, and so this breed needs access to deeper water for mating. Aylesbury fertility can be a problem, but true enthusiasts think this a premium worth paying.

◀ *Large table-type Aylesbury exhibition strains hold their breast bone, or keel, almost horizontal, and nearly touching the ground.*

Pekin

The Pekin duck, which had been bred in China for centuries, was introduced into the United States in 1873. Often referred to as the Long Island duck, it became widely popular there. Soon British breeders were importing these birds directly from China. The Pekin is only slightly smaller than the Aylesbury, is a better layer and is more fertile. However, although it is well-fleshed and matures quickly, largely due to a prejudice against yellow skin and other pigmentation it has always been considered to be inferior to the Aylesbury in terms of meat.

The Aylesbury-Pekin cross became the breed favoured by commercial breeders, who supply the market for table fowl. It remains the strain used to produce most of the world's duck meat, and Chinese Pekin duck remains a popular speciality dish.

The Pekin has white plumage with a hint of yellow running through it. With a bright orange bill and legs, it is an attractive bird. The legs are placed well back, giving the bird an upright stance with a characteristic turned-up rump. Some exhibition examples of Pekins have an almost primrose hue. Like exhibition Aylesburys, commercial birds have more flesh and the birds can reach up to 5kg/11lbs.

Commercial Pekins make prolific egg layers, though broodiness has been largely bred out of the stock. Often the ducks may abandon their eggs before they hatch, so hatching eggs in an incubator is a preferable method of ensuring the next generation survives.

ESSENTIAL CHARACTERISTICS
Size: Drake 4kg/9lbs.
Duck 3.6kg/8lbs.
Varieties: White, with exhibition strains having a primrose tint.
Temperament: Placid.
Environment: Needs plenty of space and a large house.
Egg yield:150–200 white eggs. Exhibition strains lay fewer white, blue or green eggs.

◀ *Exhibition Pekin ducks have a shape that appears far heavier than they actually are.*

Both exhibition Pekins and Aylesburys are less well-fleshed than their commercial ancestors. Yet they remain a useful genetic resource as the commercial gene pool becomes ever more interbred.

Cayuga

Coveted for its beautiful iridescent black plumage, which is tinted beetle-green, the Cayuga duck is an ornamental breed that is also kept for its meat and eggs. In appearance it has a black bill, shanks and toes.

ESSENTIAL CHARACTERISTICS
Size: Drake 3.6kg/8lbs.
Duck 3.1kg/7lbs.
Varieties: Black.
Temperament: Quiet but active.
Environment: Happiest where it can have access to a large pond.
Egg yield: 100–150 blue, green or white eggs per year.

Adults typically weigh up to 3.6kg/8lbs. Originating in New York and considered rare, this breed is increasing again in popularity.

It is a docile and hardy breed that needs plenty of space. Cayugas are quieter than other ducks and so they may be a good choice if the noise from your pond may disturb neighbours.

◀ *In the right light, both male and female Cayugas can appear an almost iridescent green colour.*

Muscovy

The domesticated descendants of the wild Muscovy duck are found throughout most of the developing world, originally hailing from Mexico and Central America. They were often kept as part of the farmyard scene for their meat. These are the only domesticated ducks not descended from wild Mallard.

Wild Muscovy ducks are either black or white, while domesticated Muscovy ducks can be found in many different varieties. The heads of each variety contain the identifying red crest around the eye, which in some instances can spread across the face. In the wild, Muscovy ducks fly and sleep in trees, and their domesticated cousins have retained the strong claws needed to hold their place among the branches.

◄ *Selected clones or colour forms of the domesticated Muscovy are generally treated as sub-varieties rather than individual varieties of duck.*

ESSENTIAL CHARACTERISTICS
Size: Drake 4.5–6.3kg/10–14lbs. Duck 2.2–3.1kg/5–7lbs.
Varieties: Black and White, but there are many colour variations including Lavender and Blue.
Temperament: Can live almost as feral populations. Large males can appear to be quite aggressive.
Environment: May sleep on a fox-free duck island, but when housed requires plenty of room.
Egg yield: Seasonal, can lay large batches of big white eggs in quick succession.

Rouen

In spite of claims that the Rouen had the most distinctive flavour of any duck, even when the market was dominated by pure breeds, its main commercial use was confined to supplying large, late-season ducklings at a time when Aylesburys would have been in short supply. The Rouen was bred in France for centuries as a utility table duck, although it is not really suited to that purpose. It resembles a large mallard, albeit heavier, reaching up to 5.4kg/12lbs in weight. The modern exhibition form suffers from poor fertility. However, the slightly smaller and equally attractively marked Rouen Clair breed may be a more appealing breeding option. The larger type may be kept as exhibition birds or as a statuesque addition to the garden pond, lake or stream.

◄ *The drake Rouen (left) will lose its iridescent black head and most of its distinctive markings during the summer when it moults.*

► *The drake adopts the same muted brown hues as its duck (right) when it moults.*

ESSENTIAL CHARACTERISTICS
Size: Drake 4.5–5.4kg/10–12lbs. Duck 4–4.9kg/9–11lbs.
Varieties: One only.
Temperament: Slow and ponderous on land.
Environment: Requires plenty of room on land and water and a large house with a shallow ramp to a large door.
Egg yield: Can be a poor layer of large white, blue or green eggs.

Silver Appleyard

The Silver Appleyard is a manmade British breed of duck developed in the 1930s and 1940s by well-known breeder Reginald Appleyard. It is a heavily set bird with a broad breast, erect stance, and back that slopes from the shoulder to the tip of the tail. It was intended to be a good utility bird, laying plenty of eggs and providing good meat as well as being attractive. The drakes, weighing up to 4kg/9lb, provide fine-tasting meat, and the slightly smaller females may lay 80 or so large white eggs per season. This bird is available in large and miniature versions. The miniature version is a recent addition, appearing in the late 1970s and 1980s, and is now far more plentiful than the original large version. The duck has an

▶ *Miniature Silver Appleyard ducks are expected to display the same strong fawn flecking to the back and shoulders as the large version.*

ESSENTIAL CHARACTERISTICS
Size: Large drake 3.6–4kg/8–9lbs.
Large duck 3.1–3.6kg/7–8lbs.
Miniature drake 1.3kg/3lbs.
Miniature duck 1kg/2lbs 8oz.
Varieties: One only.
Temperament: Active and lively.
Environment: Large and miniature versions are at their best where they have room to wander and forage.
Egg yield: Large and miniatures can lay 100–150, usually white, but occasionally blue or green, eggs.

active and lively temperament, and remains alert. The female has a silvery-white body with flecks of fawn over the flanks. The male is darker with a beetle-green head. Both have yellow beaks, orange legs and feet.

Black East India

Also classed as a bantam duck, the little Black East India was described in the first book of standards in 1875 and is known from a decade earlier. The bird, later standardized as a bantam version, is expected to weigh no more than 0.9kg/2lbs. Despite its name, the Black East India has nothing to do with East India and was, in fact, developed in the USA. Confusingly, it is also known as the Labrador duck, but no relationship to the extinct bird of that name, or to the Labrador region of Canada, is known. As with all active light-breed ducks in which breeding males have a heightened sexual drive, it is best to keep a ratio of at least two ducks to one drake. True to its name, the Black East India is black in colour, with a wonderful, almost iridescent, green sheen to its feathers. The bill should be black, and eyes, legs and webs as black as possible. Females may have white tail feathers. When kept as a pet or in a domestic environment they can be docile. The duck and youngsters make excellent exhibition birds. When kept on a pond as a breeding population, some strains can, at some times of the year, revert to a behaviour pattern not dissimilar to that of the wild mallard, and adolescent males may take to the wing in search of new mates.

ESSENTIAL CHARACTERISTICS
Size: Drake 0.9kg/2lbs.
Duck smaller than male.
Varieties: Black.
Temperament: If handled and treated as a pet, the breed can be quite docile.
Environment: Will want rather more room than the Call ducks that they are often kept with.
Egg yield: A good, if seasonal, layer of small to medium size eggs.

◀ *The Black East India has unrivalled iridescent green-black plumage.*

Khaki Campbell

This is another manmade British breed, developed at the turn of the 19th century by a female breeder intent upon producing a bird with good all-round utility qualities. The first Khaki Campbell was created by

▲ *A Khaki female with its modified mallard plumage.*

crossing a Runner duck with a Rouen and the offspring with a mallard. The Khaki Campbell was to revolutionize early 20th-century duck farming. When, in 1901, Mrs Adele Campbell, of Uley in Gloucestershire, purchased a Fawn and White Runner duck because she had heard it had laid 182 eggs in 196 days, and crossed it with a Rouen drake, she could have hardly been aware that she was starting a process that would eventually lead to the creation of what was to become the world's best-known domestic duck. She called the product of this cross the Khaki Campbell, after its colour, and in honour of the soldiers who were returning from the Boer War in South Africa wearing the new khaki uniforms. That colour became a utility standard. Later, exhibitors chose to breed and select strains in Light and Dark forms. Over the years, both have formed the basis of some of the most successful laying strains. As with some poultry, Campbell ducks that are exhibited differ in appearance from the utility types, some of which are smaller and, in the females, have a less even colour than the exhibition Khaki. The White Campbell should probably best be seen as a separate breed.

ESSENTIAL CHARACTERISTICS
Size: Drake 2.4kg/5½lbs.
Duck 1.8–2.2kg/4–5lbs.
Varieties: Khaki, Dark and White.
Temperament: Reasonably quiet but when in lay, utility strains are intolerant of disturbance.
Environment: Likes reasonable space and access to water, but utility strains are used to being kept very intensively.
Egg yield: Good utility birds will produce in excess of 300 eggs per year, though those kept as ornamental pets may not have such prolific egg-laying ability.

Saxony

The Saxony was created in Germany in the early part of the 20th century, and is named for the region where it originated. In the 1930s, it was first bred by Albert Franz of Chemnitz in Saxony. The species was almost wiped out in World War II, but was recreated in post-war Germany. It has only recently been recognized by the American Poultry Association. It has Pekin, Rouen and Pomeranian duck breeds in its ancestry and is a heavy breed, with males weighing up to 3.6kg/8lbs. The colouring of the drake is softer than a mallard, while the female has plenty of buff in its plumage, with blue shading. The breed is a utility bird, with the female laying approximately 200 eggs per year.

This attractive, medium to heavy duck re-established the idea that a potentially useful dual-purpose utility duck could also be selected as an attractive addition to the garden

◄ *Saxony ducks lay beautiful large, white eggs.*

ESSENTIAL CHARACTERISTICS
Size: Drake 3.6kg/8lbs.
Duck 3.1kg/7lbs.
Varieties: One only.
Temperament: Easily handled, ideally suited for the garden as a pet.
Environment: Requires a largish space and area of water.
Egg yield: More than 150 large, usually white eggs.

pond. The drake's head and neck are blue. A white ring completely encircles the neck. It has rusty-red natural mallard markings, which, along with the duck's buff head, neck and chest, provides a subtle variation on natural mallard markings.

Hook Bill

An ancient breed known in Holland in the 17th and 18th centuries, the Hook Bill has a curiously shaped curved bill which may have evolved to assist foraging in mud. The breed is likely to be descended from early Indonesian ducks crossed with the local Dutch mallard population. The bird is bred in

ESSENTIAL CHARACTERISTICS
Size: Drake 1.8–2.2kg/4–5lbs.
Duck 1.3–1.8kg3–4lbs.
Varieties: One only.
Temperament: Seems happy with other domestic ducks. Could make an interesting pet.
Environment: Enjoys a watery environment where it can follow its inclination to forage for food.
Egg yield: Egg numbers are variable. Some ducks lay well.

examples of the breed, which is relatively new to the show scene, seem to follow the same bibbed pattern that is so often a feature of feral populations of pond ducks.

◄ *The Hook Bill duck has a natural bib rarely standardized in other breeds.*

several varieties today, though it is mostly kept for exhibition purposes, where the shape and form of the distinctive hook bill are seen as more important than exact coloration. In fact, many

◄ *The Hook Bill drake has an attractive natural colour pattern, but the type and shape of the bill is considered the more important exhibition feature.*

Indian Runner

While European ducks were being selected on the basis of the quality of their meat, a far lighter duck capable of laying more eggs could be found over wide areas of the Far East. The breed soon to be named the Indian Runner was first imported in the

ESSENTIAL CHARACTERISTICS
Size: Drake1.3kg/3lbs.
Duck 1.2–1.8kg/3–4lbs.
Varieties: At least eight are known.
Temperament: Edgy and sometimes excitable.
Environment: Requires room to swim and forage and has a natural inclination to run.
Egg yield: Utility strains are recorded as laying more than 280 eggs, but exhibition strains lay far fewer eggs.

middle of the 19th century, when a sea captain brought some birds into Cumbria, England, from the East Indies. These were probably typical of many of the ducks that were bred or had evolved in Malaysia and Indonesia over the centuries. Not only were they taller, lighter and possessed a far more upright carriage than European ducks, they also laid far more eggs. While they gained a local reputation as wonderful layers, they remained practically unknown beyond Cumbria and the Scottish borders before the turn of the 19th century. Yet the breed was eventually to have an enormous impact on duck breeding and farming throughout the Western world, through the

commercial success of descendants such as the Khaki Campbell.
Few exhibition ducks compare with the elegance of a slim Indian Runner. The length of the neck is expected to make up one-third of the bird's total height of 66–81cm/26–32in in a drake and 61–71cm/24–28in in the duck. Slim shoulders and a lean and streamlined head complete the outline. In a show pen nothing compares with a column of bold upright Indian Runner ducks.

◄ *A slim bird with good proportions and elegance are more important than excessive height in the exhibition Runner.*

Call

Weighing only 0.6-0.7kg/21–24oz, call ducks are known as the true dwarves of the duck world. They are noisy and companionable, and make a perfect bird to keep in the back garden. With round heads, short deep beaks, puffy cheeks, and available in an increasing range of colour combinations, they have a cute appeal and a character that becomes obvious when they are kept as pets.

Originally it was their small size and the female's loud call that made them the breed of choice for their original role as "call" or decoy ducks. Once referred to as Dutch Decoys, they are still kept in Holland in large numbers, where they are aptly named "Kwakers". Call ducks were used to assist hunters in luring larger wild birds into traps. The loud call of the small bird was known to carry some distance. Once caught, the larger birds would also call, attracting even more birds to the trap.

The new interest in Call ducks has seen many new colours being developed and bred. The large quantity of show classes for the breed, combined with increased numbers kept, means that a broad range of colours is exhibited. Several subtle variations on the wild mallard colouring seen in continental varieties of Call ducks may in the future add interest to the exhibition scene. Not every duckling hatched will have the desired show characteristics. A percentage of ducklings turn out to be long-beaked. Nearly all make friendly garden pets, though their loud and talkative behaviour may make them unwelcome in built-up areas.

Call ducks are active birds, chirpy by nature, with their plumage at its best in late autumn and early spring. Not all birds bred for show will have the desired exhibition points.

The huge increase in Call duck numbers is a result of successful breeding of exhibition birds. The breed provides would-be owners with perfect pets which, with care and understanding, can be kept in a small area. The breed learns to interact with humans more readily than any other duck.

◀ *This all-white Call duck displays the appealing characteristics for which the breed is recognized.*

ESSENTIAL CHARACTERISTICS
Size: Drake 550–700g/19–24oz. Duck 450–600g/15–21oz.
Varieties: Plenty including Apricot, Apricot-silver, Bibbed, Blue-fawn, Black, Butterscotch, Chocolate, Dark Silver, Dusky Mallard, Khaki, Magpie, Mallard, Pied Mallard, Silver, White.
Temperament: Vocal and friendly.
Environment: Small area will suffice.
Egg yield: 25–75 eggs per year.

◀ *Call ducks are ideal birds to keep if you have a small garden pond.*

◀ *As ornamental birds, Call ducks make appealing garden companions.*

GEESE

Geese make interesting and unusual pets, and there are plenty of reasons to keep them if you have the land available. Perhaps your concern is in keeping geese for meat or eggs for the table, or you may be interested in breeding geese to sell either their eggs for hatching or the resultant goslings. Plenty of people keep their birds as ornamental garden companions, since those birds that are used to being handled from a young age can make docile and amusing pets that add colour and interest to the garden all year around. Remember, however, that geese will eat vegetation of all descriptions, and setting them near a prized flowerbed will almost certainly result in serious damage. Historically, geese have been used as guard animals, since they are guaranteed to set off a clamorous racket the minute visitors appear. By nature they are strong, and can be aggressive and intimidating birds. Geese have been recorded to live to a ripe old age, so making a commitment to keeping a goose can be a responsibility.

The appearance of all domesticated geese is the result of human intervention. Wild geese have a slim build, horizontal body shape and the ability to fly. Domestic geese, on the other hand, are much more upright, since they have been bred to lay down body fat around their girth, which pushes them into a much more upright stance. Most domestic breeds have lost the ability to fly, despite their great wingspans.

Embden

Embden geese were established in Britain by the 1820s, though they are widely believed to have originated in Northern Germany and Holland. They were selectively bred with native British white geese, and soon gained a reputation as one of the most useful farmyard breeds. Crossbreeding is thought to have improved the original stock, and 50 years after Embdens arrived in the UK, they were one of the first breeds to be bred to a written standard, and were reported as being re-exported to northern Europe.

▼ *The Embden goose is a large bird which requires a lot of space.*

ESSENTIAL CHARACTERISTICS
Size: Gander 12–15kg/28–34lbs.
Goose 10–12kg/24–28lbs.
Varieties: One only.
Temperament: Bold and active, but not difficult to manage.
Environment: As good grazers they require a sizeable area of grass.
Eggs: Some strains can be good layers of large eggs.

The ganders were in demand to improve the nondescript flocks that were an important part of the village economy. These all-white ganders improved local populations without interfering with their valuable trait of auto-sexing. Male goslings are white and females are grey.

While the slightly heavier Toulouse became the favourite market bird, the Embden has probably had greater influence on traditional goose breeding than any other breed.

Commercial crosses have since taken over some of their traditional role and the Embden may no longer be as common as it once was, but for those wanting a useful, large, solid breed with an upright and defiant carriage, hard and tight plumage and strong, bold head, the Embden still takes some beating.

◄ *The Embden or Bremen goose is a massive bird, up to 1m/3ft in height, with a sturdy and powerful build. Embden geese are best kept by those with some experience of poultry keeping, since the male can be over-protective and aggressive.*

African

Hailing from China, the inappropriately named African goose evolved from a cross between the Chinese goose and the Toulouse in the middle of the 19th century. Aspects of its appearance resemble both breeds, since it has the beak knob of the Chinese and the coloration of the Toulouse. The breed descends from the wild swan goose

ESSENTIAL CHARACTERISTICS
Size: Gander 9–12kg/22–28lbs.
Goose 9–11kg/20–26lbs.
Varieties: Brown, Grey, White.
Temperament: Can be far more friendly than they look.
Environment: Will need plenty of space.
Eggs: Not the best of laying geese.

species. A huge African gander, which may reach up to 1m/1yd tall, can be just as impressive as the largest Toulouse. This is one of the heaviest geese breeds, reaching up to 9kg/20lbs in weight, yet despite its great size, the breed is known to have a docile temperament. The head and neck are thick-set, even in the young. The head has a pronounced knob centred on top, which should be as broad as the head, and a dewlap hanging below the beak. The body tips at a gentle angle. African geese

are bred for meat and eggs. Brown, grey and white varieties exist.

◄ *An African gander may look intimidating but on acquaintance can turn out to be quite as friendly as any other 12kg/28lb giant.*

Chinese

Just as European breeders generally selected their birds for size and table qualities, Asian breeders developed their geese along different lines, particularly those originating in China. The Chinese breed is lighter in weight and is naturally capable of laying more eggs than the European and American heavy breeds. The pure Chinese are so different from other breeds of geese that many authorities suggest they descend from a cross that included either the wild or domesticated form of Asiatic swan geese (*Anser cygnoides*).

White and Brown-grey varieties are available, each with a long neck and

identifying knob on top of the bill. The Brown-grey colour pattern of the Grey variety is not found in any other domestic variety, but is close to that found in the wild species. These geese are vocal and their loud voice and vivacious character sets Chinese apart from other geese. Two personality types appear to develop with these geese; either they become tame and used to handling, or they become ferocious birds that may take an instant dislike to a human. Many strains kept by conservationists and exhibitors are fine-boned and smaller than the

◄ *Chinese geese are instantly recognizable by the knob at the base of the bill. They are vocal and loud.*

ESSENTIAL CHARACTERISTICS
Size: Gander 5–10kg/11–22lbs.
Goose 4–9kg/8.8–20lbs.
Varieties: White, Brown-grey.
Temperament: Feisty, will take on small dogs.
Environment: These geese are adpatable but are sensitive to extreme cold.
Eggs: Will yield at least 50 eggs per season, with 100 being known.

Chinese of previous years. Chinese can make excellent, if noisy, guards or feathered watchdogs. They rarely fly and make flexible all-rounders. Crosses between Chinese geese and other breeds are unlikely to lay well or fatten as economically as modern industrial crossbred or hybrid geese.

Brecon Buff

The original Brecon Buffs were kept on Welsh hill farms for generations before being recognized as a pure breed in 1934. This breed is unusual in that it originated in the UK. These birds were probably typical of several variously coloured regional populations. Light in bone with tight plumage and maximum flesh, Brecon Buffs are an active breed that can be expected to lay far more eggs than many of the heavier breeds. This is possibly one of the best dual-purpose utility breeds developed for farms or smallholdings. The pink bill helps to distinguish it from the larger American breed, which has an orange bill and is among the heaviest of today's geese. Brecon Buffs are hardy birds, used to free-ranging conditions, but they are in need of protection from foxes and other predators. They are kept for their meat, although they are also known to make good mothers. In a small-scale setting, the breed will quite quickly become used to handling by a familiar human.

◀ Brecon Buff geese may make useful and attractive additions to smallholdings and larger gardens.

ESSENTIAL CHARACTERISTICS

Size: Gander 7–9kg/16–20lbs. Goose 6.3–8kg/14–18lbs.
Varieties: One only.
Temperament: Active.
Environment: Requires a fair amount of space.
Eggs: Is one of the best-laying pure breeds.

American Buff

A large all-American goose that the Americans can be justly proud of; this breed shares a similar plumage pattern with the smaller British Brecon, which has caused some confusion in those countries where both are found. Apart from its larger size, the light orange bill and feet should help to distinguish it from the pinker shades standardized in the Brecon Buff. This is a hardy breed that generally lays more eggs and is easier to breed from than some other large breeds. As a useful and attractive goose that some American authorities have described as possessing a pleasant disposition, the breed may find many new friends among fanciers with enough room to accommodate a large and active bird. The breed makes good parents for their young.

◀ The orange bill and pronounced dewlap help to distinguish this from the smaller and neater Brecon Buff.

ESSENTIAL CHARACTERISTICS

Size: Gander 9–12kg/22–28lbs. Goose 9–11kg/20–26lbs.
Varieties: Buff.
Temperament: Has a pleasant disposition.
Environment: A large active goose that requires plenty of room and, like all buff-coloured waterfowl, will fade in sunlight. Exhibition specimens will need extra shade.
Eggs: Up to 25.

Pilgrim

Pilgrim geese are a lightweight breed, and one of the few types of goose where the sex of the bird can be identified by the colour of its down upon hatching. Male goslings are typically creamy yellow and females are grey. The colour difference continues into adulthood. The male turns white, while the female develops grey plumage. Both have orange beaks, legs and feet. Thought to have been developed in the 1930s, the breed is fast-growing and will become tame with handling. The females can make reliable broodies and attentive mothers. Similar self-sexing geese populations, with some relationship to the native breeds, seem to have been part of British poultry-yards for centuries. These may be the origin of strains developed in the USA in the 1930s, which hatch as grey females and white males.

◄ *Pilgrim geese have a strong flocking instinct, and make sociable birds with a companionable disposition.*

ESSENTIAL CHARACTERISTICS
Size: Gander 6.3–8.1kg/14–18lbs.
Goose 5.4–7.2kg/12–16lbs.
Varieties: Subvariety has been described as West of England.
Temperament: Active, likes to range.
Environment: Suitable for most domestic and farm situations.
Eggs: Good layers of fair-sized eggs.

Pomeranian

The ancient German Pomeranian breed is a regular winner at poultry shows. Its popularity has increased in line with the current boom in small-scale poultry keeping. This breed could be of interest to those with time and room to accommodate a family of geese. Females are good egg layers, regularly producing 60 or so eggs per season. White birds with a grey head, back and wings are available. The striking solid-coloured saddle and head was developed in the breed's native Germany where, in spite of importations of other breeds, it remains popular. Its appeal is twofold, stemming from its usefulness and attractive appearance, with striking markings. The blue-grey back markings have been described as heart-shaped. The Pomeranian is a large bird, weighing in at up to 10.8kg/24lbs, and in appearance it has a heavy build. Individuals make good guard birds. This is one of several European breeds of goose that is now becoming increasingly popular in both Britain and the USA, whereas in continental Europe, they are found in Buff-backed and solid White forms.

◄ *Solid coloration of the neck and heart-shaped back markings distinguish the German Pomeranian breed.*

ESSENTIAL CHARACTERISTICS
Size: Gander 8–10.8kg/18–24lbs.
Goose 7–9kg/16–20lbs.
Varieties: Buff-backed and solid White forms.
Temperament: Docile but can make a noisy watchdog.
Environment: Requires plenty of room and a large house.
Eggs: Variable numbers of large eggs.

Sebastopol

Long trailing or frizzled feathers identify the Sebastopol goose, the only breed with this unusual feathering. The soft, curling feathers start at the base of the neck and cover the entire body; those on the head and neck are smooth. A variation is a Sebastopol with smooth breast feathers. White and Buff birds are known. The curly feathers are a result of a mutation and mean that the bird cannot fly, so it would not survive in the wild. Sebastopols are mid-weight geese, with the gander weighing in at a minimum of 5.4kg/12lbs. Females are reasonably layers producing 25–35 eggs per year. Some strains produce good table geese.

The Sebastopol came to prominence in the mid-19th century. It was sent to England from the port of Sebastopol in the Ukraine, but is known around the Danube. In Europe it has the alternate name Danubian, which accurately reflects its point of origin. Often two intensely frizzled birds will not breed

▼ Sebastopol geese are found in both frizzled and long trailing feather forms. Skilled breeders often use both forms to obtain exhibition examples.

true. The best pairing is a smooth-breasted Sebastopol with a frizzle-feathered bird.

ESSENTIAL CHARACTERISTICS
Size: Gander 6.4–7kg/12–16lbs. Goose 4.5–5.4kg/10–12lbs.
Varieties: Self white and Buff.
Temperament: Reasonably quiet.
Environment: Long trailing feathers will need to be kept out of muddy conditions.
Eggs: Egg numbers can be variable.

Toulouse

The Toulouse is still the best-known heavy goose breed in Europe. These grey geese had been bred in the Toulouse district of France for centuries where they were used in the production of pâté de foie gras. Like the Embden, they were used to improve the British flocks. Later, they provided the accepted female partner in the classic Embden-Toulouse cross that became the basis of many farmyard flocks. The exhibition Toulouse is less heavy than its profusely

ESSENTIAL CHARACTERISTICS
Size: Gander 11.8–13.6kg/26–30lbs. Goose 9–10.8kg/20–24lbs.
Varieties: Grey, Buff and White.
Temperament: Slow and stately. May not be as long-lived as some lighter breeds.
Environment: Needs lots of space.
Eggs: Exhibition strains can be poor layers.

◄ The Toulouse makes an excellent show exhibit and an impressive picture when seen in a grassy paddock.

▲ The thickset head and large dewlap add to the overall impression of a massive bird.

feathered outline would suggest, and it lays fewer eggs than would be commercially acceptable. There is no more impressive sight than a group of deep-keeled Toulouse resembling a galleon in full sail; as they move slowly and majestically across a grassed paddock.

TURKEYS

Turkeys are very distinctive-looking birds, with their large size, scrawny necks, ugly facial features and bulbous bodies on relatively thin legs. They are reared for their meat in many parts of the world, both on a commercial scale and, in some regions, by small-scale farmers. In the USA the male is called a tom, in Europe a stag. The female is a hen and the chicks are known as poults. The fleshy protuberance on top on the head is known as the snood, while the one beneath the beak is a wattle. Turkeys are vocal birds and, when kept as pets, have been known to be responsive and companionable animals.

Many species are not seen at exhibition partly because of their size. Turkeys are large birds and are difficult to transport to shows. In addition, their feathers break easily, making the birds appear less attractive and damaging their chances of gaining maximum points. Breeders who keep small flocks of pure-breed turkeys in order to supply a distinctive, quality product have an important role to play in maintaining a wider gene pool. Nearly all of these more serious breeders will use incubators rather than broodies in order to hatch sufficient poults for further breeding at the optimum time of year.

Black

The Black turkey, also known as the Norfolk Black and Spanish Black, is a medium-sized bird weighing up to 10.4kg/23lbs. It was developed in Europe from birds brought from North America in the 16th century, and is now widespread in Europe. In the 17th century, the breed was returned to North America where it was bred to develop the Slate, Narragansett and Bronze breeds. As its name suggests, it is covered in black plumage with an iridescent green sheen. It has a bright red wattle and yellowish

> **ESSENTIAL CHARACTERISTICS**
> **Size**: Stag 10.4kg/23lbs.
> Hen 5.9–6.8kg/13–15lbs.
> **Varieties**: One only.
> **Environment**: This is a large bird that needs plenty of space.

skin. Young turkeys, known as poults, may have white or bronze feathers as they grow, but these are lost with successive moults. This bird is relatively slow to mature, taking up to six months, and as such it is not a favoured commercial breed. Its yellow skin is also a factor in its unpopularity, since the public's preference is for smooth white flesh. Having said that, the texture and flavour of the Black are unrivalled in turkey meat.

This turkey breed is known for having a calm nature and likes a large area for free-ranging. However, it is in danger of becoming extinct because of its less commercial appeal. Unlike other turkey breeds the Norfolk Black can breed naturally. This breed has been crossed with other heavier breeds to produce a larger, more commercial turkey, and as such, the pure breed may be difficult to find.

▶ *The Norfolk Black is an ancient breed of turkey with plumage that is black offset by a red head.*

Bronze

The Bronze is a giant among turkeys. For a long time it was the main commercial breed, dominating the market for several decades from the mid-20th century. The breed developed from turkeys taken to America by immigrants from Europe. For many people, these are the typical farmyard turkey, with their iridescent bronze sheen. Later in its history, the breed divided into two strains: the Standard Bronze and the Broad-breasted Bronze. Thanks to industrial breeding for exaggerated type and the public's preference for white birds, the Bronze strains had practically ceased to exist by 1976, and only survived because of the efforts of fanciers and a few small-scale producers.

While large bronze turkeys are now bred in fair numbers for the table, most of those seen at shows are kept closer to a weight of 5.4–10.8kg/12–24lbs.

▶ *The copperish-bronze feathers terminate in a narrow black band.*

ESSENTIAL CHARACTERISTICS
Size: Stag 13.6–18kg/30–40lbs.
Hen 8–11.7kg/18–26lbs.
Varieties: Standard, Broad-breasted.
Environment: Space required.

Cröllwitzer

This is a relatively small turkey with unusual and attractive colouring. The Pied and American Royal Palm turkey breeds have similar colouring, though the Pied breed is an old breed that dates back to the 1700s, while the Royal Palm was first recorded in the 1920s.

This bird is kept for its eggs rather than as a meat bird to be fattened for celebrations, and is less likely to be kept as a commercial proposition because of this. The breed makes a good bird for a small farm or for dedicated breeders keen to show at exhibitions. It is an active breed and its lighter frame make it visually different to other commerical turkey breeds. However, its meat can rival the taste of other commercial breeds. The head is red; the neck feathers are white with a black tip, while the saddle feathers are black with some white fringing. The tail feathers, when opened out, appear to have a broad black band running across them. It can take dedicated breeders years to perfect the colour markings of the feathers on this particular breed. The breed has heritage status.

◀ *This breed has an active disposition and requires a reasonable amount of space in which to live.*

ESSENTIAL CHARACTERISTICS
Size: Stag 7.3–12.7kg/16–28lbs.
Hen 3.6–8.7kg/8–18lbs.
Environment: Space required.

Glossary

Addled A fertile egg in which the embryo died during the early stages of incubation.

Atavism The resemblance of progeny to their grandparents, not parents.

Autosomes Chromosomes, other than sex chromosomes.

Back-cross Mating an offspring with one of its parents.

Barred A plumage pattern of black and white stripes across the feathers.

Beard Feathers under the throat, found in breeds such as Faverolles, Belgian bantams and Sultans.

Boule An unusually thick neck with a rounded, mane-like appearance, as seen in exhibition Belgian bantams.

Blue A feather colour that usually describes blue-grey; in reality it is a dilute black.

Brassy A yellow tinge to the feathers of white birds that can be caused by weather. It is genetic when found on the shoulders of roosters of other-coloured fowl.

Broiler A fast-growing table fowl, usually mass-produced and that may be killed as young as 42 days old.

Candling Examination of the condition of the inside of the egg during incubation, by passing a strong light through it.

Caponizing Surgical removal of the testes. Chemical caponizing: the

▼ Light Sussex bantam hen.

▶ This bird has a single comb.

administration of drugs that have a similar effect to surgical caponizing.

Chick Refers to birds from birth until removal from brooding area or broody hen.

Chromosomes Cells responsible for the transmission of characteristics to the progeny.

Clean-legged Having legs that are free of feathers.

Cloddy Inclined to be heavy in the hand.

Closed flock A flock of birds of the same breed kept by one breeder. Continuation of the flock is maintained by breeding birds within the group without the addition of outside bloodlines.

Cobby Having a compact, rounded body shape.

Cock A male bird that has completed one or more breeding seasons. Also known as a rooster.

Cockerel A male bird that is in its first breeding season, or one wearing the current year's leg ring.

Columbian A colour and the name of a variety of fowl. The neck hackle has a darker stripe, usually black surrounded by white at the edge, or buff in those varieties described as Buff Columbian.

Columbian restriction A breeding selection which results in the black being restricted to the hackle, wings and tail. It resulted in the now iconic "Light" in Light Sussex, and became a major influence in colour selection in commercial poultry production.

Cramming Forcible feeding, now illegal in the western world.

Crest A bunch of feathers on the head, or in case of the Poland breed, a full globular crest of feathers.

Cross-breeding The mating of two different breeds or varieties.

Cuckoo Feather marking similar to, but less distinctive than, barring, as found in the Marans.

Cushion A mass of soft feathers on the rump of the female. This feature is usually well developed in the Cochin.

Cull Removing an unsuitable bird from the flock.

Dominant Of characteristics that appear in the first hybrid generation when each parent shows different characteristics, eg rose comb is dominant to single. For example, the gene for the rose comb is dominant over the one for single comb, so first-generation offspring of a rose comb-single comb cross would have rose combs.

Drawing Removal of the intestines when preparing a bird for the oven.

Dressing Preparing a bird for the oven.

Dubbing Removal of the comb and wattles.

Duckwing A plumage colour where the normal red-brown, is replaced by white, or in the case of the gold duckwings, yellow or straw colour.

F1 Generation The first filial generation of a specific mating.

F2 Generation The progeny

produced by mating the F1 generation.

Fancier A person who breeds or keeps poultry for exhibition or for their exhibition points.

Feathered legs Legs completely covered in feathers, including the outer toes as in the Cochin, or just to the outer shanks as in the North Holland Blue or Modern Langshan.

Flight feathers The large primary feathers of the wings.

Flock mating Introducing a number of males to mate with a flock of females from the same pen.

Fluff The soft feathers covering the body.

Frizzled Plumage in which the feathers are turned back.

Furnished Fully feathered; a rooster with fully-grown sickle and saddle hackle feathers.

Genes Hereditary factors carried by the chromosomes.

Genotype The genetic composition of an animal. The genetic constitution for a character which may or may not be expressed.

Hackles The long-pointed feathers of the neck and saddle in male birds.

Hen A female bird older than 18 months old.

Henny or Hen-feathered The absence of neck and saddle hackle and sickles in males, standardized in the Sebright and a variety of Old English Game.

◄ *A true bantam.*

Heterozygous A bird formed by the union of a male and female germ cells which are unlike for a given character.

Homozygous When a bird is derived from the union of male and female germ cells, each containing a factor for a specific character, it is homozygous for that character and will breed true for that character.

Hock The knee joint.

Hybrid A bird produced by a program of inbreeding or recurrent reciprocal selection; or an incross or incross breed achieved only with inbred lines of which the coefficient of inbreeding is not less than 50 per cent.

Inbreeding Mating very closely related individuals such as father to daughter, or mother to son.

Incross breeding Mating of highly inbred strains of different breeds.

Incrossing Mating of highly inbred strains of the same breeds.

Keel The breastbone.

Lacing When the edging around a feather is a different colour from the ground colour. Lacing can be single as in Silver-laced Wyandotte, or double, as in the Indian Game and Barnevelder.

Lavender A paler but true breeding form of the colour "blue".

Leader A single spike at the back of the comb. It can be long and thin leading to a point, and follow the line of the comb base as in the Hamburg, or it can follow the line of the neck as in the Old English Pheasant Fowl.

Leaf-comb A comb resembling a leaf as in the Houdan.

Line-breeding Breeding within a family but avoiding the repeated use of closely related individuals.

▲ *A Game fowl.*

Mealy Describes a defect in buff-coloured birds in which the feathers are speckled with white.

Mottled Having a white tip to the end of the feathers as in the Ancona, or black spots on the legs.

Moult The shedding of the feathers prior to the growth of new plumage.

Muffled The muff and beard of the Faverolles, Houdan and Belgian Bantam.

Outcrossing The practice of introducing unrelated genetic material to the breeding pen in an attempt to add desirable characteristics to the breed. In the first crossing it reduces the chances of disease and abnormalities that can result from excessive inbreeding, but can later promote the introduction of recessive genes to a wider gene pool.

Partridge The natural wild pattern of red jungle fowl, in which the male has a black breast and red or orange hackle and the female has a light brown body. Alternatively the more complex variation found in the Cochin or Wyandotte, for example, in which the female's feathers are pencilled with concentric rings of a darker hue.

Pea comb Three small, single ridges joined at their base.

Pencilling Small stripes on the feather that may either follow its

▲ *A New Hampshire bantam pullet.*

outline or run across it. Different to barring.

Phenotype The appearance of an individual; the production record of an individual fowl is termed its phenotype for the particular character.

Primaries or Primary feathers The ten feathers of the wing lying between the finger-feathers at the wing-tip plus the small axial feather that lies between the primaries and secondaries.

Pullet A female in her first year of egg laying. In exhibition terms this also means either a bird bred after November 1 of the previous year, or wearing a closed ring issued for the current year.

Pyle or Pile A partridge pattern in which white feathers replace the standard black in the male and brown in the female.

Reachy The carriage of a bird that is held aloft.

Recessive Refers to characteristics that are suppressed in the first generation.

Rose comb A broad comb in which the surface is more or less covered by small pimples or protrusions.

Saddle The back of the male bird in front of the tail.

Sappy or Sappiness A yellow tinge in birds with white plumage which arises from excessive pigmentation. It should not be confused with

brassiness, which occurs on the surface of the feathers.

Scales The overlaying rows of horny skin tissues covering the legs.

Secondaries or Secondary feathers The set of quill-feathers in the wing between the axial feather and the body.

Selection Choosing specific birds from which to breed because they have a desirable characteristic.

Self colour All one colour.

Semi-intensive A housing system in which birds have limited access to an outside run.

Shaft The stem of the feather.

Shank The part of the leg between the hock joint and the foot.

Sickles The long curved feathers in a rooster's comb.

Single comb A flat comb which has serrations along the edge. It is held vertically in male birds and sometimes falls to one side in female birds.

Sitting The number of eggs sufficient for one bird to cover in a nest.

Spangling A spot of colour at the end of a feather that is a different colour to the rest of the feather.

Spikes The serrations on a comb.

Sport When a new characteristic appears in one generation and is transmitted to succeeding generations. The White Wyandotte originated as a sport of the Silver-laced Wyandotte, for example.

Spur The horn-like growth on the shank of a male bird, occasionally seen in females.

Squirrel tail The tail-feathers sloping forward over the back.

Stag A male bird, more commonly used to describe turkeys, but sometimes used by exhibitors.

Strain A group of birds constituting a family within a breed or population.

Top crossing Mating an inbred, selectively bred male with an unrelated, less selectively bred female.

Type Body conformation or shape.

Breed-type refers to the shape and size of the breed. A "good type" means a bird that closely conforms to the breed standard.

Under-colour The colour of the lower part of the feather that is hidden by overlapping feathers.

Utility Poultry bred for egg production and/or for the table.

Variety Different feather colours standardized within the same breed. Occasionally it refers to two different standardized comb types.

Vulture hocks Stiff feathers that grow down from the hock joint.

Wattles The red fleshy appendages hanging from the throat at the base of the beak.

Web (of the feather) The barbs of the feather on each side of the shaft.

Wing bars A line of differently coloured feathers that appear across the middle of the wing in the plumage of some varieties.

Work or working The small bumps or protrusions that are found on the top of a rose comb.

▼ *A breed with distinct comb, wattles and ear lobes.*

INDEX

A
African goose 242
aggression 66–7
Aldrovandi, Ulisse 149, 185
Alison, Dr Enid 145
American Bronze turkey 129–30
American Buff Goose 243
American Mammoth turkey 129
American Poultry Association 206
American Poultry Standard 215
anatomy 14–15
Ancona 68, 159
appendages 16–17
Appenzellar Spitzhauben 146
Appleyard, Reginald 221, 237
Araucana 89, 208
Aseel/Asil 167, 168, 170, 176
Asian hard feather fowl 136, 170–3
Asian soft feather fowl 136, 160–6
Asiatic poultry 9, 18–19, 136
Assendelft 212
auctions 29, 76

▼ A Fayoumi hen.

Australian poultry societies 219
Australorp 219, 220
auto-sexing breeds 88–9, 90–1
Ayam Kapan 193
Aylesbury duck 116, 117, 118, 120, 234, 235

B
bantams 179, 180–1
    breeds 182–93
Barbary Fowl 229
Barbu d'Everberg 184
Barbu d'Uccle 183, 184
Barbu de Grubbe 185
Barbu de Watemael 185
Barnebar 89
Barnevelders 89, 161, 209, 210
Bateson, William 16
battery hens 34–5
beak trimming 76, 110
beards 18
bedding 63
behaviour 65, 66
    feather pecking 67
    ruling the roost 66–7
Belcher, Sir Edward 11, 160
Belgian bantams 18, 183–5
Belgian d'Anvers 184
Beltsville White turkey 131
Bethnal Green Utility Poultry Society 210
Bielefelder 91
Black East India duck 237
Black Minorca 216
Black Orpington 216, 217, 218, 219, 220
Black Plymouth Rock 201, 216
Black Spanish 149
Black Sumatra 225
Black turkey 129, 131, 246
Black-blue Australorp 219
Black, John 199
Black, Thomas 199

▲ A White-crested Black Poland.

blackhead 81, 132, 133
Blue Andalusian 87, 156
Blue Dun Game 156
Blue Orpington 217
Boks, Dr 147
Bolton Bay 139
Bolton Grey 103, 139
Booted Bantam 182
Braekel 150
Brahma 11, 16, 41, 55, 102, 136, 162–3, 199
Brecon Buff goose 243
Breda 147
breeding 85, 86–7
    auto-sexing breeds 88–9
    barred breeds 88
    double mating 87
    ducks 120–1
    geese 126
    sex-linked breeding 88, 89
    turkeys 133
breeds 6–7, 12–13
    conservation 105–6, 131, 133
    ducks 234–40
    essential characteristics 137
    geese 241–5
    retaining integrity 33
    turkeys 246–7
    written breed standards 102–3

British Poultry Club 212
British Rare Poultry Society 147
British Rhode Island Red Club 206–7
British Welsummer Club 211
Broad-breasted Bronze turkey 129
Bronze turkey 129, 131, 247
brooding 46, 92–3, 94, 98
Buckeye 205
Buff Cochin 201, 202, 205, 218
Buff Leghorn 201
Buff Orpington 108, 152, 216, 217, 218, 220
Buff turkey 128
bumble foot 78
Burnham, George P. 11
    Hen Fever 162
business 7
buttercup combs 18
buying poultry 27, 28–9, 118, 124

C
Call duck 240
Cambar 88, 89, 90, 150
Cambridge Bronze turkey 129
Campbell, Adele 238

▼ An African goose.

▲ *A Mottled Java.*

Campine 88–9, 90, 149, 150
Carlisle Game 169
Carlisle Game Club 167
carrying cases 71
Cayuga duck 235
Chacalaca 208
Chantecler 176
chicks 24, 28
 brooding units 98
 chick feed 73, 75
 growth 99
 handling 69
 hatching 95–6, 97
 incubators 94–6
 rearing under hen 92–3
children 6, 179
Chinese goose 124, 126, 242
Chitterpats 139
Chocolate Orpington 217
Chu Shamo 171
climate 39
Clown-faced Spanish 155
clubs 32, 76
coccidiosis 59, 81
Cochin 11, 19, 41, 102, 142, 147, 160–1, 166, 198, 217
Cochin bantams 181, 182, 190–1, 202
cockerels 38, 46, 66
cockfighting 10, 167, 171, 173, 176, 225
Colloncas 208
combs 16–18

commercial poultry rearing 34–5
 terminology 35
commitment 29, 38
conservation 105–6, 131, 133
contour feathers 23
Cook, William 216, 218, 219
Corals 139
Cornish Game 17, 176, 199, 205, 221
Creels 139
creeper gene 145, 188
crests 18
Crevecoeur 149, 209, 213
Croad Langshan 164–5
Croad, Major 164
Cuckoo Maran 214
Cuckoo Orpington 217

D
Dandarawi 154
Danish Waddler 145
Dark Brahma 202, 203, 213
Dark Dorking 213
Darwin, Charles 8
daylight 38–9
deep litter systems 35
Derbyshire Redcap 17, 68–9, 106, 140
diarrhoea 79
diseases 29, 30, 62, 77–81
 wild birds 39, 132
DIY housing 48
 assembling 53
 droppings board 51
 external features 52

▼ *A Black Cochin.*

▲ *A Brahma.*

internal features 52
 nest boxes 50
 perches 51
 practical considerations 49
 recycling materials 48
domestication 8–9
Dominique 198, 200
Dorking 17, 19, 136, 141, 161, 176, 209
double mating 87
Double-laced Barnevelder 210
dropped abdomen 79
duck breeds
 Aylesbury 234
 Black East India 237
 Call 240
 Cayuga 235
 Hook Bill 239
 Indian Runner 239
 Khaki Campbell 238
 Muscovy 236
 Pekin 235
 Rouen 236
 Saxony 238
 Silver Appleyard 237
ducklings 120–1
ducks 115, 116, 231, 232
 bathing water 119
 breeding 120–1
 breeds 234–40
 buying 118
 cleaning ponds 119
 down 116
 eggs 117
 feeding 119, 121

 handling 118
 housing 118–19
 meat 116–17
dust baths 37, 55–6
Dutch Bantam 186–7
Dutch Decoy 240

E
eggs 6, 24
 blood spots 83
 candling 96–7
 colour 113
 ducks 117
 eggshells 82–3
 exhibitions 112–13
 geese 123
 keeping clean 62
 turkeys 128
Embden goose 122, 241
Entwistle, J. W. 190
evolution 8–9
exhibition birds 108
 breeding 86–7
 clipping the beak 110
 final preparation 110–11
 geese 123
 washing and drying 108–10
exhibitions 7, 101, 105–6
 agricultural shows 107
 classes 104
 eggs 112–13
 judging 107, 113
 local shows 106
 preparation 108–11

F
Faverolles 18, 19, 141, 213
Fayoumi 108, 157, 159
feather colours 20–1
feather patterns 22
feather pecking 67, 76
feather structure 23
 contour feathers 23
feathered feet 18–19
feeders 55
feeding 37, 72
 chick feed 73, 75
 ducks 119, 121
 food problems 75

formulated feed 72–4
geese 125
grit and oyster shell 74
pullet feed 75
turkeys 131
vegetation 72
water 74
five toes 19
fleas 37, 57
foundation breeds 135,
    136–7
    Asian soft feather 160–6
    British 138–47
    European 146–52
    Mediterranean 153–9
foxes 42, 60–1
free range 35, 43–4
Friesian 152
Frizzle 87, 228

G
Gallus domesticus 8
    gallus 8, 16
    gigantus 9, 162
    lafayettii 8, 16
    sonneratii 8, 16
    varius 8, 16
game birds 167–77
geese 115, 122, 231, 232–3
    breeding 126
    breeds 241–5
    buying 124
    eggs 123
    feeding 125

▼ A Blue Andalusian.

▲ A Jubilee Indian Game fowl.

housing 124
meat 122–3
walking to market 122
Gold-laced Orpington 217
Gold-laced Sebright 203
Gold-spangled Hamburg
    218
grass 46, 72, 75
goose breeds
    African 242
    American Buff 243
    Brecon Buff 243
    Chinese 242
    Embden 241
    Pilgrim 244
    Pomeranian 244
    Sebastopol 245
    Toulouse 245
Greenaway, Lord 214
Grey Old English Game
    220
Greylag Goose 232
grit 37, 73, 74
growers 28, 58–9
guinea fowl 115, 127, 231

H
Hambar 89
Hamburg 17, 68, 104,
    138–9, 149, 192, 198,
    202, 216, 221
handling 68–9
    ducks 118

▲ A Rumpless bantam.

picking up fowl 68
preparing for exhibitions
    107, 108
removing from cage 69
hatching 95–6, 97
health 65, 76–7
    diseases 77–81
    egg problems 82–3
    health checks 29
hens 24–5, 28, 67
    ageing hens 25
    battery hens 35
    broody hens 92–3
    discouraging broodiness
    93
Hook Bill duck 239
horned combs 17
Houdan 17, 18, 19, 141,
    209, 213
housing 37, 38
    building your own 48–53
    changing bedding 63
    choosing 40–1
    cleaning 62
    combined house and
    run 43
    daylight and climate 38–9
    ducks 118–19
    essential additions 54–6
    exhibition birds 46–7
    free range 43–4
    geese 124
    hen and chicks 93
    hygiene 57, 59

maintenance 62–3
permanent runs 44–5
secondary housing 45–6
security 60–1
semi-intensive systems
    42–3
site 38
static systems 44
turkeys 132
young poultry 58–9
hybrids 13, 29
    breeding 86
    choosing 30
hygiene 57, 59

I
Illustrated London News 11
incubators 94–6
    hatching 95–6, 97
Indian Game 16, 50, 55,
    176, 205, 221
Indian Runner duck 117,
    232, 239
infectious bronchitis (IB)
    78
intensive housing 35
introducing new birds 70
Ixworth 216, 221

J
Japanese Bantam 188, 193,
    224
Java 166, 199, 200
Jersey Giant 166, 199
Jubilee English Game 221
Jubilee Orpington 217
jungle fowl (*Gallus* spp.)
    8–9, 146

▼ A Sicilian Buttercup.

▲ *A Croad Langshan.*

K
Kent 142, 216
Khaki Campbell duck 117, 232, 238
Ko Shamo 171
Kruper 145
Kuro Gashiwa 224

L
La Fleche 17, 149
Labrador duck 237
Lackenvelder 150, 152
Lancashire Moonie 139
Langshan 19, 164–5, 199, 216
Legbar 89
Leghorns 16, 17, 89, 153, 157, 158, 220, 221
lice 29, 37, 57, 80
life cycle 24–5
Light Brahma 201, 213
Light Sussex 91, 197

▼ *A French Marans.*

Rhode Island Red x Light Sussex 197
lighting 56
Lincolnshire Buff 218, 220
long-tailed Japanese breeds 222–5

M
Macomber, John 206
Malay 172, 173, 176, 206, 221
males 24, 28, 66, 86
Maline 212
mallards 232, 234, 236, 238, 239
Manchester 103
manmade breeds 103, 195, 196–7
 American 198–208
 British 216–21
 European 209–15
 Japanese long-tailed 222–5
 modified feather 226–9
 Rhode Island Red x Light Sussex 197
Manx Rumpy 177
Marans 89, 113, 214, 161, 209, 212
Marek's disease 77
Marsh Daisy 216, 221
McKeen, Joseph 202–3
meat 176, 199, 209, 213, 229
 ducks 116–17
 geese 122–3
 turkeys 128–9
Mediterranean breeds 31, 153–9
Mendel, Gregor 16, 87, 156, 228
Minorca 110, 153
mites 57, 80–1
 housing 40
 red mite 56, 62–3
Modern Game 173, 174
Modern Langshan 165
Mooneye 103
Moss Pheasant 103
Mottled Leghorn 159

▲ *A Modern Game bird.*

moulting 25, 76, 107
muffs 18
mulberry combs 17
Muscovy duck 116, 120, 232, 236
mycoplasma 77–8
Myhill, Fred 220

N
Nankin Bantam 187
Nanking Shamo 171
neighbours 29, 38, 60, 128
nest boxes 37, 54
 making 50
New Hampshire Red 31, 89, 91, 204
Norfolk Black turkey 129–30, 131
Norfolk Grey 220
North Holland Blue 212

O
O Shamo 171
Ohiki 224
Old English Game 167, 176, 177, 221
Old English Game bantams 174–5
Old English Pheasant Fowl 140
Onaga-dori 223, 226
organic rearing 35
ornamental fowl 117, 123

ornaments 16–17
Orpington 41, 47, 55, 108, 199, 216–17
Owen, W. Powell 212
Oxford Game 168
Oxford Game Club 167
oyster shell 73, 74

P
parasites 56, 79
Partridge Barnevelder 210
Partridge Cochin 202–3
pea combs 16–17
Pease, Michael 88, 90
pecking order 66–7
Pekin bantams 181, 190–1
Pekin duck 116, 117, 232, 234, 235
perches 37, 54–5
 making 51
pets 6, 115, 117, 123, 179
Pheasant Fowl 139
Phoenix 222–3
Pile Old English Game 221
Pilgrim goose 244
Plymouth Rock 88–9, 90, 91, 166, 198, 200–1, 205
Poland/Polish 17, 18, 41, 148–9, 192, 209, 213
Polder fowl 149
Polo, Marco 226
Pomeranian Goose 244
Poultry Club 86, 102
"poultry mania" 11, 102, 160, 162
poults 128, 130–1

▼ *A Cayuga duck.*

▲ *A Bronze turkey.*

housing 132
rearing 133
prolapsed oviduct 78–9
pullets 24–5, 56, 77
pullet feed 75
Punnett, Professor 88, 90
pure breeds 12, 29
breeding 86
choosing 31

Q
Quetros 208

R
Rare Breed Society 220
rare breeds 6–7
choosing 32
rats 57
Red-faced Spanish 153
Red-saddled Yokohama
222, 223
Redbar 89
Redcap 139
Rhode Island Experimental
Institute 204, 206
Rhode Island Red 91, 102,
197, 199, 204, 206–7
Buckeye 205
Rhode Island Red x Light
Sussex 197
Rhodebar 89, 90, 91
Richardson, A. W. (Red)
204
Riseholme College,
Lincolnshire 222
Rockbar 91

roosting 37
Rosecomb 189, 192
rose combs 17
Rouen duck 116, 120, 236
Rumpless Game 177
runs 43, 44–5
Russian Orloff 18, 215

S
Sablepoot 182
Salmon Faverolles 213
salmonella 30, 77
Saxony Duck 238
Scots Dumpy 144–5, 188
Scots Grey 144, 145
Sebastopol goose 245
Sebright 111, 192, 202
security systems 60–1
semi-intensive systems 35,
42–3
Serama 72, 193
sex-linked breeding 88, 89
Shabo 188, 224
Shamo 55, 171
Shanghai 160, 161, 198
Shokoku 223
showing *see* exhibitions
Sicilian Buttercup 167,
221
Sicilian Flower 157
Silkie 18, 19, 193, 225,
226–7
Silver Appleyard Duck
237
Silver-spangled Hamburg
202
single combs 16
slugs 75
Spangled Orpington 217

▼ *An American Buff goose.*

▲ *A Jersey Giant.*

spur trimming 76
Standard Bronze turkey 129
strains 12–13
strawberry combs 18
Suffolk Chequers 91
Sultan 17, 18, 19, 147
Sumatra 16, 225
Surrey 142, 216
Sussex 19, 47, 74, 102,
136, 141, 142–3, 176,
216
Swan goose 232

T
table fowl see meat
thieves 42, 60
Thuringian 151, 215
toenail trimming 76
Toulouse goose 126, 245
transporting 71
Transylvanian Naked Neck
229
Tripp, William 206
Turken 229
turkey breeds
Black 246
Bronze 247
White 247
turkeys 115, 128, 231, 233
blackhead 81, 132, 133
breeding 133
breeds 246–7
eggs 128
feeding 131
franchises 130
housing 132
intensive farming 130–1

meat 128–9
old breeds 131
pure breed farming
129–30
University of New
Hampshire 204

V
vaccination 30, 31, 77
varieties 13
vegetation 37, 72
vent gleet 79
Victoria, Queen 11, 147,
160, 162, 164, 217
Vorverk 152
vulture hocks 18

W
walnut combs 18
water 37, 74
Wee Yean Een 193
Welbar 89, 90
Welsummer 89, 90, 113,
161, 209, 211
White Australorp 219
White Orpington 217,
221
White turkey 131, 247
White-faced Black Spanish
110, 155
wings, shortening 61
World Poultry Congress
210
worm infestations 29,
79–80
worms as food 38, 75
Wright, Charles 221
Wright, John 221
Wright, Lewis *Illustrated
Book of Poultry* 11
Wyandotte 16, 91,
202–3
Wybar 89, 90–1

Y
Yamato Gunkei 171
Yokohama 222–3
Yorkshire Hornet 103,
146
Yorkshire Pheasant 140

ACKNOWLEDGEMENTS

The publishers would like to thank all the poultry owners who generously brought their birds to be photographed, and to the show organisers who allowed the photography to take place. Every effort has been made to trace poultry owners of all poultry photographed and we apologise for any ommisions made to this list of contributors.

G Abraham, Will Allen, Brian Anderton, K Arnold Dennis Ash, R A Axman, Sue Baker, Keith Barnes, Frances Bassom, H A and S Beardsmore, Richard Bett, Tim Biela, S Black, Laura Bovingdon, G D Brearley and Son, K Britten, Alan Brooker, H W Broomfield, Alan Brown, Sue Bruton, T and J Buck, Callum Burney, Andy Capel, Samantha Carr, J Christopher, Len Clark, Christine Compton, Robin Creighton, Emma Crook, M Crowther, Sandy Cummin, A and J Cumming, C Curtis, Angela DuPont, A J Davies, P E Davy, R Eden, Celia Edmonds, Derrick Elvey, B Evans, Mrs G Evans, R A Everatt, Carle Faiers, James Firth, Mr R Fontanini, R Francis, Mr and Mrs Frizzell, Steve Fuller, Caryl, Steve Gilliver, S Goodwin, Zoe Gracey, Lee Grant, Terry Gregory, Griffin and Gifford,

Colin Gullon, Mike Hadfield, L Hampstead, Fred Hams, Louise Hidden, Mandy and Barry Hobbs, Graham Hodge, Derek Howells, Derek Hoyland, C Hughes, David Iley, Anita James, C Joiner, J Kay and Sons, Stuart Kay, Alan Kemp, Mr Kemp, M Kennedy, Andrew Kerr, M R Knowles, P Knowles, R J Lomas, P Lutkin, Jim Marland, C Marlies, Trevor Martin, Gary McKinstry, Michelle van Meurs, Lorna Mew, Priscilla Middleton, Jason Millward, Pedro Moreira, Nigel Morgan, J Nibs, J P Oakley, J Owen, Harry Pannell, Jack Partridge, Mark Perkins, J Pickles, William Pimlott, Alan Pollington, Mr Power, David Pownall, Alan Procter, John Pummell, Craig Ramus, Robin Ramus, Antoinette Reese, John Rich, C Roberts, Richard Rowley, Brian Sands, W and J A Sharp, R and C Shepherd, Ian Simpson, Ian and L Simpson, Ian Sissons, Tony Smith, John Soper, Sylvia Soper, Tamsin Spicer, Anthony Stanway, Eddie Starkey, Clive Stephens, Margaret Stephens, Martin Stephenson, D Stone, Penny Strutt, O'Sullivan, A and J Tacey, P B Tasher, C F Taylor, N R Taylor, J Tickle, G Tinson, Mrs Troth, David Vicente, Team Wakeham, Hugh Wallace, B G

Ward, P Watkinson, N Watson, R Watts, Lesley Webdale, John and P Wilde, A Wilson, Mrs Wincott, Rodney Wood, Steve Woodcock, Sue Woods, Chris Woolley, Simon York.

The publishers and author would like to thank the following for allowing photography:

The National Federation of Poultry Clubs show at Stafford. The help of the Poultry Club of Great Britain members and judges at the Poultry Club of Great Britain. Affiliated shows run by Arun Valley Poultry Fanciers Society, Hants and Berks Poultry Fanciers Society, Kent Poultry Fanciers Society, Norfolk Poultry Club, Reading and District Bantam Society, Surrey Poultry Society.

Thanks to Forsham Cottage Arks, Mr and Mrs Raymond and Angela May, Derrick Elvey, Andrew and Lorna Mew, Jane Booreman, Priscilla Middleton, Mandy O'nions and Mark Hobbs, Neil Weller, Philip Lee Woolf at Legbars of Broadway.

Thanks to the following photographic libraries and individuals for permission to use

their images: (c = centre, l = left, r = right, t = top, b = bottom) Alamy: page 8t, 9tr, 10t, 40t, 44tr, 60, 69tr, 94tr, 114, 117b, 121tr, 122r, 123b, 125b, 130t, 178, 201, 208b. Ardea: page 121b, 132t, 133t, 181tl, 208t, 238t. Clare and Terry Beebe: page 33t, 78bc, 78br, 79tl, 79tc, 79tr, 79b, 83tc, 83tr, 94tc, 131bl, 131bc, 196t, 197tc, 197tr, 233t, 233br. Bridgeman Art Library: page 9tl. British Hen Welfare Trust: page 34–35. Corbis: page 9b, 11b, 122b, 125t, 130b, 131t, 223t. Fotolia: page 57, 115, 128bl, 161t. GAP: page 117t. Istock: page 10b, 21 br, 123t, 124b, 126b, 231. Dave Scrivener: page 33b, 91br, 131r, 173b, 177br, 182t, 182c, 232b, 233bl, 241l, 241r, 244t, 245t. Roger Sing: page 88b. Superstock: page 56. Philip Lee Woelf: page 76b, 195.

This edition is published by Lorenz Books an imprint of Anness Publishing Ltd Blaby Road, Wigston Leicestershire LE18 4SE Email: info@anness.com Web: www.lorenzbooks.com; www.annesspublishing.com

Publisher: Joanna Lorenz
Editorial Director: Helen Sudell
Editor: Simona Hill
Photographers: Robert Dowling (poultry directories, Mark Winwood (pp 23–113) and Mark Wood (pp 94–99)
Illustrator: Stuart Jackson-Carter
Designer: Nigel Partridge
Illustrator: Stuart Jackson-Carter
Production Controller: Bessie Bai